Know That I AM God

Bible Study

Patty Mason

Know That I AM God: Bible Study

Copyright © 2013 by Patty Mason

ISBN 978-0-9829718-4-0
Printed by Liberty in Christ Ministries
To order: www.LibertyinChristMinistries.com

Unless otherwise indicated, Scripture is taken from (NIV) the
HOLY BIBLE, NEW INTERNATIONAL VERSION® Copyright © 1973, 1978, 1984
by International Bible Society. Used by permission of Zondervan Publishing House.
All rights reserved.

Scripture quotations marked (NASB) are taken from the
NEW AMERICAN STANDARD BIBLE®, Copyright ©1960, 1962,
1963, 1968, 1971, 1972, 1973, 1975, 1977, 1995 by Lockman Foundation.
Used by permission. (www.Lockman.org)

Scripture quotations marked (AMP) are taken from THE AMPLIFIED BIBLE®
Copyright © 1954, 1958, 1962, 1964, 1965, 1987 by The Lockman Foundation.
All rights reserved. Used by permission. (www.Lockman.org).

Scripture quotations marked (NLT) are taken from the
HOLY BIBLE, NEW LIVING TRANSLATION®, copyright © 1996.
Used by permission of Tyndale House Publishers, Inc. Wheaton, Illinois 60189.
All rights reserved.

Scripture taken from *THE MESSAGE*. Copyright © 1993, 1994, 1995,
1996, 2001, 2002. Used by permission of NavPress Publishing Group.

All rights reserved. No part of this book may be reproduced, stored in a
retrieval system, or transmitted by any means, electronic, mechanical,
photocopy, recording, or otherwise, without written permission from
the author, except as provided by USA copyright law.

To request permission, please send your request to: Patty@LibertyinChristMinistries.com

Dedication

This Bible study is dedicated Carol Tanzinski and to all those who will not settle in their pursuit of Christ—to all those who hunger to know Him at all costs and will not give up or give in until they have won the prize for which God has called them heavenward in Christ Jesus.

"I consider everything a loss compared to the surpassing greatness of knowing Christ Jesus my Lord, for whose sake I have lost all things" (Philippians 3:8, NIV).

About the Author

"I am a wife and mother who is madly and passionately in love with Jesus. As a writer, speaker and Bible teacher I love sharing Jesus, and it is the zealous cry of my heart to show you how to *know* Jesus in a richer, more intimate way." —Patty

Patty Mason is an award-winning author, speaker, and the founder of Liberty in Christ Ministries. Through the power of God's Word she has been teaching, mentoring and inspiring women of all ages, helping them find hope, healing and freedom for their souls. Her worldwide ministry has reached audiences in 170 countries through Sisters on Assignment, Salem Communication's Internet Broadcasting Channel LightSource.com, Christian TV, and WLGT Blog Radio LIVE. Patty continues to speak at women's luncheons, events, workshops and conferences; and has appeared on numerous television and radio programs, such as The Bridges Show, Crusade Radio with Willie Drake, 94.7 WFIA Just Ask Joyce, and CBN 700 Club.

Her books include *Transformed by Desire: A Journey of Awakening to Life and Love; Finally Free: Breaking the Bonds of Depression without Drugs*, and *Experiencing Joy: Strategies for Living a Joy Filled Life*.

To learn more about the author, her books or ministry, visit www.libertyinchristministries.com

Foreword

To "Know God" is the highest pursuit of man. As a bible teacher, pastor, elder, and friend, I was happy to read Patty's manuscript as she was preparing this study. What I was not prepared for was the depth and biblical insight that Patty has brought to this study. With each chapter, one is engulfed with solid teaching, the blessing of personally "mining" the biblical texts for oneself, guidance for practical application, and then devotional prayer. That is a combination that will lead the reader from a *head* knowledge of God to a *heart* knowledge of Him (John 20:31).

In Leon Morris' introduction to his classic commentary on the Gospel of John, he described John as "a pool in which a child can wade and an elephant can swim." Meaning that it is at the same time both simple and profound. I believe that this study has a similar attribute and quality. So whether you are a beginning seeker of God, a new believer in the Lord Jesus, or a seasoned bible student and Christ-follower, this study will reach, teach, and touch you wherever you may find yourself on your journey to "Know God" better. And if that is your heart's desire, then I encourage you to take this trip with Patty and know God as Father, Friend, Bridegroom, Shepherd, Redeemer, Healer, Warrior, and King. Bon Voyage!

Tony Dupree, Pastor
Franklin, Tennessee

Table of Contents

Introduction 6

Week One: *The Challenge to Know God* 8

Week Two: *Know That I AM Your Father* 38

Week Three: *Know That I AM Your Friend* 64

Week Four: *Know That I AM Your Bridegroom* 94

Week Five: *Know That I AM Your Redeemer* 122

Week Six: *Know That I AM Your Shepherd* 152

Week Seven: *Know That I AM Your Healer* 180

Week Eight: *Knowing the Name of God* 210

Week Nine: *Know That I AM Your Warrior* 232

Week Ten: *Know That I AM Your King of Glory* 258

References 284

Leader's Guide 286

Introduction

"Many have undertaken to draw up an account of the things that have been fulfilled among us, just as they were handed down to us by those who from the first were eyewitnesses and servants of the word. Therefore, I myself have carefully investigated everything from the beginning, it seemed good also to me to write an orderly account for you…so that you may know the certainty of the things you have been taught" (Luke 1:1-4, NIV).

I am ecstatic and utterly grateful that you have made the decision to join me on a quest to know God more deeply. The premise for this study was taken from Isaiah 43:10, "You are my witnesses,' declares the LORD, 'and my servant whom I have chosen, so that you may know and believe me and understand that I am he." The endless desire of God's heart is that we know Him intimately, believe Him unconditionally, and understand who He is and that He alone is God. The primary way God fulfills this desire is through close, personal relationship. For this reason, each week of study (with the exception of Week One which will lay the groundwork for our quest) will focus on a different aspect of the relationship with God, giving us a fresh perspective of His character, power, glory, and beauty. It is up to each of us, however, to diligently pursue Him so that we may be given the opportunity to witness, for ourselves, the wonders of His majesty and glory through the power of His Word and manifest presence in our everyday lives.

I am overcome with awe and wonder as we begin to prepare for our journey together. It is my hope and prayer that this study, through the power of the Holy Spirit, will challenge us to take the road less traveled, daring us to radically expand our view of God. I pray that the Holy Spirit would apply this study in such a way that it would whet the appetite of anyone who is in hot-pursuit of God. Although there are some who would contend that many believers today are not ready for such an intense pursuit. The lack of zeal and developing complacency that seems to be settling on the hearts of many have convinced some that such a study will be too much for the average believer. Perhaps, only a few are on a daring quest to know, believe, and understand the true heart of God; but I believe, deep within my heart, there are people who desire to *know* God and desire to have the unimaginable privilege of witnessing Him in the most profound ways. I believe there is a cry rising up among believers today that begs for the revelation: "I want to know God!" I am convinced there are people today who yearn to embrace a relational knowledge of God that goes far beyond the basic concepts of Christianity—a people who want to take knowing and experiencing God to the extreme.

This extreme level of relationship goes well beyond our human capabilities and is a connection, an intertwining of relationship with God that goes so deep it reaches into the deepest part of our inner being. This is not your average head-knowledge we are talking about, but a profound awareness of the Person and personality of God that consumes every aspect of our everyday lives, to the point that it changes our view of God, the world around us, the church, and ourselves.

This study is not about the pursuit of information in order to help us discover new facts about God we didn't know before. It's not about reviewing definitions in the Greek and Hebrew language, drawing from supportive commentary, and offering various viewpoints in order to understand the theological weight of certain terms which emphasize their importance and varying degrees of significance. I do agree that knowing facts and obtaining information about God is important, however, knowing facts will not draw us closer to

God. If we want to know God, we must allow what we know about God to become the reality of what we experience with God. This level of knowledge only comes through the heartfelt, zealous pursuit of personal experience through intimate relationship.

What we are after is extreme revelation, the wisdom of the Lord, and it comes no other way than through the application of personal relationship. You can spend countless hours, even decades, reading your Bible and doing Bible studies (which I am not discouraging you from doing—you need to fervently be in God's Word); but if you only read and study without applying what you have learned about God in an intimate relationship, you will know facts, but you will not know Him. Jesus said, "You diligently study the Scriptures because you think that by them you possess eternal life. These are the Scriptures that testify about me, yet you refuse to come to me and have life" (John 5:39-40, NIV). First and foremost, in order to know God, to believe and understand Him and receive the revelation of His wisdom, you must seek Him in intimacy through the aspects of relationship. And as you ardently chase after Him, God promises that if you seek to know Him, you will (see Deuteronomy 4:29). For God rewards those who intently and intentionally seek after Him— they are the ones He reveals Himself to.

Beloved, doing this study, or any Bible study, for that matter, will not help you know God unless you are willing to put the application of personal relationship into practice. For this reason, at the end of each week, you will find a section called: **Apply the Knowledge**. This will give you an opportunity to put the application of God's Word, and what the Holy Spirit impresses upon you, into action. Take these opportunities to share the longings of your heart with Jesus, to cry out for greater revelations of His Person, and to pray and ask the Holy Spirit to take what He has revealed to you each week and make it a life-changing reality in your life.

Now, if you're ready, please join me in prayer with great expectation, as we prepare our hearts to seek and know God.

"Lord, we pray that You will open wide our hearts as we earnestly seek to know You. Increase our hunger for more, so that as we approach each aspect of relationship with You as Father, Friend, Bridegroom, Redeemer, Shepherd, Healer, Warrior and King, we may behold the wonders of Your majesty and glory through the power of Your Word and manifest presence. We pray, as we seek you through Your Holy Word, that we will find the treasures that You graciously offer to us. We pray that we, by the power of your Holy Spirit, are given the power to pursue You with all our heart, soul, mind, and strength, so we may know how incredible You are. Lord, we pray to be given the ability to comprehend and recognize your Person and personality well beyond our own natural capabilities. Father, give us the strength and power of the Spirit of wisdom and revelation, so that we may know you better (see Ephesians. 1:17). May this journey only be the start of our quest to know You. May we never stop searching with a burning heart that cries out for all of the riches of Christ. May we come into deep personal union with you through intimate relationship. And may our continual prayer be: "If you are pleased with me, teach me your ways so I may know you and continue to find favor with you" (Exodus 33:13, NIV). In Jesus' Name we pray—Amen!

Knowing God—is it even possible to begin to grasp such an immeasurable concept? In this life we will never fully know or understand God, for His wisdom and ways are far beyond our own (see Isaiah 55:8-9); yet, in this pursuit, we are going to reach for higher revelations of His Person. Through the power of the Holy Spirit, we will press onward and take hold of every opportunity to embrace all we are permitted to know in this lifetime. Beloved, I am excited and greatly humbled to have the privilege and opportunity to take this adventure with you. I cannot wait another minute—let's begin!

Week One
The Challenge to Know God

The phrase *"know that I am"* appears in Scripture seventy times and emphasizes the validity that God wants you to *know* Him. He wants to share the familiarity and closeness of an ongoing and personal relationship. The inconceivable truth of the matter is if you are willing to pursue God, He is more than willing to reveal His glorious treasures. God tells us in Isaiah 45:3, "I will give you treasures hidden in the darkness—secret riches. I will do this, so you may *know that I am* the LORD, the God of Israel, the one who calls you by name" (NLT, *emphasis mine*). It is He, the God of Israel, who extends this invitation, wanting you to enter into a profound relationship, so He might reveal the secret riches of Himself, the unimaginable wonders of His Person and personality.

Please understand, however, there will be some things we need to realize. First, we need to recognize that knowing God takes time; still, we must keep forging ahead, putting one foot in front of the other day-by-day, never willing to stay content in our pursuit of Deity. Also, keep in mind, that some things we seek to know will remain unknown. It is impossible to totally know everything concerning God in this lifetime. Here on earth we can only begin to wrap our minds around the holiness, power, and mystery of God. "Now we see but a poor reflection as in a mirror; then we shall see face-to-face. Now I know in part; then I shall know fully, even as I am fully known" (1 Corinthians 13:12, NIV).

We will greatly desire to know some things, but God in His infinite wisdom will withhold them, primarily because we are not ready for the higher revelation. Jesus told His disciples, "I have much more to say to you, more than you can now bear" (John 16:12, NIV). "There are secret things that belong to the LORD our God, but the revealed things belong to us" (Deuteronomy 29:29, NLT). Nevertheless, if we call on Him with honest hearts, He will answer us and tell us great and unsearchable things we do not know (see Jeremiah 33:3). With this in mind, let us inquire with confidence, believing that as we seek to know He will open to us His wisdom and revelation based on where we are in our present journey with Him. And as we continue to pursue Him and grow in intimacy, He will eagerly disclose more and more.

I want to know God. I want to know Him every day in a fresh way, recognizing and understanding the wonders of His character, heart, and plans. I want to know not only the warm-hearted and tender parts, the parts I feel comfortable with, like the gentle Shepherd or the endearing Friend. I also want to know Him as the Lion of Judah—that great Warrior and King whose holiness and righteousness makes me tremble before Him. I want to know Him—all of Him! I want to love Him—all of Him, even the parts that scare me. How about you? Do you ache and long to know more? Do you yearn with an unquenchable hunger and thirst to know the One who knows you and longs to have an intimate and personal relationship with you?

In Jeremiah 9:23-24, the Lord said, "Let not the wise man glory in his wisdom, let not the mighty man glory in his might, nor let the rich man glory in his riches; but let him who glories glory in this, that *he understands and knows Me*, that I am the LORD, exercising loving kindness, judgment, and righteousness in the earth. For in these I delight." (NKJV, *emphasis mine*)

In our quest to know God more intimately we will need to go about our pursuit in the right way. It is not in our own knowledge, might, and wealth that we will come to know God the way He desires for us to know Him. We cannot rest on the assurance or assumption of what we think we know about God. The pursuit to gain a higher revelation of Him will go beyond what we are capable of, what we can think, recognize, or imagine. Therefore, I encourage you to keep an open heart and mind, and prepare, each day, to draw closer to God in a fresh way.

During our first week together, before we dive into our ultimate quest to know and understand God, let's take some time to lay a little groundwork. This week we are going to look at what it will take to know God, understand our motives for pursuing Him, and come head-to-head with some of the fears that can hinder our quest, or keep us from jumping in with both feet. And finally, in Day Five, we will examine the fruit that is birthed through a person who knows God.

Isaiah 43:10-13, NIV

"'You are my witnesses,' declares the LORD, 'and my servant whom I have chosen, so that you may know and believe me and understand that I am he. Before me no god was formed, nor will there be one after me. I, even, I, am the LORD, and apart from me there is no savior. I have revealed and saved and proclaimed— I, and not some foreign god among you. You are my witnesses,' declares the LORD, 'that I am God. Yes, and from ancient days I am he.'"

This week we will strive to:

Begin our pursuit with a firm foundation
"Devote yourselves to prayer" (Colossians 4:2, NIV).

Understand that knowing God begins at the cross
"Now this is eternal life: that they may know you, the only true God, and Jesus Christ, whom you have sent" (John 17:3, NIV).

Examine our motives
"All a man's ways seem innocent to him, but motives are weighted by the LORD" (Proverbs 16:2, NIV).

Understand the difference between appropriate and inappropriate fear
"The fear of the LORD is the beginning of knowledge" (Proverbs 1:7, NIV).

Determine the evidence of knowing God
"If a man remains in me and I in him, he will bear much fruit" (John 15:5, NIV).

Day One
You are My Witnesses

"You are my witnesses,' declares the LORD, 'My servant whom I have chosen that you may know and believe me, and understand that I am he" (Isaiah 43:10, NIV).

The endless desire of God's heart is that each of us know Him intimately, understand Him emotionally, and believe Him unconditionally. This is the will of God, and it has been the relentless pursuit of many who have sought to know Him. The Bible, both Old and New Testament, are filled with personal testimonies of those who knew God. Moses, David, Isaiah, John and Matthew, Paul and Peter—all penned firsthand accounts through the inspiration and empowerment of the Holy Spirit (see 2 Peter 1:20-21), recording the experiences of the One they came to know and recognize as their Father; their Bridegroom; their Shepherd; their Healer; their Redeemer; their Friend; their King, and their God. Like these men, and many others, we, too, are to be witnesses of God so we may know Him personally, believe Him with absolute resolve, and understand His heart.

Let's begin with a prayer to the One we desire to know, and then read Acts 1:1-9 and answer the following.

What did Jesus call His apostles in verse 8?

My witnesses

The apostles witnessed many things when Jesus was with them. What did they witness from these verses alone? Be specific.

Jesus presented himself alive to them after His suffering, appearing to them 40 days, spoke to them, stayed with them, spoke of the kingdom of God, commanded them to wait for the promise of the Father which was the Holy Spirit

As witnesses, what were they to do?

Share the good news of Christ. Share their first-hand knowledge of Christ to draw others to Christ

A *witness*, according to *Webster's Dictionary*, is "testimony; one who, or that which, furnishes evidence or proof; one who has seen or has knowledge of incident; …to be witness of or to; to give evidence; to testify"[1] A witness is someone who has seen, heard and experienced for themselves. A witness is not someone who reads an article in the newspaper and then takes the witness stand to give evidence on behalf of a case or person. That would be ridiculous, wouldn't it? Yet, this is exactly what we do when we only read our Bibles void of the relationship, and then say, "We know God."

The Bible is full of wonderful, firsthand accounts of the glory, majesty, strength, and love of God, but unless we experience these things for ourselves the Bible can simply be words on a page. We can learn incredible truths about God's character in studying the testimonies of those who have witnessed, and then lived to tell about it. But, reading and studying is only part of the equation. The apostles saw, heard, and, as in the witness of John—touched God.

Read 1 John 1:1-3:

How do these verses give us testimony of firsthand accounts?

They saw, looked on and touched with their hands Life made manifest, testify to it, seen & heard is repeated.

What was the reason for John's proclamation? What was he hoping the reader would gain?

That others would have fellowship with Christ & His Father

Who had John and the other disciples witnessed? Who was their fellowship with?

Jesus Christ and God the Father

John testified to what he and the other disciples witnessed. He shared their experiences so that, we, too, may come to know for ourselves the richness of fellowship with God. The word *fellowship* according to *Vine's Concise Dictionary of Bible Words*, *(koinonia)* means "communion, fellowship, sharing in common;" *(koinonos)* means "a partaker or partner; to become; that ye should have communion with."[2]

In what ways do you partake of communion fellowship with God?

Prayer, reading & study of His word

Although it is possible to have fellowship with God in a variety of ways, there are two primary ways we commune with God: Prayer and His Word. Without these two critical elements the relationship will not grow. Therefore, let's look at each of these two essentials for fellowship, so we may be challenged to grow in our communion with God, increasing our awareness to witness Him for ourselves.

Prayer:

Through prayer, the Holy Spirit opens the door for intimate communion by opening our hearts to receive God's love. We will look more intently at the word communion and what it means to commune with God through the Holy Spirit in Week Four; but, for now, understand that communion is vital to our relationship with God.

What instructions do the following verses give us about prayer?
Ephesians 6:18: *To do it at all times; on behalf of fellow Christians*
Colossians 4:2: *steadfast, watchful, thankful*
1 Thessalonians 5:17: *without ceasing*

Day One: You are My Witnesses

Learn to see prayer for what it really is—a gift from God. Too often many of us treat prayer as a sacrifice, a duty, something we're supposed to do as Christians. We don't see the value of prayer, because it has become a burden rather than a delight.

If you haven't already learned how to devote yourself to prayer and pray without ceasing, ask God to teach you. Consciously make the choice to connect with God throughout your day in prayer. Prayer does not always have to be formal. Pray while you drive in your car, do the dishes, shop, stand in line at the store, whatever you are doing, in your heart talk with the Lord. Also, keep in mind, like any form of communication, prayer is a two-way dialogue. Don't approach prayer with the attitude that you need to do all of the talking. Do pour your heart out to the Lord, but also take the time to listen.

Record the words of Psalm 46:10 below:

Be still and know that I am God I will be exalted among the nations I will be exalted in the earth.

All too often we quit praying the minute we finish rattling off what is burdening us. If we want to *know* God we must learn to be still, silent (NLT), and cease striving (NASB) so we will know that He is God. We need to quiet ourselves before Him and listen as He imparts His love and wisdom into us.

My life radically changed when my prayer life changed. When I began to pursue God in intimacy through the wonders and ecstasy of communion prayer, my passion and zeal for the Lord increased greatly. As a result, I began to pray more. I began to travail more. I began to experience God more. Because of the change in my prayer life, my relationship with Jesus skyrocketed, taking us to new highs of closeness, producing a level of power I never knew existed.

How has your life radically changed as a result of intimacy in prayer?

Total dependency; knowing that nothing happens unless I do w/ Him first.

Jesus was very passionate about prayer. In John 2:12-17 and Matthew 21:12-13 we see two accounts of Jesus coming into the temple courts only to find many other things going on—things other than prayer.

Read both of these accounts, and in your own words, explain why you think Jesus became angry when the people turned away from using the temple as a place for prayer.

They defiled the purpose of the temple.

If we are to truly know God, we must, first and foremost, get a revelation about prayer. J.I. Packer wrote in his book, *Knowing God*, "People who know God are before anything else people who pray, and the first point where their zeal and energy for God's glory come to expression is in their prayers."[3]

In Psalm 69:9 the psalmist states: "... zeal for your house consumes me."
How about you? Does the zeal of prayer burn in your heart? Why or Why not?

Hunger for God. Yes, because d/Knowing is the way the Truth and the Life.

Let us challenge ourselves every day to strive for deeper levels of intimacy in prayer. Let us endeavor to accept nothing short of deep, passionate prayers of pure worship. Prayer and worship go hand-in-hand—we cannot have one without the other. If we separate them, all we offer God is a list of demands. If we only come to God to offer up our petitions and requests, we are missing out on the most wonderful part of prayer. God is the source of all pleasure; and through prayer, we experience the pleasure of His love. Prayer is one of the most profound instruments of worship that we have been given. Let's utilize it to the max!

God's Word:

The second primary element of communion with God is Scripture.

Read Psalm 19:7-11 and complete this sentence checking all that apply.

God's Word is…

- ✓ Perfect
- ✓ Sweeter than honey
- ✓ Worth more than gold or silver
- ✓ Gives sight
- ___ Incomplete
- ✓ Trustworthy
- ___ Confusing
- ✓ Gives joy to the heart
- ___ Hard to understand
- ✓ Wisdom
- ✓ Right
- ✓ Steadfast

Read Psalm 1:2-3:

What insight does verse 2 give us about the Word of God?

It is a delight, we should meditate on it day and night

What are the benefits for following these instructions in verse 3?

Ever flow of God's love, drawn others to Him (Christ) and will not wither - or go away.

Meditating on the Word that is perfect, trustworthy, right, and sweeter than honey, means to chew on it, take it in, savor it, and allow it to dwell within you. You can meditate on the Word while you sit quietly before the Lord pondering and concentrating on a particular verse. And you can meditate on the Word as you go about your day. The main goal is to allow the seed of God's Word to take root by allowing the verse(s) to penetrate every part of your being, applying it to your life and letting it change you. If you want to be like that tree planted by steams of water that prospers, yields fruit, and does not wither, you need to come every day to feast on, delight in, and savor the Word of God.

Day One: You are My Witnesses

The Bible gives us all the information we need to know God. However, part of the problem is many of us do not take the time to dive into the Word; or, we divorce Scripture from the Holy Spirit, who is the great Interpreter of the Word. Only by putting the two together can we hope to know and understand God.

When you sit down to read and study your Bible, do not come with only your book—come with God. Then as you read, find great joy in the Word of God. Look at the Scriptures and cut them up into little pieces. Look up definitions and dissect each word for clarity and insight. And, as you do this, pray for the Holy Spirit to open your spiritual eyes, so you may see more of His wonders as you delight in knowing Him better.

Perhaps right now, you may be thinking: *Why are we covering basic topics? I thought this study was going to be challenging.* Beloved, without the fundamental basics we cannot hope to know God and draw near to Him. Without the steady diving into God's Word and the intimacy found only in prayer, our pursuit of God will be limited.

Through the wonders and joy of intimate prayer and Scripture, we have the two main elements necessary for intimate fellowship, and an incredible opportunity to know God. Therefore, let's take this journey together without hindrance or assumption. Let's take up our shovels and dig in His Word together in order to find the answers we seek to know. Let us dare to know God more through the fellowship of intimate prayer with the Father and the Son through the Holy Spirit.

Beloved, this is just the beginning. As we come after God with all our heart and soul, He will be faithful to give us the revelations of His person, and He will share the secrets of His heart. He will give us tender opportunities to snuggle up to Him the way John did at the table during the last supper (see John 13:23), so that we may experience the tender-hearted and loving Christ. As we cry out for wisdom and seek it as for hidden treasure (see Proverbs 2:2-6), the Holy Spirit will open our eyes to see the riches of His glory, so we may behold the wonder and majesty of His magnificence. And as we humble ourselves before Him, yearning to surrender to the power and omnipotence of our awesome God, I believe He will knock us off our axis in complete awe and wonder as we *witness* the authority and magnitude of His greatness.

> End today's lesson by meditating on Romans 11:33-36. Share with God your longing to know Him more, and to fellowship with Him in intimate communion.
>
> *The words of these verses are my prayer and desire to know the ways. To gain the riches of wisdom thy Lord has for me. To chase what He is calling me to and to live in reckless abandon for the One who gave it all to me & for me.*

Day Two
They Will Know Me

"Now this is eternal life: that they may know you, the only true God, and Jesus Christ, whom you have sent" (John 17:3, NIV).

Yesterday we began our pursuit of knowing God with the basics—prayer and the Word. We must understand that without the fundamental basics, our fellowship with God will be limited, and we will not become the powerful witnesses God desires for us to be. Today, as we continue to lay the groundwork for our quest to know God, we will recognize that it is impossible to know God the Father without first knowing the Son.

> Pray for God to increase your fellowship with Him through intimate prayer and His Word, then read Matthew 11:27 and John 6:44-46. What do these verses tell us about knowing God the Father and His Son?

_____

_____

According to *Webster's Encyclopedia of Dictionaries* the word *know* means "to be aware of; to have information about; to have fixed in the mind; to be acquainted with; to recognize; to have experience; to understand..."[4] A synonym for the word know is "be familiar with." According to *Webster's* the word *familiar* means "intimate; ...free; unconstrained; well-known; current; covenant with; close acquaintance."[5]

> Based on these definitions, how would you describe your relationship with God? How *familiar* are you with God the Father and God the Son?

_____

_____

_____

The Holy Trinity (Father, Son, Holy Spirit) know each other with great familiarity, and they desire to share this same kind of familiar relationship with us. God desires for us to recognize and experience Deity to the point that we are so familiar with Him that it becomes intimate. To the point where we are free in our relationship with Him; unconstrained and unhindered to worship Him, understanding Him and His heart to where we never doubt Him. Continually believing that He has our best interest at heart, even if we don't understand what He is doing. And finally, He wants us to embrace a covenant with Him—the ultimate union—a bond of extreme relational connection.

> According to Psalm 105:8, how long will the Lord remember His covenant?
> ____ A thousand years
> ____ Until we mess up
> ____ Forever

Read Jeremiah 31:31-34:

What is the promise the LORD made? (v.31)

_____

How will this new promise be better? (v. 33)

_____
_____

What statement does the LORD make in verse 34? Check the correct response:

____ "Man is ignorant and unable to teach his neighbor or brother about me"

____ "Man is wicked, his teaching of me would be impure"

____ "Man will know me, from the least to the greatest"

According to Ezekiel 36:26-27 and 1 Corinthians 2:9-16, how will God fulfill His promise made in Jeremiah 31:33-34 to know Him?

____ By giving us everything we desire

____ By filling our heads with facts

____ By giving us His Holy Spirit

What does 1 Corinthians 2:14 tell us about the man who does not have the Spirit?

_____

This is not to say we no longer need the wisdom of our Pastors or Bible study teachers, those who help us grow in the Word and mature as a disciple of Christ. What I am saying is: We need God to know God. The covenant relationship that the Holy Trinity offers us is unfathomable. It is a relationship of fellowship that God was determined to have with mankind since the beginning of the world. But, if we are to truly know God, we must first recognize the covenant relationship that He desires to share with us through His Holy Spirit.

Adam and Eve were the first to ever experience knowing God in covenant relationship.

Read Genesis 2:18-25:

How did God form the original covenant marriage? What took place?

_____
_____

What specifically happened to Adam?

_____

What took place between Adam and Eve?

_____

Compare the covenant marriage between Adam and Eve in Genesis 2:23-24 with Ephesians 5:31-32. How is the first marriage covenant similar to the New Covenant? What does the original marriage covenant represent in relation to the New Covenant?

_____

Who is this New Covenant between?

___ Adam and Eve

___ Christ and His church

___ God and the Israelites

Now compare Genesis 2:21-23 with John 19:34 and Luke 22:19-20. What similarities do you witness between Adam and Jesus? Check all that apply:

___ Both of their sides were pierced

___ Both had their flesh broken

___ Blood poured from both of their sides

What was the result of their broken bodies, pierced sides and spilt blood?

_____

Eve came from Adam, and the Bride came from Christ. "For this reason a man will leave his father and mother and be united to his wife and the two will become one flesh. This is a profound mystery—but I am talking about Christ and the church" (Ephesians 5:31-32, NIV).

Fill in the blanks according to Hebrews 7:22 (NIV):

"Because of this oath, _____ has become the _____ of a better _____."

Fill in the blanks according to Ephesians 1:13 (NIV):

"And you also were included in Christ when you heard the word of truth, the gospel of your _____. Having believed, you were marked in him with a seal, the _____."

We were created to know God (Father, Son and Holy Spirit) through a personal, covenant relationship formed in the heart of God, set in place upon the cross of Calvary, and sealed with the Holy Spirit. Upon the cross, through the broken body, shed blood and pierced side of Jesus Christ, God put the New Covenant into place and made a way for sinful men, who do not know him, to come to Him. All men—young and old, Jew and Gentile, from every tribe, tongue and nation—now have an opportunity to know God (the Trinity) through the sacrifice of Jesus. And by giving those who repent and fully embrace salvation through Jesus' sacrifice (see Acts 3:19; 4:12) the indwelling Holy Spirit (see Ephesians 1:13), God (The Trinity) made a way for us to know Him personally, a relationship that can be so familiar, so intimate, that we begin to know Him like we know no other. Jesus said, "Now this is eternal life: that they may know you, the only true God, and Jesus Christ, whom you have sent" (John 17:3, NIV).

This covenant relationship, which is written on our hearts and minds by His Spirit, should be our ultimate aim. Knowing God should be the best thing in life. Knowing God the Father, God the Son, and God the Holy Spirit in every aspect of relationship should be our greatest joy. Remember, I am not speaking about knowing *of* God. We may have been reared in the church, even learned about God through our parents and other family members, but until we make Him our own, until we come to know Him for ourselves through intimate relationship, we do not know Him at all.

If you desire to know God (Father, Son and Holy Spirit), you must first come to the cross and know Jesus Christ as your One and Only Savior and Lord (see Romans 10:9-13). In order to know God, the deep things of God, the mind of God, the heart of God through His Holy Spirit, you must first come to God the Son.

> If you have not yet come to the cross to repent of your sins and turn to God by receiving His grace through faith in Jesus Christ, please do so now. The Bible says, if we repent and be baptized in the name of Jesus Christ for the forgiveness of sins, we will receive the gift of the Holy Spirit (see Acts 2:38). And First John 1:9 says, "If we confess our sins, he is faithful and just and will forgive us our sins and purify us from all unrighteousness" (NIV). Use the space below to earnestly share your heart with Jesus and confess your need for Him. You will not know God any other way than through Jesus Christ.
>
> _____
>
> _____
>
> _____
>
> If you have already committed yourself to Jesus as your personal Savior and Lord, please recommit to knowing God through this innermost and ultimate covenant relationship. There is far more to this relationship with God than we could ever ask or imagine, and utter submission and complete surrender is key to discovering more. Pen your heartfelt prayer below:
>
> _____
>
> _____
>
> _____

If this is your first time responding to Jesus at the foot of the cross, receiving God's gift of grace through faith (see Ephesians 2:8-9), please contact me or share with someone who can help you grow in faith. I am grateful beyond words to have this opportunity to help you know God through this Bible study; however, this is just the beginning of a lifelong journey of devotion with Jesus. It is important that you learn how to "continue to live in Him, rooted and built up in Him, and strengthened in the faith" (Colossians 2:6, NIV). You must now begin to receive sound doctrine, from both God's word and a local body of believers, so that you may "grow in the grace and knowledge of our Lord and Savior Jesus Christ" (2 Peter 3:18, NIV).

Day Three
Getting It Straight

*"All a man's ways seem innocent to him, but motives are
weighted by the LORD" (Proverbs 16:2, NIV.)*

We have spent the last two days laying some foundational groundwork, reiterating the importance of daily fellowship with God through initiate prayer and the Word, and understanding that the path to knowing God, and sharing in covenant relationship with God, begins at the cross of Calvary. Today, we are going to evaluate the purpose for our pursuit.

> Before we begin, let's pray for the Holy Spirit to reveal the true motives of our hearts, then spend some time meditating on and answering the following questions.
>
> Why do I attend church? What am I searching for?
>
> _____
> _____
>
> Why do I pray? Why do I read my Bible?
>
> _____
> _____
>
> What is it I hope to get out of this Bible study?
>
> _____
> _____
>
> Why do I desire to know God?
>
> _____
> _____

We, as believers, all have some kind of connection with God. Most of us pray, read our Bibles, and even go to church on a regular basis, but many of us still have no depth of relationship with God. Why? Before we begin our pursuit of God, it is important to determine what we are after.

Today's lesson may ruffle a few feathers, including mine, but let me begin by saying that I believe each of us desires to have a closer relationship with God. God has implanted, in each of our hearts, a hunger—a deep longing to know Him—that is why we are now in "hot" pursuit of Him. However, we cannot allow our pursuit of God to be merely for our personal gain.

God wants us to know Him, to pursue Him, to love Him in spirit and in truth (see John 4: 23-24); but, all too often, our quest for "spiritual growth," if not tempered with God's love, can turn our hearts cold with religious attitudes, turning our desires to know

God into misconceptions about our relationship with Him. When this happens it is because we are pursuing Him with wrong motives.

Fill in the blank according to James 4:2-3, NIV:

"You want something but don't get it. …You do not have, because you do not ask God. When you ask, you _____ _____ _____, because you ask with _____ _____ _____, that you may spend what you get on your pleasures."

Our pursuit of God is not, and never will be, about us, so that we may receive from God purely for our own personal gratification. If we are, in any way, approaching our quest with wrong motives, we will not receive what we long for, the relationship will be hindered, and we will not become the witnesses God intends for us to be. This is not to say He doesn't want to reveal Himself to us in our needs or desires. God greatly delights in being our soul's wellspring of satisfaction. What I am saying is that none of us can be selfish or self-focused in our pursuit. With this in mind, let's consider each of the questions you answered at the beginning of this lesson.

"Why do I attend church?" and "What am I searching for?"

Just the other day I met a woman who claimed that she and her family have been looking for a church for eight years, for as long as they have lived in the area. My first thought was to invite her and her family to my church, and I did invite her son to join us at our VBS the following week; but still, even with my invitation, my spirit felt unsettled. What I should have asked was: "What are you searching for?"

Anyone who has been church hopping for eight years is looking for something and not finding it. Some may have a specific need, others may not even be aware they have a need, they just feel empty.

Hear my heart; I am not discouraging anyone from seeking out a church family. And there are genuine reasons to leave a church. What I am saying is we must stop running from church to church expecting them to fill us. That is not the role of the church. Only God can fill us and feed us. Church is not a shot in the arm, quick fix, and I'll see you next week program. We must cease looking for some kind of experience, some spiritual rush, a Sunday morning fix that will sustain us until next Sunday, because when we do not receive what we are hoping to find, we will leave hungrier and more dissatisfied than when we arrived.

Read Ephesians 4:1-16:

In your own words explain what you believe Ephesians 4:1-4 is communicating to the church.

___

___

What does Ephesians 1:22-23 call the church? Check the correct answer.

___ A waste of time

___ A building

___ Christ's body

As different parts of one body, what is each member given and why? (v.11-13)

How is the church held together? (v.16)

What is the purpose of unity and why is it important?

Gauge your response: How often do I go to church and expect the pastor, my Sunday school teacher, or leadership to feed me and fill my spiritual needs?

Every Week

Never

So, if there is one body, one Spirit, one Lord, one faith, one baptism, one God and Father of all, then why are we running from church to church? And once we get there, why do we think the church is supposed to fill us and feed us? We are fitted for God's purposes. He has equipped each of us to be a functional part of the church, His body, for a specific reason. As a church we are to come together corporately to pray and worship in unity, to encourage one another and build each other up in love. We come together as a body to be equipped for the benefit of giving to others and to glorify God (see 1 Corinthians 12:7-11). Yes, we do want to be challenged by the Word on Sunday mornings, but this should be happening all week. We don't eat once a week to sustain our physical bodies, so why do we think we should eat once a week to sustain our spiritual souls? Church should be the cherry on top of the incredible Sundae we have shared with God all week.

Our attitudes about church can keep us from knowing God. If we are spiritually hungry, and complaining the church is not feeding us, we have a misconception about the role of the church. It is great to be hungry—we need to be hungry for God. However, in order to fill this hunger, we need to be in communion with God, receiving from Him all week. Then, as we receive from Him, we need to allow what He deposits into us to find an outlet through church service and community outreach. Church is not a "bless me" club. Church is intended to help us become more like Jesus, so through us Jesus can reach a lost and hurting world.

"Why do I read my Bible?" and "Why do I pray?"

Another wrong motivation can be how we treat the Bible and prayer. As we saw in Day One, these are the basic fundamentals for solid communication for fellowship with God, helping us grow closer to Him in intimacy. We must search the Scriptures to know God, not just to receive from God. We must spend time in prayer so that we can draw closer in fellowship, not just offer up our petitions and requests. We must stop treating God's Word and prayer with pomp and pretense, outwardly looking like we are in pursuit of God when we really aren't. When we do this, when we simply go through the motions in order to make others think that we are in pursuit of a godly life, we forsake the joy found in intimate communion and revelation.

What does Isaiah 29:13 say about those who pursue God outwardly but do not pursue Him inwardly?

_____

_____

Read Revelation 3:14-18:

What does the Spirit of Christ say to the church of Laodicea in verses 15-16?

_____

_____

The church at Laodicea thought they had it all together. They thought they were spiritually content, thinking they didn't need anything, so they didn't pursue it. Yet, what does Christ call them in verse 17? Check all that apply:

___ Beautiful ___ Righteous ___ Wise
___ Wretched ___ Pitiful ___ Blind

Don't fool yourself. As long as you are on this earth, you should never be fully content in your pursuit of Christ. Don't think for one minute you can kick back and relax in your pursuit of Deity. Also, don't think this pursuit will be some kind of joyride and that the journey will be easy. The pursuit to know God is not like some get rich quick scheme. Reading your Bible infrequently, or spending five minutes a day throwing out popcorn prayers of want and need will not do. This is going to take an investment of time and energy, on all our parts, to know the richness of His sweet companionship, coming to know Him in the covenant familiarity we talked about in Day Two. We have got to take our pursuit seriously and not be lukewarm about it.

"What is it I hope to get out of this study?" and "Why do I desire to know God?"

What you hope to gain from this study, most likely, will be a personal thing, one that is just between you and God. But do analyze your heart. Are you taking this study for personal gain? Do you desire to know God for your benefit or for His? Do you want to get something from God? Are you pursuing Him in order to genuinely know Him, or are you only after what He can give you? You know when you are seeking the benefits of God, and not God Himself, when you turn away from Him when things don't go your way. When you get angry because God doesn't respond the way you want or think He should, or He doesn't give you what you desire when you want it, then your motivation is in the wrong place.

Seeking God as a means for getting things from God will not work. God wants to be your one and only treasure. Not one of many treasures, or even the most important treasure. God desires to be your all-in-all, anything short of that is what the Bible calls idolatry. Anything you take away from this Bible study, or any Bible study, must be for the glory of God and for the joy of knowing Him intimately. Anything He graciously deposits into your spirit, whether through His Word or His Holy Spirit in fellowship, is for the glorious purpose of truly knowing Him, and so that others may witness Christ through you.

> Remind yourself what Jesus called His disciples in Acts 1:8: _____
>
> What was the purpose of them being His witnesses?
> _____
> _____

God calls us His witnesses so we may know Him, believe Him, and understand that He, and He alone is God (see Isaiah 43:10-12). God is our heavenly Father, our Bridegroom, our Shepherd, our Friend, our Redeemer, our Healer, our Warrior and our Coming King, but do we truly understand what God is after in sharing all of these relational connections with us? He wants and longs for us to strive daily for the sheer delight of getting to know Him the way He knows us. Then, we are to take what we have witnessed through our relationship with God and tell the world, so that, they, too, may know, believe, and understand that He is God.

Beloved, God should be your life's pursuit. He is what you are searching for. He is the reason you read your Bible. He is the reason you pray, the reason why you go to church—it is about Him—all about Him! If you are in pursuit of God for any other reason, you are completely missing the mark.

You might be feeling a little hammered right now, but let me encourage you—the pursuit of God will not be easy, but it will be worth it. Please do not think that I am condemning you. Paul tells us in Romans 8:1, "There is now no condemnation for those who are in Christ Jesus" (NIV). The point is: If you desire to know God, you must take your pursuit seriously. You must indulge in the fellowship of prayer and the delight of digging in His Word, and you must stop expecting the church to do all the work. In your pursuit of Deity, you must get your priorities straight.

> End today's lesson by recording anything the Holy Spirit has revealed to you. Are there any areas in which falseness of relationship or wrong motives have crept in? Pray and ask Him to help you overcome, and to set you on the right path of knowing God for His purposes and glory.

Day Three: Getting It Straight

Day Four
The Fear of the Lord is the Beginning

"He will be the sure foundation for your times, a rich store of salvation and wisdom and knowledge; the fear of the LORD is the key to this treasure" (Isaiah 33:6, NIV).

Yesterday we took a little time to examine our hearts and ask ourselves some tough questions. Today we need to take a little time to look into our hearts to see if there is anything else that is keeping us from fully embracing our quest to know God. I don't mean sin, unforgiveness, or even legalism. Most of us know these things will keep us from the communion fellowship John described in 1 John 1:1-3. Rather, I am referring to fear. The Bible tells us that perfect love drives out fear, and that if fear exists in us, then we have not been made perfect in love (see 1 John 4:18). In other words, we haven't received a revelation of Christ's love.

Let's begin by asking Christ to help us overcome any fear that is hindering us by revealing His perfect love to us, in us, and through us.

During the course of my journey with Christ, I have come to realize that knowing God will cost me something. Even in writing this Bible study, before I began, I sensed that the privilege would come at a great cost. Going deeper with God comes with a price. In order to go up, we must first go down. We must be willing to dig deep, to set aside everything that hinders, and devote ourselves to our pursuit.

Sometimes, when I stop and think about what this quest will cost me, it overwhelms me—even terrifies me—but one thing is greater than my fear: My desire to be close to Him. The truth is, no matter the cost, I am willing to pay the price because I have experienced enough to know that nothing—absolutely nothing—is better than drawing closer to God.

> How about you? Are you willing to allow your desire to know God to be greater than your fear? Are you willing to pay the price? Take the risk? Invest the time? Are you willing to do whatever it takes to know God intimately?
>
> ___ YES   ___ NO   Why or why not?
>
> _____
>
> _____

Building a relationship with God, like any relationship, will take commitment and time. The sad reality is not everyone will be willing to take the risk or make the commitment, because fear will overrule their desire to know God. Not everyone will be willing to make the investment of time that is required to come closer to God; because, in their minds, it will cost them more than they are willing to give.

The depth of your relationship with God is in your hands. How close you come to Him will depend greatly on how much you are willing to risk for the sake of your pursuit. The quality and satisfaction of your pursuit to know God will be determined by the level of commitment and priority that you give it. Therefore, if you allow fear and other excuses to come between you and your relationship with God, you will not achieve the deep satisfaction of knowing Him in intimacy.

Fear, whether appropriate or inappropriate, will affect our pursuit of knowing God. *Webster's Encyclopedia of Dictionaries* defines *fear* as "alarm; dread; anxiety; reverence toward God; to regard with dread or apprehension; to anticipate a disaster; to hold in awe; to be afraid."[6] I find it interesting that sandwiched in between inappropriate fears, we find appropriate fear.

> What do the following verses teach us about the appropriate "fear of the Lord"?
>
> Proverbs 1:7: _____
>
> Proverbs 15:33: _____

The word *knowledge* according to *Webster's Dictionary* means "direct perception; understanding; well informed." The word wisdom according to Webster's means "knowledge and the capacity to make use of it."[7] Knowledge is what we know, and wisdom is the ability to use what we have learned. Through an appropriate fear of the Lord we are given a level of knowledge and wisdom we would not possess otherwise. This is why approaching God with appropriate fear is the beginning of knowing God.

> What do these verses teach us about the fear of the Lord? Fill in the blanks according to Proverbs 10:27 and 14:27 (NIV):
>
> "The fear of the LORD _____ _____ _____"
>
> "The fear of the LORD is a _____ _____, turning a man from the snares of death."

The fear of the Lord not only brings wisdom and the knowledge of God, but it also brings life. According to these scriptures, appropriate fear is like a fountain, a wellspring of life gushing up from inside of us. Appropriate fear of the Lord helps us to experience the abundant life Jesus spoke of in John 10:10.

On the other hand, inappropriate fear, our own man-made fears, can cause us great harm and distress; trapping us, holding us prisoner, keeping us from the freedom to be all of who we are meant to be in Christ.

> What man-made fear is listed in Proverbs 29:25a? What does this fear bring?
>
> _____
>
> _____
>
> What question does Galatians 1:10 ask?
>
> _____
>
> _____

The fear of man, in any shape or form, is an inappropriate fear. Jesus said, "Do not be afraid of them. Do not be afraid of those who kill the body but cannot kill the soul. Rather, be afraid of the One who can destroy both soul and body in hell" (Matthew 10:26; 28, NIV).

Day Four: The Fear of the Lord is the Beginning

There are two distinct types of fear: appropriate fear and inappropriate fear. List examples of both.

Appropriate fear:

_____
_____
_____
_____
_____
_____
_____
_____
_____
_____
_____

Inappropriate fear:

_____
_____
_____
_____
_____
_____
_____
_____
_____
_____

However, there is something else we need to recognize and understand, just as there is appropriate fear of the Lord, there is also inappropriate fear of the Lord. An inappropriate fear of the Lord will hinder us and keep from drawing near to God.

Read Exodus 19 and Exodus 20:18-21:

From these verses we can see examples of how both appropriate fear and inappropriate fear of the Lord can manifest in our lives. From the list below, place an "A" for appropriate fear and an "I" for inappropriate fear, next to each statement.

____ Obeying the Lord and honoring His covenant (19:5)

____ Preparing for your encounter with the Lord (19:9-11)

____ Following the Lord's instructions (19:12-16)

____ Trembling in fear (19:16; 20:18)

____ Staying at a distance (20:18)

____ Receiving teaching from the pastor or Sunday school teacher but not desiring to hear from God yourself. (20:19)

____ Letting the fear of the Lord keep you from sinning (20:20)

The Lord does not want us to be terrified and afraid of Him as the Israelites were when they stayed at a distance in Exodus 20:18-21. Rather He wants us to know Him with awe and wonder (see Psalm 33:8). He wants us, in the Holy Spirit's power, to obey Him and keep His covenant, so that, we, like Moses, may have the privilege of approaching the cloud where God is. Our goal is to know God, and according to Psalm 25:14, God "confides in those who fear him; he makes his covenant known to them" (NIV).

Ponder Proverbs 8:13. Why can God trust His covenant secrets to those who fear Him? Check all that apply.

____ They hate what He hates

____ They resist pride and arrogance

____ They are in tune with God

An appropriate fear of the Lord cultivates in us the heart and mind of God. Appropriate fear of the Lord will give us the opportunity to know Him as never before, because it will bring us so close to the heart of God that we will develop His nature and character.

Beloved, the fear of the Lord is not apparent in some kind of spiritual facial expression. It is not evident in the way we dress, or the tone of voice we use in prayer; nor is it displayed through various acts of religious rituals. God is after covenant fellowship. He wants us to hate what He hates, to resist the things that will cause separation, and to be in tune with His heart.

End today by pondering 1 John 4:18. Identify any inappropriate fear(s) you are carrying that is keeping you from a closer relationship with God, then pray and ask the Holy Spirit to cultivate in your heart an appropriate fear of the Lord.

_____
_____
_____
_____
_____
_____
_____
_____
_____
_____
_____
_____
_____

No inappropriate fear is worth holding onto if it stands in the way of you drawing near to God. Right now, stop and ask the Holy Spirit to help you let go of every hindering fear. I know this may be difficult, but remember it will be worth it. Witnessing that sacred mountain on fire with His manifest presence may look scary, the sound of His voice may seem intimidating, but know what Moses understood—His presence is glorious!

God is a wellspring of life, a storehouse of wisdom and knowledge, and He desires to share it with you. But remember, the key to obtaining this treasure is the fear of the Lord (Isaiah 33:6). Now, if you are with me, let's continue forging ahead, zealous with an appropriate fear of the Lord (see Proverbs 23:17), so that we may *know* God.

Day Five
The Evidence of Knowing God

"We know that we have come to know him if..." (1 John 2:3, NIV).

For most of my life I went through the religious motions of saying the right things at the right time. I stood when they told me to stand, and knelt when they told me to kneel. I memorized prayers, took communion, and even confessed my sins; yet, in reality, there was no tangible evidence that I knew God.

Today we are going to consider the evidence of knowing God. How do we know we are on the right track? What fruit is produced in our lives that offers proof that we know God?

Let's pray to exhibit the fruit of knowing God in our lives, and then please read John 15:1-8 and answer the following:

How are we able to bear fruit?

___

What happens if we do not remain connected to the vine? (v. 6)

___

What is the evidence of remaining connected to the vine? (v. 8)

___

Once again we see that the basics for communion fellowship are essential. Remain in me (prayer) and my word remains in you (Word of God) and you will produce much fruit. So, what is the fruit that will be produced? What evidence will be revealed in us and through us that reveals we know God?

Who do you know who you believe knows God? What characteristics do you see in this person that leads you to believe that he/she knows God?

___

J.I. Packer, in his book, *Knowing God*, claims that the evidence of knowing God is great energy for God; having great thoughts of God; showing great boldness for God; and having great satisfaction in God.[8]

What truth and insight! Anyone who is in earnest pursuit of an intimate relationship with the Lord God Almighty is going to be passionate for Him with a high level of energy. I have seen people, in the midst of the assembly, worshiping God with their entire being. I have listened as some believers proclaim the word of God with vast vigor and zeal. These people, who have great energy for God, seem to never grow weary or tired of pursuing God and proclaiming His goodness. And this enthusiasm shows through their worship and work for the Lord.

I can see how anyone who knows God is going to continually ponder His greatness, and be consumed by persistent thoughts of His splendor. They are awestruck to the point that their view of God goes beyond words. They are overcome by His majesty and humbled by His omnipotence.

Beloved, our perception of God is everything. How well we know God will be determined by what we think of Him. How we think of Him will determine how we proclaim Him, praise Him, and pray to Him.

People who know God are going to be bold for God—not perfect—but bold in the Holy Spirit's power. Scripture offers us unbeatable examples of this kind of boldness in the Spirit. There were many men and women, mere mortals, who, in the Spirit's power did great things. One of the things I love best about the Lord is how He uses ordinary people to do extraordinary things. None of the people in the Bible were any different than you or me. They were ordinary people, full of weakness, insecurities and failures; yet, God made them bold instruments of His glory.

And finally, Packer tells us that knowing God will bring "great satisfaction in the Lord." In Psalm 43:4, David called God "his joy and delight." Therefore, yes, I would have to agree—those who know God take great pleasure in God, and find fulfillment for their souls. They seem to radiate with His joy and abound in His goodness. This is not to say that these people do not have any problems; rather, they have come to a place in their pursuit of God where He has become their ultimate and complete source of fulfillment (see Psalm 63:5).

Knowing God is wonderful; and I agree with Packer—those who know God intimately will produce the evidence of knowing Him. Yet, one day, as I pondered the fruit that is obvious in the life of a person who knows God, the Lord took me into His Word and showed me another list, other examples of proof that will reveal whether or not someone knows God.

> First John will be our main text today. You may wish to mark this place in your Bible since we will refer to it often in our study.
>
> Read 1 John 1:1-10:
>
> Earlier this week we determined that the Apostle John was a valid witness who saw, heard, and testified to the Word of life. With this in mind, let's consider his testimony as evidence.
>
> Fill in the blanks according to 1 John 1:5, NIV:
>
> "God is _____; in him there is no _____ at all."
>
> What does John say about the person who walks in darkness, yet claims to have fellowship with God? (v.6)
>
> _____
>
> In verse 7, what is John's first proof of evidence that a person knows God?
>
> _____
>
> What did the Apostle John testify about Jesus in John 1:4-5?
>
> _____
>
> Why do you think those who walk in darkness do not understand the light?
>
> _____

"There it was—the true Light [was then] coming into the world [the genuine, perfect, steadfast Light] that illuminates every person. He came into the world, and though the world was made through Him, the world did not recognize Him [did not know Him]. But to as many as did receive and welcome Him, He gave the authority (power, privilege, right) to become the children of God…" (John 1:1-10; 12, AMP). If we know God, we are not going to walk in darkness; we are going to walk in the light. We are not going to look like the world who does not know Him.

According to 1 Corinthians 3:1-3, who is acting worldly?

___ Nonbelievers   ___ Some Christians

How can this be? If we claim to be Christians, followers of the Lord Jesus Christ, how can we still be walking in darkness? If we know Him, we are going to begin to reflect His light and take on His appearance—we are going to look like Him. Jesus said, "I am the light of the world. Whoever follows me will never walk in darkness, but will have the light of life" (John 8:12, NIV).

Read Matthew 5:14-16:

What does Jesus call His disciples in Matthew 5:14?

_____

What does He tell us to do with the light?

_____

What will happen as a result of the light produced in us? What is the evidence or fruit?

_____

Please turn back to 1 John and continue reading verses 2:3-6. What does John tell us is the second evidence of knowing God? (v.3)

_____

What does John call the man who says, "I know God," but does not reveal this evidence?

_____

Fill in the blanks according to 1 John 2:6, NIV:

"Whoever _____ to live in him _____ _____ as _____ did."

According to Philippians 2:5-8, to what degree did Christ Jesus walk in obedience?

_____

What was Christ's attitude?

Are we picking up a theme here? The Apostle John tells us, if we know God we are going to take on the characteristics of God. We are not going to look like the world; instead, we are going to look like Jesus who is the Light of the world. And now John tells us that if we know God, we are going to have the same attitude as Christ and be obedient to His will and commands.

John states in his epistle: "Whoever says, I know Him [I perceive, recognize, understand, and am acquainted with Him] but fails to keep and obey His commands (teachings) is a liar…. But he who keeps (treasures) His Word [who bears in mind His precepts, who observes His message in its entirety], truly in him has the love of and for God been perfected" (1 John 2:4-5, AMP).

John made it clear. Those who know God will have a deep desire to be obedient to His Word—period. This doesn't mean they will be perfect in their walk with God and never make mistakes, but it does mean that those who know God will produce the evidence of keeping His commands and will yearn to walk in His ways—just like Jesus.

What is the next evidence of knowing God that John names in 1 John 4:7-8?

The characteristics of obedience and love actually tie together. Look again at 1 John 2:5, "But he who keeps (treasures) His Word [who bears in mind His precepts, who observes His message in its entirety], truly in him has the love of and for God been perfected" (AMP, emphasis mine). If we love God, we are going to obey God—if we obey God, we show our love for God.

How does John 14:23-24 confirm this?

How do you see the evidence of obedience as a type of love language between you and God?

Obedience is one of God's primary love languages (see John 14:23). If we are truly passionate for God, truly desiring to know God, then we will want to make decisions that please Him. We will want to be obedient. Not out of duty or obligation, but out of love for Him. If we do not have the desire to please Him, we are not showing God we love Him—we are not revealing the evidence of knowing Him. According to the Apostle John, if the characteristics of Jesus are not evident in our lives, in the way we love God and others, then we do not know God.

Day Five: The Evidence of Knowing God

What command did Jesus give in John 15:12?

_____

This command can be overwhelming, I know, but let me take the pressure off of you. We are to love as Jesus loved us. He tells us in John 15:9, "As the Father has loved me, so have I loved you, now remain in my love" (NIV). With the love we receive from God we are to love others, even the unlovable. We can only do this in the power of God. We are able to love beyond ourselves only because God first loved us and revealed His love to us (see 1 John 4:19). Beloved, you need God to love God and others. Only through the power of the Holy Spirit working in you can you hope to love and be obedient.

The Apostle John said that if we know God, then the love of God will be evident in us, because God is love (v.4:16). If we claim to know God, and claim to know the love of God, yet, we do not show love, then, again John calls us liars (v.4:20).

According to Galatians 5:22, what is the first fruit of the Spirit?

_____

Paraphrase what you think John is communicating in 1 John 4:13 and 16:

_____

Basically, John is saying, "If a person does not bear the fruit of the Spirit (love), then he/she does not know God because he/she either does not have the Spirit of God dwelling in them or he/she is not submitted to the Spirit, because God is love and anyone who knows God loves.

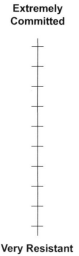

Gauge your level of commitment to obedience:

Extremely Committed

Very Resistant

Before we conclude, we need to recognize one more important reason for obedience to God. What other motivation do we have for being obedient just like Jesus? Check the best response:

____ So we can know that God is in control

____ So we can have joy all of the time

____ So we may receive God's power and authority

Do you realize that one of the greatest purposes of obedience is authority? One of the reasons God asks us to obey Him is so that He can give us His power. Scripture bears witness to great power and authority in Jesus' earthly life and ministry, because He was completely submitted to the Holy Spirit, fully committed to doing the will of the Father. Immense power and divine intercession await those who are obedient to the Word of the Lord.

God entrusts His invincible power to those who submit to His Spirit, because they are the ones who demonstrate that they love Him.

List the evidence of knowing God according to the Apostle John.

1. _____
2. _____
3. _____
4. _____

According to John, the evidence of knowing God is revealed when we look and act like Jesus. So, let us follow Jesus and strive to walk as He did (v.2:6). Let us put ourselves in a posture to receive from Jesus, being filled with Jesus, so that we may look like Him. Jesus said, "If you remain in me and I remain in you, you will bear much fruit." (see John 15:5). When we fellowship with God, abiding in Him and He in us, as John testified, we will bear the fruit of His likeness. We will become like Jesus, and this will give great glory to God. Then, my friend, you can testify that you know God.

End today by meditating on John 15:5, 8. List the fruit that is being produced in your life as evidence of knowing God. Thank God for His desire to reveal Himself to you and through you.

_____
_____
_____
_____
_____
_____
_____
_____
_____
_____
_____
_____
_____
_____
_____
_____

Apply the Knowledge

In my pursuit of God this week, the Holy Spirit has shown me …

_____
_____
_____
_____

The verse that spoke to me the most this week is…

_____
_____

In order to make this verse a reality in my life, I…

_____
_____
_____
_____

The changes I need to make in order to make knowing God more of a priority in my life are… Lord God, help me to…

_____
_____
_____
_____

The hidden treasure (see Isaiah 45:3) of His Person and personality God revealed to me this week is… This higher revelation of God's presence profoundly awakens me to…

_____
_____
_____
_____

Witnessing God this week has changed my perspective of God from… to…

Holy Spirit, help me to apply what I've learned to my everyday life, so…

Prayer for the Journey

Lord, God, I want to know You in the richness of deep genuine fellowship. Give me a deeper understanding of the longings of Your heart to know and to be known in a covenant relationship. Help me to recognize the cost involved in drawing close to You; yet, at the same time, show me the priceless and unfathomable value of relationship with You through the bonds of intimate communion. Give me wisdom and revelation to know You better, that I may bear the fruit of our relationship for Your glory…

Apply the Knowledge

Session One
Called to be a Witness

Ezekiel 1:1; 4-5; 22-28—2:1-8—3:1-11

*"This was the appearance of the
likeness of the glory of the LORD.
When I saw it, I fell facedown, and heard the voice
of the one speaking (Ezekiel 1:28b, NIV).*

To be faithful witnesses we…

1.) Must keep God in His _____

_____ . (Ezekiel 1:22-28)

2.) Must testify with _____ and

_____ . (Ezekiel 2:1-8)

3.) Must testify with what God _____ us. (Ezekiel 3:1-11)

4.) Cannot allow our _____ to get in the way of our testimony. (Ezekiel 3:14)

5.) Cannot give way to being _____ or allow those feelings to _____ us. (Ezekiel 3:15)

Week Two
Know That I AM Your Father

One of the greatest joys I have discovered in my journey with God is His role as my heavenly Father, and my role as His princess daughter. This may sound silly because I am an adult now, but I still need to be a little girl—a daughter who is honored and adored. One who finds joy in the presence of a Father who takes great delight in simply being with her. You might even come to the conclusion that I am crazy, if I were to share with you some of the tender moments the Father and I have shared. Nevertheless, I see myself as that little girl, a princess of privilege, a precious daughter who is absolutely treasured by her heavenly Father beyond all the riches of earth.

It wasn't always this way. I didn't always see myself as a princess of the Most High God. I didn't feel the liberty in our relationship to snuggle close to His heart and delight in the sound of His voice. For many years, I kept my distance from my heavenly Father, certain that He was anything but pleased with me. I was afraid of Him—and not with that appropriate fear we talked about in Week One. I often believed He was angry with me, or that He was watching me with a keen eye, just waiting for that moment when I would misstep so He could bring down the hammer of conviction.

But the truth of the matter is, God the Father is nothing like what I made Him out to be. He is not an angry Father who can't wait to pounce upon one of His children the minute he or she makes a mistake. Rather, He is a tender-hearted and caring Father who knows exactly how to reach each of His children in the midst of heartache and pain. He knows how to draw each of us into His loving embrace and make us whole.

In order to reach me, Papa (that's what I call Father God), takes me in His arms and tells me stories. When this happens, I am like a little girl lost in His hugs. As I close my eyes and sit quietly, I feel the warmth of His embrace. It is then I can see myself in the Spirit sitting on Papa's lap as He holds me close and speaks tenderly to me. His delightful stories, which always seem to fit the present season I am in, capture my heart as I listen intently. It is here that I begin to feel safe and loved, valued and treasured as a daughter.

At first, one may not understand, or see the value of such child-like stories. After all, why would the Sovereign God of the Universe take the time to tell someone, anyone, a story? But the truth is Papa is a storyteller. He told stories while He was here on earth in the form of His Beloved Son, and He still tells stories today. Frankly, at first I didn't understand the whole reasoning behind the stories myself; until one day, as I heard the sound of my own laughter I realized—He was healing me.

Father God longs for each of His children to receive the revelation of how special they are to Him. He longs with great tenacity for the moment when one of His beloved children finally let's go of his fear long enough to reach out to a Father who loves him and cherishes him. He waits with great anticipation for the day when one of His darling daughters receives the wisdom that she, too, is a princess in His presence, as she finds the freedom to come and curl up in His arms next to His heart.

You are that cherished child of God. Let go of whatever misconceptions you might be holding on to and draw near, so that you may know Him as your loving and tender heavenly Father.

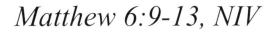

Matthew 6:9-13, NIV

*"Our Father in heaven, hallowed be your name,
Your kingdom come, your will be done
on earth as it is in heaven.
Give us this day our daily bread.
Forgive us our debts, as we also have forgiven our debtors.
And lead us not into temptation,
but deliver us from the evil one."*

This week we will attempt to:

Know the Father through Jesus
"No one comes to the Father except through me"
(John 14:6b, NIV).

Witness the Father's purpose
"This is to my Father's glory that you bear much fruit…"
(John 15:8, NIV).

Understand the Father's heart
"I have longed to gather your children together,
as a hen gathers her chicks under her wings…"
(Matthew 23:37, NIV).

Recognize a Father's love
"…the LORD disciplines those He loves…"
(Proverbs 3:12, NIV).

Receive the Father's gift
"…wait for the gift my Father promised,
which you heard me speak about"
(Acts 1:4, NIV).

Day One
Jesus—the Only True Witness

*"No man has ever seen God at any time; the only unique Son,
or the only begotten God, Who is in the bosom [in the intimate presence]
of the Father, He has declared Him [He has revealed Him and
brought Him out where He can be seen; He has interpreted Him
and He has made Him known]" (John 1:18, AMP).*

As we begin our pursuit this week to know God more intimately as Father, let's begin with prayer and ask the Spirit of Truth to reign in us, so we may be true witnesses of the Father.

Read 2 Peter 2:1-19:

What do each of the following verses in 2 Peter tell us about false witnesses?

2:1: _____

2:2: _____

2:12: _____

2:15: _____

2:18: _____

2:19: _____

Taking into consideration what we determined in Day Five of last week, and the verses found in 1 John 4:5-6, how can we know the difference between a false witness and a true witness of God?

_____

_____

Fill in the blanks according to Proverbs 12:17, NIV:

A _____ _____ gives _____ testimony, but a _____ _____ tells _____.

What does our opening verse, John 1:18, tell us? Check all that apply.

___ It is impossible to see God

___ No one has seen God the Father except the Son

___ Jesus has made the Father known

Jesus is the true witness (see Revelation 3:14). He is the only begotten Son of God, who has seen and heard, from the most intimate place of His presence, and His ultimate mission is to make the Father known. Jesus desires to declare Him, to reveal Him, to interpret

Him, so that, we, too, may truly *know* the Father for ourselves, becoming, like Jesus, a true witness of God.

According to *Webster's*, the word *declare* means "to proclaim; to make clear; to state publicly; to state in the presence of a witness."[9] The word *reveal* means, "to make known; to expose; to make public." And the word *interpret* means "to explain the meaning of; to translate orally for the benefit of others."[10]

With this in mind, read John 14:5-14, our main text for today.

What is the only way we have access to the Father?

_____

How did Jesus say we would know the Father? (v. 7)

_____

What did Philip ask of Jesus? (v. 8) Why do you think he asked this?

_____

_____

Paraphrase Jesus' response to Philip's request?

_____

_____

What does Jesus' response to Philip tell us about Jesus and the Father? Check the best response:

____ Jesus longs to make the Father known

____ Jesus and the Father are one

____ Jesus only makes the Father known to those who believe Him

Jesus said, "Don't you know me, Philip!?" Isn't it amazing how we can walk with Jesus, talk with Jesus in prayer, go to church and study His word, and still not know Him? And according to Jesus, if we do not know Him, we do not know the Father. Jesus said, "Anyone who has seen me has seen the Father" (v. 9).

What question did Jesus ask Philip in John 14:10a? Check the correct response:

____ Didn't you hear what I said?

____ Don't you recognize me?

____ Don't you believe?

In response to Philip's query to see the Father, Jesus first responded to Philip with, "Don't you know me?" And then He asked, Philip, "Don't you believe…?" The word *believe* means "to regard as true; to trust; to have faith."[11] In order to know God, we must believe

Day One: Jesus—the Only True Witness

God. In Week Three, as we discover more of God as our Friend, we will go into more detail about believing God; but, for now, understand that in order to truly know God as Father, or in any aspect of the relationship, you must believe. It is not enough to believe *in* God, you must *believe* God. Believe what He reveals to you, and then, have the faith to put that revelation into practice in your everyday life.

Jesus said, "Believe me when I say that I am in the Father and the Father is in me; or at least believe on the evidence of the miracles themselves" (v. 11). During His earthly ministry, Jesus performed many miracles—everything from turning water into wine at the wedding in Cana (see John 2:1-11) to raising the dead (see John 11:38-44; Luke 8:40-56; Luke 7:11-17). And everything He did brought glory to God the Father in order to make Him known. I believe Jesus still performs miracles today, and one of His greatest miracles is the uniting and transforming work of the Holy Spirit in the lives of those who believe Him.

What miracle is taking place according to 2 Corinthians 3:18?

___

Look again at John 14:11-14:
What did Jesus say anyone who believed Him and had faith in Him would do?

___

How is this possible? (v. 12b)

___

What is Jesus' ultimate goal? (v. 13)

___

To know God is to become one with God through Christ, who is the true and faithful witness. I am not saying we become God or that we have equality with God, but as we submit more and more (dying to self) to the Spirit who is at work within us we become more and more like Jesus. By the power of the Holy Spirit we become one with God in Christ which gives us the power and ability to be Jesus to those around us, doing even greater things, all for the glory of God the Father.

The word *glory* means "renown..."[12] Renown is fame, recognition, reputation, character. The purpose of every miracle Jesus did was to point to the Father and make Him known—His character and reputation—so others could know Him and praise Him.

And now Jesus, the only true witness who is the image of the invisible God (see Colossians 1:15a), is at work within us by His Holy Spirit, consuming all who believe Him and have been crucified with Him (see Galatians 2:20), transforming them into His image (see 2 Corinthians 3:18) becoming one with them in Spirit (see 1 Corinthians 6:17). "For in Christ all the fullness of the Deity lives in bodily form, and you have been given fullness in Christ..." (Colossians 2:9-10, NIV).

In Christ, by the power of the Holy Spirit, you are given the power to know the Father and become His witness, so that you may declare, reveal, and interpret the Father to others, just like Jesus.

> Read John 17:20-26:
> How do these verses pull it all together for us? Check all that apply:
> ___ Jesus, the only true witness, who knows the Father intimately, comes from the Father
> ___ Jesus and the Father are one
> ___ Jesus makes the Father known
> ___ Believers become one with God through Jesus Christ (also see Colossians 3:3)
> ___ Believers come to know God and make Him known to the world through Jesus Christ

"You are my witnesses,' declares the LORD, 'and my servant whom I have chosen, so that you may know and believe and understand that I am he'" (Isaiah 43:10, NIV). Therefore, let us ask to be completely consumed by the Spirit and transformed into the image of Jesus, so we may know the Father. Let's submit to the miracle that is taking place within us, and then let's take Jesus up on His promise in John 14:14, "You may ask me for anything in my name, and I will do it."

> End today by sharing with the Father your desire to know Him better, to know Him in the intimacy of His presence, so that you may become a true and faithful Christ-like witness for the sake of His glory.

Day One: Jesus—the Only True Witness

Day Two

My Father the Gardener

"I am the true vine, and my Father is the gardener" (John 15:1, NIV).

Let's begin today's lesson by praying for the pruning work of the Father to be done in our lives, and then read John 15:1-8.

In verse one, what does Jesus call the Father?

_____

What does a gardener do? List as many things you can think of:

_____   _____
_____   _____
_____   _____

I do not know much about gardening. I am not a gardener. The landscaping in my front yard was put in by professionals, and my backyard boasts of almost no landscaping at all. I simply do not know what to do. I was not born with a green thumb. Plants do not always do well in my care. I know I need to water them, and when I have the time I go out into the yard and pull weeds—basic stuff. But when it comes to creating, designing, and really making the garden look beautiful, I'm at a loss. I have, however, watched gardeners in action. When my family and I lived in Dayton, I had a neighbor who was meticulous about his yard. Whenever I was outside, I would see him in his yard weeding, watering, trimming, tying up the plants that had gotten too large—it was a lot of work!

In this parable found in John 15, Jesus compares the relationship with the Father through the aspects of gardening. Jesus is the vine, we are the branches, and the Father is the Gardener. This gives us the mental picture of a garden, or at least a very large bush. The Father is the one who does the work tending to the garden (or bush), caring for all of its agricultural needs. We, the branches, need the Father's loving care, and we need the nourishment of the vine.

What is the spiritual implication made in John 15:4-6? What happens to a branch that is not connected to the vine?

_____

Building on what we studied yesterday in Day One, how do these verses in John 15 give us another interpretation of oneness with God through Jesus Christ?

_____
_____

According to verse 8, what is the purpose of fruitfulness?

_____

Recall from Day One, what was the definition for the word glory?

_____

If we are not connected to the Vine—joined with Christ—submitted and yielded to His will, we will not produce fruit or the evidence of knowing God. In other words, we will not bring the Father glory (renown), making Him known.

Oh, what a beautiful picture this parable portrays of the Father's loving care and tenacity, all for the benefit of producing fruit in our lives that will ultimately bring Him glory. Jesus is the vine and each of us are the various branches, and together we make up the Father's garden (the church). And like any garden, we come with an array of colors, textures, and beauty. We are oaks of righteousness, plantings of the Lord for the display of His splendor (see Isaiah 61:3b); yet, at the same time, we need constant attention in order to keep the garden full of productivity, and to keep the weeds and other unwanted debris to a minimum. The good news, the Father is a dedicated gardener and fully up to the task.

With our mental picture of a garden in place, taking into consideration its many needs, let's look at the Father's gardening style. In verse 2, what did Jesus say about the Father? What is the purpose of pruning?

_____

_____

According to *Webster's* the word *prune* means "to cut off the dead parts; to remove any thing superfluous."[13] Pruning sounds painful, doesn't it? But as painful as it may be, pruning is necessary. Think about an overgrown garden; it's not very pretty is it? Some bushes tend to be so large you can't see some of the other plants in the garden. The garden's appearance is messy, cluttered, and revealing little fruitful vegetation. In the same manner, the Father's garden needs to be cleaned up in order to remove anything that does not beautify and enhance the garden.

Consider Colossians 3:5-17, what are some of the things that must be pruned from the garden (the church). Then list some of the things God desires to grow in His garden.

Prune	Grow
_____	_____
_____	_____
_____	_____
_____	_____
_____	_____

As a result of the Father's gardening, what will come forth and bring glory to God? (vv. 15-17). Check all that apply:

____ Peace

____ Thankfulness/gratitude

____ A joyful heart

____ Praise to God

____ Other: _____

For this lesson, due to my lack of gardening skills and knowledge, I needed to do a little extra homework. As I studied tips on gardening, I learned some new terms, such as, "pinch back." In this procedure, the gardener pinches off the growing tips of the plant which forces new growth.

Jesus said, "He cuts off every branch in me that bears no fruit, while every branch that does bear fruit he prunes so that it will be even more fruitful" (v. 2). Pruning not only removes the unwanted and unnecessary parts of the plant, but it also allows the plant to produce new growth, making it even more fruitful.

Pruning transforms our lives and the lives of others. What needs to be pruned in your life or ministry in order to make it even more fruitful?

_____

_____

_____

_____

As we grow and mature in the Father's garden, we also need to understand that there is more work that needs to be done, other than pruning. The Gardener must also take the time to remove any unwanted weeds from the garden as well. Jesus said, "Every plant that my heavenly Father has not planted will be pulled up by the roots" (Matthew 15:13, NIV).

When I think of the weeds that clutter my life, I think about the wounds from my past—those hurts that keep me from flourishing. Yet, even though some of those wounds go down deep into my soul, God will dig just as deep, in order to get to the root of the problem. I believe that is one reason why Father God takes me back to a place of being a child again (as I mentioned in the introduction of this week). By allowing me to be that little girl curled up on His lap, He can get to the root of the problem and heal it from its point of origin.

Fill in the blanks according to Psalm 147:3, NIV:

"He (God) _____ the brokenhearted and binds up their _____."

Psalm 34:18, NIV:

"The LORD is _____ _____ _____ _____ and saves those who are crushed in spirit."

Share about a time when the Gardner pulled up an infectious weed from its roots in your life.

_____
_____
_____
_____

According to Matthew 13:24-26, where else can weeds come from?

_____
_____

Infectious weeds can also come from the enemy of our soul. If we accept the enemy's lies and allow them to grow, his lies can bear false witness and take root in our hearts. If we believe the enemy over the word of the Gardener, who plants His seeds of righteousness, we will become so cluttered our lives will not bear fruit.

I have a dear friend who has been walking with the Lord for more than 30 years; yet, she repeatedly believes and accepts the lies of the enemy. She continually makes negative comments about herself and her walk with Jesus, convinced she is no good and that the Lord cannot possibly be glorified through her life.

If you can relate to my friend in any way, use the space below to expose the lies and then allow the seeds of God's truth to abolish those lies. God's word is the only true seed, and the only seed we should allow to take root in our hearts.

_____
_____
_____

Can you think of another source where infections weeds can come in and clutter the garden?

_____

List some of the lies we can receive from the enemy that will hinder new growth?

_____
_____
_____
_____
_____
_____
_____

Infections weeds, like the seeds of a dandelion blowing in the wind, can come into our lives. The good news is we can make the conscious decision to refuse to receive those seeds, and many of the bad influences the world tries to plant into our hearts and minds.

Life change comes when we allow the Gardener to have total access to our lives, so He can beautify our gardens. Go to God in prayer and ask Him to prune you of the things that are keeping you from being abundantly fruitful. Ask Him to dig up the weeds that clutter your life.

Day Two: My Father the Gardener

The Father desires to produce abundant fruit in your life—fruit that will reap a harvest and glorify Him. His love for you is tenacious, and He will do whatever it takes to make you fruitful, revealing Himself to you, in you, and through you.

End today by meditating on John 15:5, 16. How does the parable of the Gardener, the vine and the branches help you to connect better with God as Father?

_____
_____
_____
_____
_____
_____
_____
_____
_____
_____

Day Three
The Heart of the Father

"O Jerusalem, Jerusalem…how often I have longed to gather your children together, as a hen gathers her chicks under her wings…" (Mathew 23:37, NIV).

Let's pray to know the Father's heart, then read Luke 15:11-27 and answer the following:

Shortly after the younger son had received his share of the estate he left home. Why do you think he left the care of his father's house?

_____
_____

What happened after the son was out on his own? Check all that apply:
____ He spent all of his money on immoral living
____ There was a severe famine and the son began to go hungry
____ The son got a job as a hired man feeding pigs and still didn't have any food

Verse 17 says, "When he came to his senses…" What did the son realize about his current situation? How would life have been different at his father's house?

_____
_____
_____

In verse 18, what did the son decide to do?
 ____ Stay where he was
 ____ Travel to another far off place
 ____ Return to his father's house

Based on what the son rehearsed in verses 18 and 19, what do you think he expected when he arrived home? What did he think his father's reaction would be?

_____
_____
_____

What actually happened? How did his father respond to him? Check all that apply:
 ____ His father ignored the fact he was back
 ____ His father rebuked him and told him to go back to his sinful lifestyle
 ____ His father no longer considered him his son
 ____ His father ran to him and welcomed him home with great affection
 ____ His father adorned him with garments and jewelry
 ____ His father fed him and had a great party in his honor

Why do you think the father reacted this way, even though his son left home, squandered his wealth, and did sinful things?

_____
_____

Compare the love and compassion that this father had for his wayward son to our heavenly Father, what similarities do you see? What does this story tell you about the heart of the Father?

_____
_____

Have you ever felt like the wayward son? You are under the care and protection of the Father, but the world suddenly appeared better; so, you set out for what you thought were

Day Three: The Heart of the Father

greener pastures. Or perhaps the separation happened unknowingly. One day you were enjoying the presence of the Father, and then suddenly you woke up and found yourself away from His fellowship and out from under His protection. You didn't mean for it to happen; life got busy and the relationship began to take second place. It really doesn't matter how the separation happened, or why. What matters is that the Father is waiting and longing for your return.

There are many things I love about God, but one of the sweetest things I have come to recognize is that even though I am far away I can always return. At any time, I can come to the Father, confess and repent of my sins, and He will run to me, throw His arms around me, and welcome me back home, safe and sound under the protection of His wings. This was a wonderful discovery for me to make about the Father, because I did not always feel this sense of access. I think it was because I had formed a stereotype about God. I was afraid of how He would respond to me. I believed He would be angry and harsh, so I found it difficult to go to Him.

> Have you ever felt this way? Have you ever not turned to God because you thought He would be angry or harsh? Did you ever believe the sins you had committed were too great for Him to forgive? Share your heart.
>
> _____
>
> _____

The good news is no matter what we have done, no matter how far we have strayed from the Father, by the blood of Jesus, we're always welcomed home. Christ's blood covers all our sins and waywardness. There is no sin you or I can commit where God cannot heal us, restore us, redeem us, and bring us back to Himself. However, we cannot stay away from home; if we are to receive His mercy, forgiveness and grace, we must be willing to come to Him.

> I love the compassion and tender heart of the Father expressed in Matthew 23:37. Fill in the blanks according to the NIV:
>
> "O Jerusalem, Jerusalem…how _____ I have _____ to gather your children together, as a hen gathers her chicks under her wings…" (Matthew 23:37).
>
> Read Psalm 91:1-4:
>
> How do these verses describe the protection and care of the Father's wings?
>
> _____
>
> _____
>
> What is the key to being covered by the Father's wings? What do we need to do in order to come under His refuge? (v. 1)
>
> _____

Like the wayward son who came to his senses and returned home to his father's care, we, too, must be willing to return home and dwell (NIV), live (NLT), with the Father so we can rest in the shadow of the Most High—protected, guarded, and cared for by God. Now, this is not to say we will never suffer or experience tragedy; but, when we are hit with the unexpected in life, we will be sheltered under His loving wings, held close to the Father's heart and nurtured by His constant care.

If you desire to have your heart, mind, soul and spirit protected and guarded by the shelter of His wings, then you must abide in His presence. You must walk with the Father daily, so close that you are walking in His shadow.

According to *Webster's Dictionary* the word *shadow* means "…inseparable companion; ghost; to cast a shadow over; to follow and watch closely."[14]

> With this definition in mind, paraphrase Psalm 121:5-8 in your own words.

Do you hear the heart of the Father? Listen, it is like He is saying: "Come to me and I will cover you with the shadow of my hand. I will be your inseparable companion, the Holy Ghost, who casts my shadow over you. I will follow you forever. When you come to me and dwell in my shadow I will protect you, guard you, and keep you safe from the scorching heat of the sun. I will make a vine grow over your head, and you will sit in its shade (see Jonah 4:6), nurtured by its fruit. In that day, you will delight to sit in my shade and taste the sweetness of my fruit (see Song of Songs 2:3), for my love is better than life (see Psalm 63:3). I will surround you with my over-shadowing faithfulness. I will watch over you by day and by night. I will be your constant companion who covers you and says to you, 'Do not be afraid; I will help you.'"

> End today by meditating on Psalm 63:7-8. How does the psalmist's prayer communicate the heart of the Father to you?

Day Three: The Heart of the Father

Day Four
The Love of a Father

*"My son, do not despise the LORD'S discipline and
do not resent his rebuke, because the LORD disciplines those he loves,
as a father the son he delights in" (Proverbs 3:11-12, NIV).*

I don't know about you, but understanding the Lord's discipline was hard for me. In fact, it was not always easy for me to experience the Father's discipline. Not that the chastisement made me feel unloved, quite the contrary. I think the struggle came out of my own experience with my earthly dad.

My childhood, in my eyes, was not an easy one. I was afraid of my earthly dad who was so strict and overindulgent in physical discipline I felt abused and unloved. Perhaps the punishments would not have been as bad if my dad had also revealed his love for me, too. But, in reality, I could count on one hand the number of times my dad had ever hugged me as a child. It wasn't that my dad was cruel. As it says Hebrews 12:10, NIV, "Our fathers disciplined us for a little while as they thought best...." What I realize now is my dad just didn't know a better way.

On the other hand, I am delighted to share with you that the Lord restored my relationship with my dad, and I no longer feel afraid or even resentful toward him for the discipline I received. Nonetheless, the relationship I had with my earthly dad affected how I saw my heavenly Father, and why, I think, I was afraid of being disciplined by the Lord.

How we see our earthly fathers, whether good or bad, affects our relationship with the heavenly Father. We may not always be aware of this fact; but, the relationship we share, or have shared, with our earthly dads carries a lot of weight. If we experienced negative reactions and treatment from our earthly fathers, it can cause us to shrink away from our heavenly Father. Our personal experience will turn into a mental and emotional block that can cause distance or total separation between us and the Father of love.

Briefly describe the relationship you had with your earthly dad as a child.

_____

_____

In what way(s) do you see this earthly relationship affecting your relationship with God the Father?

_____

_____

Regardless of where you are right now in your relationship with Father God, stop and pray for your relationship with Him to be made new. Ask God to help you let go of any pain you experienced from your relationship with your earthly dad. Ask Him to help you see and embrace His love for you.

Read Hebrews 12:4-11 and answer the following:

In verse 5, what did the writer of Hebrews call the discipline of the Lord when addressing his audience as sons (NIV) or children (NLT)? Check the correct answer.

____ As something to fear

____ As disheartening

____ As a word of encouragement

The discipline of the Lord is meant to be a word of encouragement. We may not see it that way when we are in the midst of a stern rebuke, but the Lord's discipline should bring us encouragement.

According to verses 6, why should we be encouraged?

_____

What does verse 8 call those who are not receiving the Father's discipline?

____ Lucky   ____ Well behaved   ____ Illegitimate

Anyone who does not know the discipline of the Lord does not belong to Him. Every human being on the face of the earth was created by God, but not everyone is a child of God.

How do the following verses distinguish who the children of God are?

John 1:10-13: _____

1 John 2:29-3:10: _____

Fill in the blanks according to 1 John 3:1, NIV:

"How _____ is the _____ the Father has lavished on us, that we should be _____ of _____! And that is what we are!"

Hebrews 12:6 told us that the Lord disciplines those He loves. Revelation 3:19 also confirms this form of the Lord's love? Write the verse below:

_____
_____

Revelation 3:19 was one of the greatest revelations of God's love for me. After a stern time of rebuke from the Lord, He sent me this verse telling me that He disciplined me because He loved me. It was like receiving a hug after being turned across Daddy's knee. And this revelation changed the way I viewed God. Because of the way I was dealt with as a child, it led me to believe that God would treat me the same way. Oh, I assure you, the discipline I received from the Lord was painful, and it lasted for two weeks. His rebuke

Day Four: The Love of a Father

came at me from every direction—from His word to the sermons at church—I could not escape it. Talk about feeling the rod of God. But after it was over, I cannot begin to tell you how a revelation of the Father's love came over me. I wept more over the revelation of His love than I did the time of discipline.

> Hebrews 12:10, NIV, says, "Our earthly fathers disciplined us for a little while as they thought best; but God disciplines us for our good, so that we may…" what? Complete the sentence:
>
> _____
>
> What will the Father's discipline also eventually produce in those who are trained by it? (v. 11) Check all that apply:
>
> ___ A resentful heart   ___ A harvest of righteousness   ___ Peace

The Lord's discipline brings forth holiness, peace, and a harvest of righteousness for those who submit to it; even though it may seem unpleasant at the time. The Amplified Bible takes this verse even further by stating Hebrews 12:11 like this: "For the time being no discipline brings joy; but afterwards it yields a peaceable fruit of righteousness to those who have been trained by it [a harvest of fruit which consists in righteousness—in conformity to God's will in purpose, thought, and action, resulting in right living and right standing with God]" (AMP).

Remember our ultimate goal is to know God. We do this by drawing near to God through His word and prayer, and by being transformed into the likeness of His Son, Jesus Christ, so that we produce His holiness, righteousness, and peace.

> What do the following verses tell us about holiness, righteousness and peace?
>
> Leviticus 20:7: _____
>
> Isaiah 32:17: _____
>
> Isaiah 42:6a: _____
>
> Isaiah 61:10-11: _____
>
> Philippians 4:7: _____
>
> Colossians 3:15: _____
>
> 1 Peter 1:14-16: _____

Holiness, righteousness and peace only come from God. He is the one who calls us to holiness and makes us holy. His peace rules in our hearts when we submit to Him, and we receive the peace of God that transcends all understanding. He adorns us with His robes of righteousness, and makes righteousness spring up in us. But this takes discipline.

One of the biggest mistakes most of us make is we do not draw near to God. And one of the reasons we do not draw near is because we think He is displeased or mad at us, and we don't want to experience His discipline. But also understand this about discipline—discipline does not always mean punishment.

The word *discipline* comes from the word *disciple*. A *disciple* according to *Webster's* is "one who received instruction from another."[15] The word *discipline*, according to *Webster's Dictionary* means "instruction; training of the mind, or body; subjection to authority; to train; to improve behavior by judicious penal methods."[16] I love the definition of *discipline* in *Vine's Concise Dictionary of Bible Words* which states: "saving the mind, an admonishing or calling to soundness of mind…a sound mind."[17] Beloved, is not peace the evidence of a sound mind? Oh, how I praise Him!

As disciples of the Lord, what else do we gain as a result of discipline?

Proverbs 12:1: _____

Proverbs 15:32: _____

When we embrace discipline, we embrace knowledge. When we heed the Lord's discipline we gain understanding. Without understanding, how else will we grasp the significance of knowing God?

How do these definitions change your attitude about the Father's discipline? What new insight have you received into the Father's heart?

_____
_____

End today by meditating on 1 John 3:1. How does knowing that the Father disciplines you because He loves you, and claims you as His son or daughter, encourage you? How has the Father revealed His love to you through today's lesson?

_____
_____
_____
_____
_____
_____
_____
_____
_____
_____
_____

Day Five
A Gift From the Father

*"If you then, though you are evil, know how to give good gifts
to your children, how much more will your Father in heaven give
the Holy Spirit to those who ask him!" (Luke 11:11-13, NIV).*

This week, in our journey to know God better, we have taken a look at the Father and our relationship with Him. We have seen that the only way we can have access to the Father is through His Son, Jesus. And we learned that in order to know the Father, we must first know the Son, who is one with the Father and makes Him known to us. We have yielded to the Father's pruning shears as He revealed His gardening style, and what He desires to produce in our lives. We witnessed the love of a father who rejoiced with great delight at the return of his wayward son, and the joy that belongs to our heavenly Father when we willingly come under the refuge of His wings, living in His shadow. And finally, we began to recognize the Father's love through discipline, so we may share in His holiness, produce His righteousness, and reap the peace that comes from a sound mind.

Today we are going to look at the most precious and powerful gift we receive from the Father—the Holy Spirit.

Let's begin by praying for the Father to increase our understanding of the work of the Holy Spirit, and then let's turn to the book of John.

> Read John 15:26-27 and answer the following:
>
> According to John 15:26, where does the Holy Spirit come from? Who sends the Holy Spirit?
>
> _____
>
> How does Jesus refer to the Holy Spirit in this verse? What do these titles or names tell you about the Holy Spirit?
>
> _____
> _____
>
> What does Jesus say the Spirit of Truth will do when He comes? (v. 26)
>
> _____

What a team. The Son makes known the Father; the Spirit and Father make known the Son. And here, in these verses, we see an example of Jesus telling us about the Holy Spirit, making known to His disciples the Spirit who comes from the Father.

> What instruction did Jesus give to His disciples in John 15:27?
>
> _____

Jesus said, "When the Counselor comes...he will testify about me. And you also must testify..." If we are to accomplish this command, we need the Holy Spirit. If we are to be the witnesses that God intends and desires for us to be, then we need be filled with the Spirit's power.

In Acts 1:8, Jesus said, "You will receive power when the Holy Spirit comes on you; and you will be my witnesses...to the ends of the earth" (NIV). This all-important gift from the Father (see Acts 1:4) infuses and inundates the believer with power. When this happens, we are able to share with those around us, testifying about Jesus with a boldness and joy beyond our human capabilities. God gives us, though His Holy Spirit, the power to know and understand Him, and He gives us the ability to be Christ's witnesses to the ends of the earth.

Read 1 Corinthians 2:6-16:

How does the Holy Spirit help us to know God?

_____

_____

"For who has known the mind of the LORD that he may instruct him? But we have the mind of Christ" (1 Corinthians 2:16, NIV). Let this verse sink in. What does it mean to you personally to have the mind of Christ through the Holy Spirit?

_____

_____

What does the Holy Spirit give to us, or help us to do? Check all that apply:

____ Discernment of spiritual truths

____ Understand the gift God has given us

____ Know and understand the things of God

____ The mind of Christ

No one knows a man's thoughts except the spirit man living within him, and no one knows the thoughts of God except the Holy Spirit. And God has given us His Spirit so we may know Him—His views, His desires, His heart, His plans, His will, His ways. Through the Holy Spirit we have been given everything we need to know God intimately. By His Spirit, God has revealed to us the secret wisdom, the wisdom that we were destined to receive before time began (see 1 Corinthians 2:7).

So, how do we live in the fullness of this all-important gift from the Father who helps us to know God, inundates us with power, and equips us to be Christ's witnesses? We know that every believer has received this gift from the Father (see Acts 2:38-39), but, not every believer is operating in the fullness of this gift. Let me put it this way: Every believer has the Holy Spirit; but, the Holy Spirit is not in control of every believer.

According to Ephesians 5:17-18, what is God's will for believers?

_____

We have a choice, to live as the world lives, under the influence of a worldly attitude; or, we can be filled with the Holy Spirit. Romans 8:5 says, "Those who live according to the sinful nature have their minds set on what that nature desires; but those who live in

Day Five: A Gift from the Father

accordance with the Spirit have their minds set on what the Spirit desires. The mind of sinful man is death, but the mind controlled by the Spirit is life and peace" (NIV).

It is the perfect will of the Father that we not only receive His gift of the Holy Spirit, but that we also come under His control, allowing His gift to flourish in our lives. Only by surrendering to the Spirit, coming under His influence, can we know the secret wisdom of God. Only by the Spirit's power can we be effective witnesses.

> What does Jesus say about the Holy Spirit in Luke 11:9-13? What instruction does He give for those who desire more of the Holy Spirit in their lives?
>
> _____
>
> _____
>
> _____

Do not settle for mediocre Christianity—ask for the Holy Spirit to infuse you with power. So much is offered to us in our relationship with Christ. The problem is many believers never ask for the Holy Spirit to overtake their lives. As a result, many do not walk in victory over sin, their minds are not at peace (see Romans 8:6), and their lives exhibit very little joy and love (the fruit of the Spirit, see Galatians 5:22).

Jesus said, "I have come that they may have life, and have it to the full" (John 10:10, NIV). Without the fullness of the Holy Spirit operating in our lives, we will not know this abundant life. Jesus wants to share everything with us—His power, His wisdom, His grace, His peace, His joy, all that He has, and all that He is. He wants us to have it—all of it—more than we could ask or imagine (see Ephesians 3:20).

> Read John 16:13-15:
>
> What did Jesus say the Holy Spirit will give us?
>
> _____
>
> _____

We really don't understand all of what we have been given through the Father's gift of the Spirit. All that belongs to the Father is Christ's, and through the Holy Spirit, Jesus will take from what is His and give it to us, if we are willing to submit and come under the control of the Holy Spirit. If we want to walk in the fullness of the Holy Spirit, then we must completely surrender our lives, coming under His influence, supremacy and authority. In order to receive all that is His, we must first come to a place in our relationship with God where we continually say, "All I have is yours."

> In John 17:10, Jesus gives us this example. Fill in the blanks according to the NIV:
>
> "_____ I have is _____ and _____ you have is _____."

In an act of submission, prior to going to the cross, Jesus says to His Father, "Everything I have, everything I am is yours; I belong to you. Therefore, everything you have, everything you are belongs to me." This is exactly the relationship Jesus wants with each of us. He wants us to daily come and offer up our mind, heart, will, and life—to completely give Him everything we have to give. Then, He, in turn, will give us all of who He is, filling us with the power of His Spirit, so we may know, believe and understand that He is God.

> End today's lesson by meditating on Luke 11:11-13. Pen your prayer to the Father. Ask Him to help you surrender everything, so you may be filled with His Spirit. Ask Him to make John 17:10, "All I have is yours, and all you have is mine" a reality in your life.

Apply the Knowledge

In my pursuit of God this week, the Holy Spirit has shown me …

_____
_____
_____
_____
_____

The verse that spoke to me the most this week is…

_____
_____

In order to make this verse a reality in my life, I…

_____
_____
_____
_____
_____

The changes I need to make, the hurts and attitudes I need to let go of, in order to embrace a more meaningful and affectionate Father—child relationship with God are… Father God, help me to…

_____
_____
_____
_____
_____

The hidden treasure (see Isaiah 45:3) of His Person and personality God revealed to me this week is… This higher revelation of God's presence profoundly awakens me to…

_____
_____
_____
_____

Witnessing God this week has changed my perspective of God from… to…

Holy Spirit, help me to apply what I've learned to my everyday life, so…

Prayer for the Journey

Father, show me who You are so that I may see You. Not as an earthly dad, but as my heavenly Father who loves me beyond words, who cares for my needs, and longs to shelter me under the warmth and protection of Your wings. Help me to know Your heart toward me. Permit me to see myself as You see me. Show me that I am Your beloved child, and that You long to hold me close to Your heart. Reverse the damage that has caused separation between us. Open my spiritual eyes so I can behold You like Jesus, the true witness of Your glory, so I may grow in the revelation of Your love for me…

Apply the Knowledge

Session Two
Love from a Father's Perspective

Ezekiel 11:8-9; 11-12; 16-20

*"I will execute judgment on you at the border of Israel. And you will **know that I am the LORD**, for you have not followed my decrees or kept my laws but have conformed to the standards of the nations around you" (Ezekiel 11:11-12, NIV).*

Four characteristics of relationship with the Father:

1.) The Father _____ or _____ away everything that is not of Him. (Ezekiel 11:8-9).

2.) The Father will _____ His children. (Ezekiel 11:17-18)

3.) The Father _____ those He loves.
(Revelation 3:19)

4.) The Father gives His children the _____ _____ _____ _____.
(Ezekiel 11:19-20).

Week Three
Know That I AM Your Friend

When I was a little girl, we moved a great deal, so it was hard for me to make friends. By the time I arrived at my new school, the kids had already formed their bonds of friendship. The kids in the neighborhood, well, they wanted to be my friend only when it was beneficial to them. I recall how the minute our pool would go up in the backyard it would draw the children in the neighborhood like flies to honey. All summer long we would have others to play with. However, the minute the pool was taken down, and put into storage for the winter months, those "so-called" friends would seemingly go into storage, too. Since we no longer had the attraction of the pool, the kids stopped coming over.

I remember one day in particular, I was nine years old and desperately longing for a friend—a true friend. I wanted a friend who would be there for me no matter what—a friend who would be sincere and not tease me or make fun of me. I wanted a friend who would come over and play even if I didn't have something to offer. That day, as I lay across my bed, sobbing into my pillow, I began to cry out, "I want one true friend; not two, or twelve, but one true friend. I want a friend I can laugh with, cry with, and share things with."

What I didn't realize, at the time, was Jesus wanted to be my friend. He wanted to be the one I laughed with, cried with, and shared everything with. Consequently, I went most of my life not realizing the longing in the Lord's heart for friendship with me.

John 15:9-15

*"As the Father has loved me, so have I loved you. Now remain in my love.
If you obey my commands, you will remain in my love, just as I have
obeyed my Father's commands and remain in his love. I have told you this
so that my joy may be in you and that your joy may be complete.
My command is this: Love each other as I have loved you.
Greater love has no one than this, that he lay down his life for his friends.
You are my friends if you do what I command.
I no longer call you servants, because a servant does not know
his master's business. Instead, I have called you friends
for everything that I learned from my Father I have made known to you."*

This week we will attempt to:

Realize God is our Best Friend
"…there is a friend who sticks closer than a brother"
(Proverbs 18:24).

Build face-to-face friendship
"The LORD would speak to Moses face to face,
as a man speaks with his friend"
(Exodus 33:11).

Witness His hand of friendship
Jesus, "a friend of tax collectors and sinners"
(Matthew 11:19).

Learn to be a good friend to God
"You are my friends if you do what I command"
(John 15:14).

Recognize His traits of friendship
"I keep asking that the God of our LORD Jesus Christ…
may give you the Spirit of wisdom and revelation,
so that you may know him better"
(Ephesians 1:17).

Day One
Embracing True Friendship

"Never will I leave you; never will I forsake you" (Hebrews 13:5b).

Friendship means different things to different people. Some have had the joy of lifelong friendships, while others know only the heartbreak of loneliness. This week, as we look into the heart of God and His desire to form the bonds of everlasting friendship, we will need to look at some tough issues. Just as our relationship with our earthly fathers affected our relationship with God, so have our earthly friendships. For this reason, we will attempt to give God the opportunity to get to the root of the matter by exposing our earthly friendships, whether good or bad, in an attempt to strengthen our friendship with Christ. This will be a beautiful week, but it may also be a challenging week. In order to experience healing, we need to face the hurt, betrayal, and heartbreak. And we must remember that Jesus is our Friend—a true Friend—who will not treat us as the world treats us.

Let's begin today's lesson by asking God to help us see Jesus more clearly as a true Friend. And then spend some time answering the following questions:

What does friendship mean to you?

What do you look for in a friendship?

Is there someone in your life you consider to be a good friend? What qualities or characteristics make this person a good friend?

What does Ecclesiastes 4:9-12 tell us about friendship? Check all that apply:
___ When two work together, more can be accomplished
___ If one stumbles, his friend can help lift him back up
___ We can find added strength when our friend is by our side

What does "A cord of three strands is not quickly broken" mean to you? (v. 12)

_____

_____

_____

The word *friend*, according to *Webster's Dictionary*, is defined as "one attached to another by esteem and affection; an intimate association; a supporter."[18] Synonyms for the word *friend* are comrade; companion; a partner. Friendship involves the idea of loving as well as being loved.

Friendship is a bond. It is an attachment to another, a joining of two hearts in intimate association. Think of a three-legged race. You know the game where two people are tied together at the leg or ankle, and together they try to move as one to the finish line. In order to be successful in the race, they must trust each other. They must lovingly guide, care for, support, and listen to each other as they work together. They need to share the responsibility in cooperating, while encouraging each other to keep moving forward.

Our partnership with God is very much like a three-legged race. In order to move forward we need to join with God in our spiritual journey. Friendship takes partnership. Friendship with God takes a divine partnership. You have your part, and God has His part. Your portion is to seek after God, to seek His face through His Word and union with His Spirit. God's role is to draw you closer, and to equip you through His Word and the divine power of His Spirit. You were created to partake of a divine friendship with God. You were fashioned just for Him, and to know Him through the intimate bond of friendship.

Regrettably, many people do not know the richness of friendship with God. This is largely due to the fact that they, in their earthly relationships, have suffered all kinds of hurt, betrayal, and adversity. What they need to understand is God is not human; therefore, He will not react like humans. People are not perfect. They can hurt us deeply; some unknowingly, but they can, through their disloyalty to the relationship, cause a wedge that can hinder our friendship not only with them, but with God. As a result, we treat God as if He were the one who hurt us.

All of us have known people in our lives who were not true, authentic friends. Consider the following verses, how can those we call friends hurt us?

Psalm 41:9: _____

Proverbs 16:28: _____

Jeremiah 9:5: _____

Lamentations 1:2b: _____

Place a star next to the disloyalty you can relate to the most.

Day One: Embracing True Friendship

I would place a star next to the last one—Betrayal. Trust became a big issue for me in the sixth grade when a friend, whom I thought I could trust, betrayed me. One day on the playground I told this friend a secret, one that had to remain private. I even stressed this critical need for secrecy upfront before I shared with her. She eagerly agreed and promised me she wouldn't tell anyone. So, I told her the secret. It wasn't one minute later when she turned to me and said, "Oh, there's Laura, let me go tell her."

"No," I cried, mortified.

"Oh, don't worry," she said, "she won't tell anyone." And off she ran to tell Laura. I stood there and watched her betray the trust I had just placed in her—helpless to do anything about it. The pain I felt in my heart was unbearable. My throat swelled as I tried to fight back the tears. Needless to say, by the end of that school day, the secret was out and the rumors were flying. Sick and cold with shame, I went home vowing to never trust another soul.

For many years after that, well into adulthood, I didn't trust anyone. I built a wall and would not let people get close to me. I hid everything, and wouldn't let anyone know what I truly thought or felt. And I certainly did not share any more private matters with the outside world. In my mind, I had created a fortress of safety, when in reality the only thing I managed to create was loneliness.

Then, one night, 30 years later, a night very much like the day I cried out as a nine-year-old for that one true friend, I began to cry out to the Lord. I was tired of being lonely. I wanted the companionship of a close friend. My heart yearned to be able to let go of the hurt and embrace friendship, just as I longed to embrace it years earlier. Then, through my sobs, a soft whisper came to my heart. "Be My friend first."

To tell you the truth, until that night, I had never thought of the Lord as a friend. I had never even considered the idea. I didn't realize how I had kept Jesus at arm's length, unwilling to draw near to Him in relationship, especially as a friend, because of how others had hurt me. Yet, here He was, reaching out His hand to me in friendship.

It took time, but as I continued to open my heart to the idea of allowing Jesus to be my friend, He began to show me how much He understood what I was going through and why I didn't trust people, even Him. It was hard to fathom, but Jesus could actually relate to me in my pain and suffering. He was able to sympathize with me in my weakness because He had been there, too (see Hebrews 4:15), and that understanding helped me let go of the hurt.

> Look up the following verses and record how Jesus Himself suffered in His earthly relationships with man.
>
> Matthew 26:47-50: _____
>
> Matthew 26:69-75: _____
>
> Isaiah 53:3: _____

Over the years, the Lord and I have become the best of friends. I tell Him everything. And guess what? He never tells a soul. Little by little, day by day, the Lord tore down that wall of protection I had built around my heart. He has since opened my soul to trust not only Him, but others. Even to the point that I can share things openly with you through this Bible study. He has healed the hurt and mended the wounds of betrayal. He has become, without a doubt, my one true Friend. The one I laugh with, cry with, and share everything with. He is my best Friend.

Interestingly, the miracle did not stop there. Since my friendship with Christ grew strong, He brought some wonderful friendships into my life. Women I know I can trust. My friend Miriam is a treasure beyond anything I could have asked for. She and I have been through a lot together. We have prayed together, shared our hearts and struggles, and we have walked through some dark and difficult times together. But, most importantly, our friendship is centered on Christ. This is what I think Solomon was talking about in Ecclesiastes when he said, "A cord of three strands is not quickly broken" (v. 4:12). When our friendships are based and centered on Christ, they are strong friendships built on truth. To really understand true friendship, we must first be friends with the One who created friendship.

Friends—true friends—are a gift from God. Treasure the true friendships God graciously brings into your life. They are priceless, because these true, authentic friendships are designed to teach you something about friendship with God.

> Who has the Lord brought into your life to teach you about friendship with Him? What makes this person a shining example of Christ's love?
>
> _____
>
> _____

Keeping in mind what we've talked about in today's lesson, coupled with all I have learned over the years, I would like to share with you my answer to one of the questions I asked you at the beginning of this lesson: *What does friendship mean to you?*

I put a very high value on friendship. Perhaps, because of the difficulties I had in making friends early in life, I consider friendship something to be greatly esteemed and treasured. And I consider friendship with God my highest priority. Then, as I continue to grow and blossom in my friendship with Jesus, He brings others into my life that develop into Christ centered friendships grounded in His love.

If you are hurting due to a past untrustworthy friendship, turn to the Lord. Share your heart with Him. Ask Him to help you overcome the pain. Ask Him to help you to forgive this person(s). Allow Jesus to be your Friend. Be still before Him and hear His soft voice whisper to you: "Be My Friend first."

> End today by meditating on Proverbs 18:24: "A man of many companions may come to ruin, but there is a friend who sticks closer than a brother." How does this verse speak to your heart? Share with Jesus—the One who longs to be your true Friend.
>
> _____
>
> _____
>
> _____
>
> _____

Day One: Embracing True Friendship

Day Two
Face-to-Face Friendship

*"The LORD would speak to Moses face to face,
as a man speaks with his friend" (Exodus 33:11).*

Yesterday we began to look at some of the pain and hindrances that can keep us from trusting God in friendship. Today, we will look at another obstacle that can keep us from friendship with God—fear. Rest assured, the Lord will not allow anything to get in the way of your friendship with Him. Not sin, not the pain of past relationships, and certainly not the inappropriate fear we talked about in Week One. If you give God access to your heart, He will right the wrongs and remove all of the obstacles that cause you to feel separated from Him. Today, as we consider the divine friendship between God and Moses, we will take a more in-depth look at how inappropriate fear can hinder our friendship with God.

Let's begin today by asking God to help us enter into face-to-face friendship with Him, and then please read Exodus 33:7-11 and answer the following.

What special place did Moses build to meet with the Lord?

_____

Where did Moses construct the dwelling?

_____

What would happen when Moses entered this place?

_____

In what manner did God speak to Moses? (v. 11)

_____

What added insight does Numbers 12:6-8 give us into the depth of friendship God shared with Moses?

_____

_____

I would not have wanted the responsibility Moses had in leading the Israelites through the wilderness. Can you imagine the stress and headache of trying to deal with such a large group of people? On the other hand, Moses enjoyed one of the most profound and incomprehensible relationships with the Almighty Creator. For that reason, I would have loved to have been Moses. Moses was a man; yet, he had a face-to-face friendship with God. And their relationship was so close that God spoke to Moses unlike any other prophet in the Old Testament, and Moses beheld the form of the LORD.

Can you imagine sharing this kind of relationship with God? ___ YES ___ NO

Why or why not?

_____

_____

God established and maintained friendships with many mortal men. God called Abraham His friend (see 2 Ch 20:7; Isa. 41:8; James 2:23). David, God considered a man after His own heart (see 1 Sam. 13:14; Acts 13:22). The Apostle John was the disciple whom Jesus loved (see John 13:23). With this in mind, let me ask you a question: Was God any less God because He chose to be friends with mortal man?

You may think I am asking a ridiculous question, but, the truth of the matter is there are many believers who have a hard time conceiving of friendship with God, because He is God and they are mortal humans. They fear that by allowing God to be their friend they somehow humanize Him. In their minds, this brings Him down to their level. This type of fear, usually brought on by feelings of unworthiness, keeps us from drawing closer to God and can even cause a separation in the relationship.

What does Isaiah 57:15 tell us about those with whom God dwells?

_____

_____

Yes, God lives in heaven, but He also lives with those who are humble and repent of their ways and seek His ways. David, for example, understood the greatness of God; nevertheless, He also understood that it was by God's humbled favor that he found friendship and help from his glorious Friend (see Psalm 18:35).

Psalm 113:5-6, says, "Who is like the LORD our God, Who is enthroned on high, Who humbles Himself to behold the things that are in heaven and in the earth?"(NASB)

God is enthroned as the God of the universe; but, and let this sink in, He humbles Himself in order to behold all He has made—that includes you. Even though God is infinitely above you, He still desires to be close to you. God will humble Himself, leaning over the very edge of heaven from His high and lofty place, just to be with you.

How does the idea of the Lord humbling Himself just to be your friend move your heart closer to His?

_____

_____

Unfortunately, we can go to the other extreme as well. It is true only focusing on God's position in a high and lofty place will keep Him at a distance in our hearts. With this perspective we will revere Him, as we should; however, we will never draw near to Him in intimacy. On the other hand, only thinking of God as a friend, that warm and cuddly companion we buddy around with, is a misconception as well. He does desire to be our friend, but He is far more. We must keep our perspective balanced. We must hold Him in

Day Two: Face-to-Face Friendship

honor and admiration; but, we must also give Him access to our hearts in the close companionship that He seeks.

So how do we do this? How do we hold God in reverence, understanding that He is the high and holy One; while, at the same time, witness Him as a close personal Friend? The answer—focus. We need to keep our perspective balanced by keeping our focus on Jesus. When we come into that face-to-face encounter with the Lord we see Him more clearly, and we begin to see ourselves more clearly. As a result, we begin to see ourselves the way the Lord sees us. As we seek after God with our whole heart, He draws us closer. By bringing us into a place of friendship, He reveals more of His heart, and we begin to see what He looks like emotionally. The closer we get the more God reveals, so we become more deeply and intimately familiar with Him.

Deep relationship is based on *knowing* God. The way we get to know God is by allowing Him to build that deep, innermost bond of friendship with us. Our job is to build that "Tent of Meeting," just as Moses did.

I realize Moses met with God on many occasions, and in many different places, and we can rest in this assurance as well. The Lord is omnipresent. He is with us all the time. We have access to Him 24-7. What I would like to suggest to you is this: Learn to create a place where you can meet privately with God. This is a place where the two of you can come face-to-face in fellowship. A quiet place where you can focus your whole being on Jesus, and He can reveal His heart to you in friendship.

Consider Mark 1:35. What can we learn from this example of finding a solitary place to be alone with God?

_____

What instruction did Jesus give in Matthew 6:6?

_____

What do you think Jesus meant when He said that the Father will reward those who pray in secret?

_____

When I come into that quiet place to spend time with the Lord face-to-face, it is as if heaven opens up, and there I am before Him, consumed in His presence and enjoying sweet fellowship with Him. In that moment love fills my heart—so much love that my soul sings, and I am like a psalmist as my spirit comes alive once more. My heart quickens, and I feel His Spirit interact with mine. As He lifts me higher and higher by His heavenly grace, my entire being is held captive by joy and pleasure. If that is not reward, then I don't know what is.

Receive the truth and abolish the fear. Every day, common, mortal men knew the pleasure of friendship with God. They were earthly friendships formed from a heavenly perspective.

Re-read Exodus 33:7-11, our main text for today. This time, let's consider these verses from the relational perspective of the Israelites.

Who was able to go to the Tent of Meeting to inquire of the Lord? (v 8b)

_____

What would the people do when Moses entered the Tent of Meeting with God?

_____

Where would they stand? (v. 10)

_____

What happened after Moses entered the tent? (v. 9) Who witnessed the event? (v. 10)

_____

_____

God was there! He came down and the evidence of His glory was in a pillar of cloud, and *all* the people saw it. Regrettably, only Moses entered in and met with God face-to-face. The Israelites remained at the entrance to their own tent and worshiped from a distance. The majority of our church services are a primary example of what we see happening here in Exodus 33:7-11. We worship through song, tithes and offerings, we even honor God through our fellowship with each other; yet, most miss the extreme pleasure of meeting with God face-to-face.

God desires for everyone to know Him in close fellowship, yet there are still some who simply will not draw near to God. Why? What makes the difference? What motivated Moses to go beyond distant relationship to one of close proximity? What kept the Israelites worshiping at a distance?

For insight into the hearts of the Israelites, reflect on Deuteronomy 5:23-29.

What had the people witnessed?

_____

_____

What choice did the people make? (v. 27)

_____

What reasons did they give for not wanting to draw near? (v. 25-26) Check all that apply:

____ We will die if we hear God's voice again

____ We will be consumed in His fiery presence

____ We will not survive the encounter

Day Two: Face-to-Face Friendship

Yet, what was God's plea in verse 29?

_____

_____

> Do you feel the way the Israelites did?
>
> Do you think that God is an angry God and is out to get you?
>
> Do you think if you came near He would look upon you with disapproval, and then strike you down with His word?
>
> If you answered "yes" to any of these questions, openly share your heart with Jesus. Tell Him about the struggles you are having in making the choice to draw near. He is a great and majestic God with a great, big tender heart.

Scripture tells us that the people saw the glory, majesty (NIV), and greatness (NLT) of the Lord. They heard His voice coming from the fire that was ablaze upon the mountain, but they made the choice to not draw near. Instead, they told Moses, "You go! You listen, then come and tell us what He said." Somehow, they had convinced themselves that God was going to destroy them if they came near. Why? Did they think He was an angry God, and if they came near He would strike them down with His word? Did they envision God annihilating them with His fiery presence? Nonetheless, God's heart was tender toward them.

Look again at verse 29; do you see the longing of God's heart? Do you feel His imploring? "Oh, if only they would fear me with *appropriate* fear and follow my commandments, so that it might go well with them…" *(emphasis mine)*. Look at how the verse begins with the exclamation, "Oh..." This implies great longing and strong desire on the part of the Communicator. God truly desired for the listener to understand and heed its message.

It grieves my heart, but many people today have convinced themselves that God is out to get them, even hates them. As a result, many believers are making the choice, even refusing to make the effort, to draw near to God. Don't be one of them. God wants your worship, and not from a distance. He wants you to behold His glory and greatness. He longs for you to hear His voice for yourself. He wants you to have face-to-face intimate fellowship with Him.

Beloved, we have a choice to make. God has already chosen us. He has chosen you. He has chosen me. And it is the greatest longing of His heart for us to choose Him in face-to-face friendship, but, we, too, must make the decision to come near. We must want that cherished friendship, desiring to draw closer than we've ever been before.

Every day do your utmost for the reward of being face-to-face in His presence. Ask Him to open your eyes so you may behold His form. Enter into that solitary place, whether it is in private or in the midst of the assembly. Focus your whole being upon the Lord in worship, and come near in intimate friendship. Seek to behold His glory! Then you will have the confidence to acknowledge Him as Friend; while, at the same time, revering His holiness.

End today by meditating on Psalm 8:3-4. How do these verses help us maintain a balanced focus of holding God in reverence, while witnessing the heart of God to draw near to man in friendship?

_____

_____

_____

_____

Day Three
Bonds of Friendship

"Greater love has no one than this, that he lay down his life for his friends" (John 15:13).

What an incredible privilege we have been given to partake of friendship with God. But do we understand this privilege and what it truly means to God to be our Friend? Do we understand all of what He was willing to sacrifice in order to give us this esteemed honor? This week, thus far, we have considered some of the hurts and hindrances that can cause us to remain distant in our relationship with God as friend. Today, as we seek to strengthen those bonds of friendship, we will begin to see the intensity of relationship God desires to share with us. We will also see the depth of sacrifice He was willing to undergo all for the sake of coming into friendship with us.

Let's dive into today's lesson by asking the Holy Spirit to help us pursue stronger bonds of friendship with Christ, and then let's read Matthew 9:9-13 and consider the following.

In this brief scene, we are given a very vivid picture. Who was Jesus having dinner with? Check all that apply:

____ The Pharisees

____ Matthew

____ Tax collectors and sinners

Why do you think Matthew invited Jesus to his home?

_____

When the Pharisees saw what was happening, what did they ask the disciples?

_____

How did Jesus respond to the Pharisees' accusation? (v. 12)

_____

_____

According to the statement made in Matthew 11:19, who did Jesus befriend? Check the correct answer:

____ The righteous and holy

____ Sinners and tax collectors

____ People who are saved

It was not the sins of the people, their actions, nor their lifestyles that Jesus befriended—it was the people themselves. Jesus dined with sinners, not to show that He agreed with what they did, not to condone their sins, or to join in as a sociable companion. No, He did this in order to show Himself to them as a friend who loved them, and desired to bring them out of their sins and draw them to Himself.

Record a time when Jesus revealed Himself to you as a gentle and loving friend in order to lead you away from sin and draw you to Himself?

_____

_____

_____

Jesus was a friend to sinners and tax collectors, the outcasts, and those who were not socially accepted. The Pharisees were exasperated that Jesus associated with such people. After all, if Jesus was the Messiah, as He claimed to be, then why was He hanging out with the riffraff? The Pharisees were blind guides (see Matthew 15:14), they could not understand why Jesus befriended those they themselves avoided. But Jesus came to earth to be a Friend to sinners, even though they were not friends of God.

Read Romans 5:6-11:

According to verse 6, what did Christ come to do?

_____

How does God demonstrate His love for us? (v. 8)

_____

_____

Though we were God's enemies, how did He reconcile us to Himself, bringing us into friendship? (v. 10)

_____

When we were utterly helpless (NLT), still powerless (NIV), Christ came at just the right time and died for sinners (NLT), the ungodly (NIV). While we were sinful, and still separated from God, anything but His friends, Christ died for us to show us His great and incomparable love (see 1 John 3:16).

Record John 15:13 below:

_____

_____

Before we even knew Jesus as Savior, He revealed Himself as a Friend. A Friend who was patient and slow to anger, compassionate, gracious and abounding in love (see Psalm 103:8). A Friend who was willing to make the ultimate sacrifice—to come to earth and lay down His life for sinful people who did not call Him Friend. "So now we can rejoice in our wonderful new relationship with God—all because of what our Lord Jesus Christ has done for us in making us friends of God" (Romans 5:11, NLT).

> How then should we to respond to such an offering of friendship and love? Reflect on John 15:12-15 as you consider your response.
>
> _____
> _____
>
> We will look at this verse in more detail in tomorrow's lesson, but for now, who does Jesus say are His friends in verse 14?
> ____ Those who love Him
> ____ Those who listen to Him
> ____ Those who keep on sinning

Jesus offered Himself as a Friend to sinners by laying down His life (v. 13), but, if we desire for Jesus to call us friend, we need to respond to His love by listening to Him and heeding His commands (see John 14:23). Jesus said, "You are my friends "if" you do what I command" (v. 14). And His greatest command is to love: To love Him and to love others as He has loved us (v. 12, also see Mark 12:28-31).

> How does 1 Corinthians 13:4-7 describe love? List as many as you can:
>
> _____   _____
> _____   _____
> _____   _____
> _____   _____
> _____   _____
>
> What instructions does Jesus give us in Matthew 5:43-48? Check all that apply.
> ____ Love your enemies
> ____ Pray for those who hurt you
> ____ Love the unlovable
> ____ Respond as your heavenly Father would respond

Day Three: Bonds of Friendship

Through sacrificial love, we are to love a lost world with Christ's love—to love as He did—to love those who do not love us in return. So, how do we do this? How do we love the unlovely? How do we move past the attitudes of the Pharisees and embrace a world who is an enemy of God instead of rejecting them?

> As you consider your response to these questions, reflect on and record the following verses.
>
> John 15:9: _____
>
> _____
>
> 1 John 4:19: _____
>
> _____

Only by allowing Christ to strengthen the bonds of friendship with His love can we hope to be obedient to His command to love. We cannot give out what we do not have. It is vital that we first become strong friends with Jesus and submit to His love, then we can bring His love to others. There are lost and hurting people in this world who need to know the divine truth that Jesus is a Friend to sinners.

How grateful I am that Jesus was willing to be my friend in spite of all I have done. In spite of all my mistakes and sinful actions God did not turn His back on me. Without the grace of God, I was no different than the tax collectors and sinners Jesus dined with. At one time, I, too, was an enemy of God. This is why I am all the more grateful and willing to share Christ's love with others. Just as Jesus offered me His hand of friendship, I, too, desire to offer others that same hope. In response to all Jesus has done for me, I long to see the world as He does— through the eyes of love.

> End today by meditating on Romans 3:22-24. Thank Jesus for His hand of friendship offered to you. Ask Him to help you to embrace His command to love Him, and to love others, by strengthening your bond of friendship with Him?

Day Four
I Call You Friend

*"And the LORD replied to Moses, 'I will indeed do
what you have asked, for you have found favor with me,
and you are my friend'" (Exodus 33:17, NLT).*

This week, in our quest to know God, we have been looking at friendship through God's eyes, and how He longs to be our friend. We saw yesterday that Jesus offered Himself as a Friend to sinners by laying down His life, and that no greater love exists (see John 15:13). Jesus is always our Friend. Even while we were still sinners, Christ came and offered each of us His hand in friendship. We can rest in the assurance that Jesus is our true and all-faithful Friend. No matter what, even in our weakness and failures, Jesus remains our steadfast Friend, but do we understand what it means to be a friend to Jesus?

More than anything, I delight in the knowledge that God is my constant Friend—I depend on His ability to remain reliable in the relationship, but what does God say about the friendship I offer to Him? I wonder, am I a good friend to God? Do I possess the characteristics of those whom God called His friends? I want to be a good friend to God. I desire to draw close to Him in that face-to-face connection as Moses did. I want to be sincere in my friendship with God and possess the qualities He seeks in those He calls His friends. But how do I do that? How do I know I am being a friend to God?

In our previous lesson, we learned that love is the most important trait of friendship. Jesus said, "You are my friends *if* you do what I command" (John 15:14). And His greatest commandment is to love: To love Him and to love each other as He has loved us (see John 15:12; Mark 12:28-31). In God's eyes there is no trait of friendship greater than love. Yet, along with love, in His Word, God offers other characteristics that He finds valuable and pleasing. So what are these additional characteristics? What does God look for in those He seeks to call "friend?"

Before we dive into the Word to examine these additional characteristics, let's pray and ask the Holy Spirit to help us develop the traits of true friendship God seeks to find in us.

Consider the following verses, record the name and what faithful trait(s) each man possessed.

	The Friend	**The Trait**
Genesis 6:9:	_____	_____
Numbers 12:3; 6-8:	_____	_____
John 15:14:	_____	_____
James 2:23:	_____	_____

"Noah was a righteous man, the only blameless man living on earth at that time. He consistently followed God's will and enjoyed a close relationship with him" (Genesis 6:9, NLT).

"Moses was a humble man, more humble than anyone on the face of the earth" (Numbers 12:3), and God developed a personal friendship with him and spoke to him face-to-face (see Exodus 33:11). Jesus considered the disciples His friends because of their obedience. And God considered Abraham a friend, not only because he was righteous, but because Abraham believed God. *Blamelessness, upright living, humility, obedience,* and *belief* were the characteristics of friendship God sought.

Let's look at each of these character traits independently with the hope of intensifying each of them in our own friendship with God.

Righteous and Blameless:

Webster's Dictionary defines the word *righteous* as "doing what is right; just; upright; godly."[19] Synonyms for the word *blameless* are "clean, guiltless, spotless, and unblemished."

According to 2 Peter 1:3-4, where does righteousness come from? How are we able to live a righteous and godly life?

_____

_____

What did Paul tell the Ephesians in verse 5:26-27? How will Christ present His church?

_____

_____

Ponder Isaiah 33:14-17. How do these verses help us experience friendship with God? List some of the character traits that describe how to fellowship with God, who is a consuming fire (see Hebrews 12:29).

_____	_____
_____	_____
_____	

God gives us everything we need to live a godly life with Him. We are not in this journey alone—God will help us live righteous and blameless lives. However, if we want to enjoy friendship with God the way Noah did, we, too, need to make the choice to come under His divine nature and walk in His ways. We need to pursue His will by turning away from evil and turning toward God with our whole heart. We need to speak the truth and do what is fair and just. We need to shut our eyes to sin and embrace what pleases God. The man or woman who makes the choice to pursue these things will dwell on the heights. He will behold the beauty of the Lord, and will enjoy a remarkable friendship with God while still here on earth. Hallelujah!

Humility vs. Pride:

Consider each of the following verses. Record how God regards humility and responds to the proud:

	Humble	Proud
Psalm 25:9:	_____	
Psalm 101:5:		_____
Psalm 138:6:	_____	_____
Psalm 147:6:	_____	_____
James 149:4:	_____	
Psalm 3:34:	_____	_____
Psalm 16:5:		_____

What did Jesus say about those who are lowly, meek, and poor in spirit in Matthew 5:3, 5? (Wording will vary in each translation.)

_____
_____
_____
_____
_____
_____
_____
_____
_____

God says, "This is the one I esteem: he who is humble and contrite in spirit, and trembles at my word" (Isaiah 66:2b). God draws near to the humble. He honors him, esteems him, gives him grace, guidance, salvation and takes great delight in him. The proud He knows, but, only from a distance, not as a close personal friend. He detests pride and will not tolerate it; in fact, He hates it. Those who are proud are not God's friends. Those who are humble, however, come into His intimate companionship.

To be humble means to be lowly, meek, and poor in spirit. Being humble doesn't mean we are weak and powerless. Being meek does not mean we allow others to take advantage of us. Being poor in spirit doesn't mean we are spiritually deprived or oppressed.

True humility comes when you reflect Christ. Being poor in spirit means to acknowledge your dependence on God, from whom all your spiritual strength comes. And being meek is grace under fire. It is being gentle and loving in a world that is often anything but kind and caring. Great power is found in the man who is meek, humble, and poor in spirit, because this is the man God empowers. This is the man that God calls His friend.

Obedience:

What did God say about David in Acts 13:22b?

_____

What character trait was evident in David?

_____

Wholehearted devotion gives way to a life of desired obedience. David was a man after God's own heart; and David's love and devotion toward God revealed itself through his willingness to do what God asked of him. David was not perfect. He did make mistakes, and some big ones; but, his heart sought hard after God's heart. Like David, we, too, will make mistakes, but God sees and honors the effort, that willing desire to please Him, even when we fall short. Obedience is not about being perfect—it's about a genuine and unwavering determination to love Jesus, even in the midst of our limitations.

Day Four: I Call You Friend

Fill in the blanks according to John 14:23, NIV:

Jesus replied, "If anyone _____ me, he will _____ my teaching."

If we love God we will want to obey God from a heart purely devoted to Him and the pleasure of doing His will.

Look at John 15:14 again. What distinguishing attribute did Jesus say His friends possessed?

___ Flexibility toward His commands

___ Complacency toward His sovereignty

___ Submission to His authority

Jesus said, "You are my friends *"if"* you do what I command" (NIV). *If*: a small word with a big impact. God calls us His friends "if" we are willing to follow His commands and make the sincere attempt to do what delights Him. Synonyms for the word *command* are "control, authority, rule, dominion, power, and supremacy." We may not always like giving up the control of our lives to God. We may often find it difficult to surrender to His will. But, "if" we want to be called a friend of God, we need be willing to listen, to hear God's voice and submit to His control, authority, rule, dominion, power and supremacy.

What area(s) of your life are you having trouble submitting to the control and authority of God?

_____

_____

Remember, we have already been given everything we need to live a victorious life in Christ (2 Peter 1:3). Stop right now and ask the Holy Spirit to help you to hear God's voice and to respond with genuine obedience, overflowing from a heart of pure devotion.

Look one more time at John 15:14-15; there is something very special we need to take note of here:

What did Jesus tell His friends? What did He make known to them? (v. 15)

_____

_____

How do you see the connection of obedience (v. 14) tying into the assurance that Jesus confides in His friends (v. 15)?

_____

_____

According to Psalm 25:14, who does the Lord confide in? What does He share with them?

_____

_____

According to *Webster's Dictionary* the word *confide* means "to entrust in; to tell a secret; to put faith in; to rely on."[20] Jesus told His disciples that He no longer called them servants, but friends. Because of their willingness to be obedient to His commands Jesus trusted them. And through this bond of trust, Jesus put faith in their friendship by entrusting them with covenant secrets. Jesus held nothing back—He told them everything He learned from His Father.

> Do you have a friend you can confide in, one you feel you can share everything with? ___ YES ___ NO If you answered YES, what does it feel like to have such a trusted friendship?
>
> _____
>
> _____
>
> What would it mean to you to know Jesus trusted you and was willing to share covenant secrets with you?
>
> _____
>
> _____

Friendship with God, like our human friendships, requires time, energy, effort, and trust. The closer we get to our earthly friends, the more they feel they can trust us. As a result, they will be more apt to divulge particular details about their lives. The same is true of God. The more we are willing to submit to His commands in obedience, the more the relationship will grow in intimacy. This increase of intimacy will bring deeper, richer times of fellowship with God.

Believing God:

> Fill in the blanks according to James 2:23, NIV:
>
> "Abraham _____ _____, and it was credited to him as righteousness, and he was called _____ _____."

Romans 4:20-21, says "Abraham never wavered in believing God's promise. In fact, his faith grew stronger, and in this he brought glory to God. He was absolutely convinced that God was able to do everything He promised." (NLT) A friend of God is someone who believes God, who trusts Him completely, and takes Him at His word.

Review Hebrews 11:

Who else believed God? List as many as you can. Place a star next to the ones we have talked about in this lesson.

_____   _____
_____   _____
_____   _____
_____   _____
_____

What did these believers gain by believing God? (v. 33-34)

_____
_____
_____

The word *believe* means "to regard as true; to trust; to have faith." *Belief* means "that which is believed; full acceptance of a thing as true; faith; a firm persuasion of the truth."[21]

We must allow our relationship with God to grow to unquestionable levels of trust. We must have faith, that unshakeable belief in God's ability to do as He promised, and to allow that belief to penetrate our connection with Him. Without faith in God, Who He is and His ability to do as He promised, the friendship will be hindered.

The one thing that set each of these men apart—Noah, Moses, David, the disciples, and Abraham—was they made a choice. They purposefully set out to live rightly before God; they walked in His ways; they were humble, obedient, and they believed God for everything. The bottom line: They were utterly consumed with God. He was their magnificent obsession; and their greatest desire was to please Him through right living, obedience, humility and firm belief.

Which characteristic do you find the most difficult to purposefully make the choice to submit to in your relationship with God? Why?

_____
_____

End today by meditating on 2 Corinthians 12:9. Pray and ask God to help you to be His faithful friend, and then claim His promise to equip you in your weakness.

_____
_____
_____
_____
_____

Beloved, once you make up your mind to firmly commit your life to wholehearted, devoted friendship with Christ, and yield to His divine power and authority, everything changes. It is Christ's relentless desire to build those bonds of friendship between the two of you. And, when you make the unwavering choice to submit to His ways He will stretch, strengthen, and develop your friendship to unimaginable levels of closeness. Then, you will be called "a friend of God."

Day Five
No Other Friend Can Compare

"This is my lover, this is my friend" (Song of Songs 5:16).

Before I sat down to write today, I had an extra sweet time in the presence of the Lord. As I prepared for the day, I felt His Spirit draw me into fellowship. In the Spirit we danced and loved each other. What a time of refreshment as I experienced His touch and tender affection. Now my heart is overflowing and my soul soars higher and higher into the heavens. My spirit is renewed, and I feel as if I am walking six inches above the floor. What encouragement the Holy Spirit brings to the soul when we fellowship with Him in friendship. He truly is a Friend beyond all other friends.

> Let's begin today's lesson by asking the Holy Spirit to reveal the treasure we have in friendship with Christ. Then, please read Song of Songs 5:9-16.
> How does the maiden describe her beloved friend? (List three)
>
> 1. _____
> 2. _____
> 3. _____
>
> Based on this description, how close would you surmise their relationship to be?
>
> _____
> _____

I love the way the maiden describes her beloved friend in these verses. His head, his hands, his face, the scent of his skin—she knows him, she completely and thoroughly knows him—and no one else in all the earth will do. She wants and longs for her most precious friend.

As I read these Scriptures I think of Christ and how valuable His friendship is to me. I want to know Him the way the maiden knew her beloved friend. I want to be able to describe Him as meticulously and fully as she did. I want to know Him—His personality, attributes, and characteristics—His whole and entire being. And when I compare Him with all others in my life I want to proclaim as she did, "He is the most lovely and valuable, far above everything else!"

In your eyes, how does Christ compare? Describe how He is outstanding among everyone and everything in your life?

___

___

___

From the moment I became a new believer, I dove fervently into the Word of God. It was like I was starving to death and couldn't get enough. I remember carrying my Bible in one hand reading, while, at the same time, going around the house cooking, cleaning, and taking care of the children. You might say, in those early days, I was obsessive, but I had lived for many years hearing about God but not knowing God. Up until that time, I had no relationship with Him. But when Jesus came into my life a hunger arose in my soul—a hunger for His Word and a hunger for Him! And as I dove into God's Word, I learned many wonderful things about Him.

For example, He is just (Hebrews 10:30-31); good (Matthew 19:17; 2 Chronicles 7:3); and holy (Revelation 15:4). He is love (1 John 4:8; 4:16); righteous (Psalm 119:137); sovereign (Isaiah 46:9-10); faithful (Deuteronomy 7:9); unchanging (James 1:17); truth (Isaiah 65:16); merciful (Ephesians 2:4); jealous (Exodus 34:14); and all-knowing (Hebrews 4:13). And these are only a few of the attributes of God's personality I read about. However, just reading that God is "compassionate and gracious, slow to anger, abounding in love" (Psalm 103:8), did not become a reality to me until I began to put the application of relationship into practice. Reading God's Word is vital, but only reading and studying God's Word is not enough.

When I was in High School, I remember doing an immense amount of research about Thomas Edison. I read every book I could find about him. I looked into his background and deliberately studied every invention he devised. I learned many facts about Thomas Edison, and I could have probably answered any trivia question you might have had about the man; but, I never knew him personally. Knowing *about* Thomas Edison did not help me to know Thomas Edison. Doing all that research never helped me develop a friendship with him.

The same is true of God. Only reading and studying your Bible, void of fellowship with God through His Holy Spirit, will not help you to *know* God or strengthen your relationship with Him. You may have intellectual knowledge as a result of doing all of that studying, but you will not experience God's personality in real friendship, until you allow the Holy Spirit to awaken your heart and soul to the reality of God's emotional heart toward you. The truth is God longs for you, is passionately in love with you, and desires an intense friendship with you, just like the one expressed through the Song of Songs.

Can you envision such a friendship? ___ YES ___ NO

If you answered no, what is keeping you from embracing a rich, deep friendship with God?

___

___

One of the things I love best about my relationship with God is that I can get real with Him. He is my one true Friend—the One I laugh with, cry with, and share everything with. I can tell Him exactly how I feel, even if I am wrong in my attitude or judgment about a situation. I can share the deepest, most hidden places of my heart. No matter if I am angry, hurt, joyful, or excited, like a wonderful friend, He listens and loves me.

I know this about God because I experience it in a cherished friendship through His Holy Spirit. I have confidence in what I know because God's Word supports these attributes. Therefore, as I read in His Word about His Person and personality, I also pray for the Holy Spirit to bring these attributes to life for me, making them a reality in my life. I want to move from religion to reality, don't you? I don't want to just read about Jesus, I want to experience Jesus in a real and practical relationship full of love and fellowship.

As you come to know God through His Word and fellowship with His Holy Spirit, which of His personality traits has moved from religion to reality in your life? From the list below, circle the qualities you have personally experienced in your relationship with God.

trustworthy	patient	caring/compassionate	loyal/faithful
kind/loving	supportive	encouraging	good listener
pleasurable	affectionate	dependable	forgiving

Now, take three of these qualities that you have experienced, and support it with God's Word. I'll give you an example:

The Characteristic	God's Word
Pleasurable	*Psalm 16:11, "…you fill me with joy in your presence, with eternal pleasures at your right hand."*
_____	_____
_____	_____
_____	_____

Match the following verses with the corresponding characteristic or quality: (Some verses will have more than one answer.)

____ Psalm 86:15	a. faithful	e. kind
____ Psalm 22:4-5	b. compassionate	f. loving
____ Galatians 5:22-23	c. gracious	g. trustworthy
____ Psalm 18:6; 16-19	d. patient	h. supportive

God is loving, caring, and trustworthy. He is loyal, forgiving, and a good listener. He is perfect. He is the best friend you and I will ever have. As I grow closer to God in friendship, He continually reveals Himself to me by spending an immense amount of time with me. As He draws me closer, I come to Him in simple child-like obedience, desiring

Loving
Righteous
Affectionate/warm
Just/Fair
Romantic/wooer
Possessive
Honest/truthful
Punctual/never late
Wise
Private/secret side/intriguing
Powerful
Passionate/zealous
Sensitive
Enthusiastic
Compassionate
Free Spirited
Understanding
Gentleman
Merciful
Friendly
Caring
Meticulous/perfectionist
Forgiving
Patient
Loyal/faithful
Insightful
Sense of humor
Leader
Playful/Joyous
Responsible
Generous/Provider/giving
Alive
Extravagant
Energetic
Creative/imaginative
Charming/alluring/irresistible
Tender/Gentle
Personable
Kind
Consistent/reliable/unfailing
Trustworthy
Thoughtful
Devoted
Sentimental
Protective
Sweet

to know Him more. Through our connection He shows me His character and nature. He builds my confidence in our relationship by rescuing me, loving me, and guiding me, as He unveils His worth and secures His position of authority in my life. He continually teaches me, letting me know who He is and how He operates.

Now, let's think even bigger! From the list in the margin, underline any of the attributes you have come to know in your relationship with Jesus; then circle the attributes you desire to know more.

Amazing, isn't it? Truthfully, there is no way we could record or experience all of the Lord's characteristics and qualities. Yet, God gives us the incredible privilege to know Him and see His magnificent personality all throughout Scripture, and in close fellowship with His Spirit.

Through our relationship with God we can see great strength of character. The more we get to know Him and trust in His promises, the more we will realize that He is indeed the best of all friends. He is a friend who will love us, guide us, and stand with us in good times and in bad. He is a friend who will not desert us or turn His back on us. Even in our own unfaithfulness and weakness, He will never leave us nor forsake us (See Hebrews 13:5).

Oh, how I praise Him for His faithful and persistent friendship with me. There is no one I would rather be with than Him. He is the one I confide in—the one I trust with my life and every aspect of it. I know He will be there when I am full of joy, and when I am drowning in the depth of despair. He is my true and constant Friend.

This week has been amazing as we have given God the opportunity to reveal Himself as a true and faithful Friend. However, as amazing as it all is, there is still more. I contend that no matter how well we may think we know Him, we will never know all of Him in this lifetime (see 1 Corinthians 13:12). One day we will see the glory of the Lord revealed in all fullness, but for now, we are given the opportunity to peek into a reflection of who God is. He is a friend; yet, as we saw earlier in today's lesson, He is also a lover (Song of Songs 5:16). As we leave this week's lessons on friendship with God, let's look with great expectation to next week's lessons on the Bridegroom. In Week Four we will give Him the opportunity to open the door to a much deeper revelation: Christ as a Husband and a Lover.

End today by again mediating on Song of Songs 5:16, "This is my lover, this is my friend." How has this verse changed, or taken on a deeper meaning, as a result today's lesson? Pray and ask Jesus to help you to know Him as the maiden in the Song, as both a Lover and a Friend.

_____
_____
_____
_____

Apply the Knowledge

In my pursuit of God as Friend this week, the Holy Spirit has shown me …

_____
_____
_____
_____

The verse that spoke to me the most this week is…

_____
_____

In order to make this verse a reality in my life, I…

_____
_____
_____
_____

The changes I need to make, the hurts and attitudes I need to let go of in order to embrace a deeper, richer friendship with God are…

_____
_____
_____
_____
_____

Lord God, I desire to be your friend, help me to develop…

_____
_____
_____
_____

The hidden treasure (see Isaiah 45:3) of His Person and personality God revealed to me this week is… This higher revelation of God's presence profoundly awakens me to…

_____
_____
_____
_____

Witnessing God as a Friend this week has changed my perspective of God from… to…

_____
_____
_____
_____

Holy Spirit, help me to apply what I've learned to my everyday life, so…

_____
_____
_____
_____

Prayer for the Journey

Lord, I long to be Your friend. Help me to exhibit the characteristics of those who knew You in intimate friendship. Teach me your ways so I may continue to grow in friendship with You. Lord, I want to know you as my Friend—my true Friend—the best of all friends. I want to speak with you face-to-face. I want to laugh with you, cry with you, and share everything with you. As a true and treasured friend, I yearn to…

_____
_____
_____
_____
_____
_____

Session Three
True Friendship

Ezekiel 13:20-23

*"I will save my people from your hands.
And then you will **know that I am the LORD**"*
(Ezekiel 13:23, NIV).

1.) A false friend _____ .
   (Ezekiel 13:20a)

   A True Friend is _____ those who

   _____ _____ . (Ezekiel 11:20b)

2.) A false friend _____
   A True Friend will _____ our

   _____ _____ .

   (Ezekiel 11:21)

Week Three: Know That I AM Your Friend

3.) A false friend _____ the righteous

And _____ the unrighteous.

(Ezekiel 11:22)

4.) A True Friend _____

And _____ us when we are wrong.

(Ezekiel 11:22-23)

Week Four
Know That I AM Your Bridegroom

Oh how I pray that the bride of Christ could truly see the heart of her Bridegroom. If only she could look into the core of a charming romantic movie and understand that the ardent love she sees is a parallel to the love that Christ carries in His heart for her. Then she could witness a glimpse of His passionate pursuit of her, and see how beautiful the love they could share would be.

In the new version of the movie *Pride and Prejudice*, I recall the scene where Elizabeth Bennett finally returns Mr. Darcy's affections. Oh, the delight that must have filled his heart at that moment. The relief and joy that must have swelled within his soul as Elizabeth made her feelings known for him. How, at long last, the pursued became the pursuer as she took hold of his hand and returned his love. This, I believe, is an indication of the heart of our Bridegroom. When, at long last, the love that He longs to shower upon His bride is finally returned with fervor and eagerness.

I realize that earthly movies are a poor example of the love Christ carries for His church. The truth of the matter is, however, reminders of His love are everywhere—not only in movies, but in love songs, fairytales, and poems. Even creation holds the heartbeat of the eternal love affair. Deep within the core of each and every story that touches our hearts and moves our souls, whispers to us the secrets of the sacred romance.

We, in this life, cannot entirely appreciate the full measure of such a romance; yet, God, in His grace and wisdom has given us wonderful and tender examples of His love, giving us glimpses of Eden every day. If only we would ask the Holy Spirit to open our hearts to receive the wonders of His great affection.

For this reason, I pray continually that the bride of Christ would one day know and understand these things. I pray that a wave of revelation would overtake her heart and she would see that He is desperately in love with her, and that He desires nothing more than her whole-hearted devotion.

If you have trouble embracing Christ Jesus as the Bridegroom, then you will have a difficult time experiencing one of the most wonderful parts of salvation. You may acknowledge Him as your Shepherd. You may love God as your heavenly Father. You may call on Him in times of trouble and heartache, and know what it is to receive His healing and grace. You may call on the Name of the Lord as Warrior, and receive great victory when life happens or the enemy attacks; but, until you learn to see Christ as a lover, you will always keep a part of Him at arm's length. As a result, you will not draw near enough to truly know and understand Him.

The Old Testament testifies that God revealed Himself to Israel as her divine Husband, and the New Testament tells us that Jesus is the eternal Bridegroom of the church. Scripture also gives us many parallels, allegories, and Christ figures to help us grasp this glorious relationship.

Therefore, this week we are going to look at a few men in Scripture, who, I believe, not only knew the love of God in the most intimate way, but also existed to be living metaphors. Each of these men are "Christ figures" to help us understand the love of God, and to give us a glimpse into the heart of our eternal Bridegroom.

Allow me to encourage you to reach for more in your relationship with God. Do not resist. Ask for the Spirit of Wisdom and Revelation to awaken your heart to the desires you have within you to the sacred romance. Only in intimacy with Christ will you ever hope to truly *know* God the way He longs for you to know Him.

Hosea 2:16; 19-20, NASB

"It will come about in that day." declares the LORD,
"That you will call Me Ishi
And you will no longer call Me Baali"
"I will betroth you to Me forever;
Yes, I will betroth you to Me in righteousness and in justice,
In loving-kindness and in compassion
And I will betroth you to Me in faithfulness.
Then you will know the LORD."

This week we will attempt to:

Witness Christ as our Husband
"I have promised you to one husband, to Christ, so that
I might present you as a pure virgin to him"
(2 Corinthians 11:2).

Observe the mediation of the covenant
"In the same way, he took the cup of wine after supper, saying,
'This cup is the new covenant between you and God,
sealed by the shedding of my blood…"
(1 Corinthians 11:25, NLT).

Witness the faithfulness of God through Hosea
"Because of the LORD'S great love we are not consumed,
for his compassions never fail. They are new every morning,
great is your faithfulness"
(Lamentations 3:22-23).

Experience Christ's redeeming love through Boaz
"Praise be to the LORD, the God of Israel, because
he has come and has redeemed his people"
(Luke 1:68).

Open our hearts to the Lover of our soul
"I belong to my lover, and his desire is for me"
(Song of Songs 7:10).

Day One
Is God Really Our Husband?

"For your Maker is your husband—the LORD Almighty is his name" (Isaiah 54:5).

Today, we will attempt to lay the groundwork for the sacred romance, as we search the Scriptures in order to answer the question: *Is God Really Our Husband?* In order to truly witness Christ as the Bridegroom of the church, we must first receive a revelation of His love and understand His desire for each of us as His beloved. With this in mind, let's begin by praying for the Spirit of Revelation to open our hearts, so we may experience more of Christ's love as we attempt to behold Him as our beloved Bridegroom.

> Record a time when you personally experienced the love of Christ and received a revelation of His love.
>
> _____
> _____
> _____
> _____
> _____
> _____
> _____
> _____
> _____

Read Ephesians 3:14-19:

What did Paul pray that the Ephesians would have the power to grasp (NIV), understand (NLT)?

_____

Paul witnessed the love of Christ, and he deeply desired for the Ephesians, plus all of the saints, past, present, and future to know this love firsthand. Paul knew the difference between the "head knowledge" that tells us Jesus loves us, and "heart knowledge" that comes only through personal experience. Paul desperately wanted the saints to know the familiarity of Christ's love, because that revelation would change their lives.

Read John 13:23-25:

In verse 23 (NIV), the Apostle John referred to himself as "the disciple whom Jesus loved." Why do you think John addressed himself this way?

____ He thought he was better than the other disciples
____ He earned the right
____ He knew the love of Christ

What evidence do you see in John 13:23-25 that testifies to the level of intimacy Jesus and John shared?

_____

John knew Christ's love in a very real and intimate way. I love the way the NASB and the KJV state verse 23: "There was reclining on Jesus' bosom one of His disciples, whom Jesus loved." This wording suggests that John was already resting his head on the bosom of Jesus prior to Peter's question in verse 24.

Beloved, until you learn to stop and savor tender moments of resting your head upon the bosom of the Lord Jesus Christ, you will not be near enough to hear His soft voice whispering into your ear. You may hear the Lord speaking to you through His word, through sermons at church, through Bible studies and other books. You may even hear His voice through other people, but until you learn to savor in the delight of coming into that quiet place with Jesus, being still before Him (see Ps. 46:10), you will have a difficult time hearing His voice from within the core of your being. Learn to be like John and you won't have to be like Peter—asking someone else to ask Him for you. Perhaps I am stretching the text a bit, but understand what I am trying to tell you: intimacy is about proximity. There is no such thing as too close—draw near, rest on His bosom and listen.

> What analogy are we given in Ephesians 5:31-32 to represent our relationship with Christ?
> ___ Potter and clay   ___ Teacher and student   ___ Husband and wife
>
> In Ephesians, Paul draws a parallel and gives us the image of Christ as the Husband of the church. Who makes up the church?
> ___ Women only
> ___ Men who are secure enough to see themselves as the bride of Christ
> ___ All who call on the name of the Lord for salvation

The bridal imagery in Scripture has been a challenge for men for centuries. They think that the feminine description of the "bride" somehow disqualifies them—that the bridal archetype should be reserved for women alone. How false! Men of God, you also make up the church. Therefore, you, too, are members of the bride of Christ. Sexuality and gender have nothing to do with it. You must stop looking at the bridal metaphor from an earthly perspective. When Christ calls the church His bride, He is sharing the passionate longings of His heart. He is communicating the height, the breadth, the width and the length of His desire and intense passion for those He loves.

All throughout Scripture, in both the Old and New Testaments, we are given the titles of "husband" and "bridegroom" to symbolize our relationship with God.

> Look up the following verses. Record whether "husband" or "bridegroom" is used to identify God, and then record the witness, the one who is making this claim of identification. Finally, record any additional information or connection we are given about this relationship.
> 2 Corinthians 11:2: _____
> John 3:27-29: _____
> Matthew 9:14-15: _____
> Isaiah 62:4-5: _____
> Isaiah 54:5: _____

"Your new name will be the City of God's delight and the Bride of God" (Isaiah 62:4, NLT). Oh, how my heart swells; yet, at the same time, I am in awe at how God, who is pure and perfect, would want to be the eternal Husband of impure and imperfect human beings.

Ann Spangler, in her book *Praying the Names of God* says: "God's passionate love for Israel is reflected in the Hebrew word *Ishi* (EESH), meaning "husband." When it is applied to God in the Hebrew Scriptures, it symbolizes the ideal relationship between God and Israel. God is the perfect husband—loving, forgiving, and faithful, providing for and protecting his people. This metaphor of monogamous marriage between God and his people is strengthened in the New Testament, which reveals Jesus as the loving, sacrificial bridegroom of the church. Our destiny, our greatest purpose as God's people, is to become his bride.

"When it comes to love and marriage, the strangest match in all of history is the one between God and his people. At first glance it looks like a complete mismatch! A holy God linked to weak and sinful human beings. Greatness linked to smallness. Wisdom linked to folly. Yet, God says: 'I will betroth you to me forever.' This is his intent, his idea, his plan. Whether you are a man or a woman, married or single, makes no difference. Because you are a member of his people, God wants you to know him as your protector, as friend and provider, as the lover of your soul—as your husband."[22]

Paraphrase Hosea 2:16; 19-20 below:

_____
_____
_____

I love the way the New Living Translation records these verses: "In that coming day," says the LORD, "you will call me 'my husband' instead of 'my master.' I will make you my wife forever, showing you righteousness and justice, unfailing love and compassion. I will be faithful to you and make you mine, and you will finally know me as LORD." (NLT)

When God says, "…you will finally know me as LORD," He is saying, "…you will finally know me as YHWH (Yahweh)." When we see "LORD" spelled out all in capital letters, we are seeing the name of God. "Lord," capital "L" with small letters following is "Adoni" which means "Lord, Master." God's communication to us in these verses is very personal. He is saying: "…you will *finally know me* intimately—as husband. You will call me by my name. God wants us to know Him intimately, to call Him by his Name, not by His title. For example, you wouldn't call your husband Mr. Smith; you would call him by his first name.

Calling God by His name is huge. I have a Jewish friend who will not, and cannot, speak the name of the LORD. God's name is so holy, so revered by his Jewish culture that he will not speak it out loud. My friend loves God, but he does not know Jesus as his Savior, he does not believe the Messiah has come yet. When we receive Christ as our Messiah, our Savior, we come into relationship with God through the New Covenant in Christ's blood. Through the New Covenant we become a member of His bride, giving us covenant access and the privilege of calling upon the Name of the LORD in intimacy—as a friend, as a lover, as a husband.

End today by mediating on Hosea 2:16; 19-20. If you are having a difficult time embracing the relationship between the Bridegroom and His bride, use the space below to share your heart with Jesus. Confess what is holding you back in receiving His intimate love.

_____
_____
_____
_____
_____
_____
_____
_____

Oh, how I pray the Holy Spirit will broaden our perspective of Christ to witness Him as an adoring and committed Husband. Today is only the beginning of a wonderful and glorious week of witnessing the heart and passion of the Bridegroom. Through those who have witnessed before us, we will experience the Bridegroom's tender heart toward His beloved bride. We will see His heartbreak over her unfaithfulness, and his delight in bringing her back to Himself, redeeming her with the highest price. It will be an exciting week. Thank you for joining me on this incredible journey.

Day Two
The Mediator of the Covenant

"For there is one God and one mediator between God and men, the man Christ Jesus" (1 Timothy 2:5).

We began our week with the Bridegroom by laying the ground work for the sacred romance, so we could receive a greater revelation of Christ's love and desire for His church. God longs to draw us into the deepest and most intimate of all relationships. And through the imagery of covenant marriage, God sets the stage for the ultimate connection of relationship—husband and wife. Today we are going to take a closer look at this divine marriage covenant between God and His people.

Begin by asking God to communicate His heart to you, and then read Jeremiah 31:31-34 and Hebrews 8:7-13.

What is the proclamation God made in Jeremiah 31:31 and Hebrews 8:8?

____ I will forget my covenant

____ I will renew my covenant

____ I will make a new covenant

Why did He make this declaration? Why was a New Covenant necessary? (Heb. 8:7-8)

_____

What parallel of relationship did the Lord draw for us? How did the Lord describe the care He offered His people through the covenant in Jeremiah 31:32? Check the correct answer:

	____ He was a Father to them

	____ He was a Friend to them

	____ He was Husband to them

According to Jeremiah 31:33 and Hebrews 8:10, what would be different about the New Covenant?

	____ God would write the law on stone tablets

	____ God would write the law on people's hearts

	____ God would do away with the law altogether

Why was this better?

_____

What was God's intention for the New Covenant? (Jer. 31:33-34) More than one answer applies:

	____ God's commands will make more sense

	____ The law will be easier to obey

	____ God will belong to His people and His people will belong to Him

	____ God's people will know Him

How does Jeremiah 31:34 and Hebrews 8:11 encourage your heart in your pursuit of knowing God?

_____

_____

At the time God declared this promise through the prophet Jeremiah, God had already made a covenant with the house of Israel and the house of Judea. This Old Covenant came with many laws and the greatest of these commandments was to: "Love the LORD your God with all your heart and with all your soul and with all your strength" (Deuteronomy 6:5). But His people forsook the covenant, because they were unable to follow God faithfully in their own strength. Even though God loved them and cared for them like a husband, His people were not able to keep the demands of the Old Covenant.

The Old or Mosaic Covenant was a foreshadow of the New Covenant to come, and was put in place to show the people their need for God. God said the New Covenant would be better, because He would write His covenant upon the hearts and minds of His people, helping them to follow Him wholeheartedly. Hebrews 7:18-19 puts it this way: "So a previous physical regulation and command is cancelled because of its weakness and ineffectiveness and uselessness—for the Law never made anything perfect—but instead a better hope is introduced through which we [now] come close to God (AMP).

There was a clear purpose in both the Old and New Covenant, and one man stood in the gap between God and the people for each covenant.

> Consider the following verses; who was the mediator of the Old Covenant and how did God use this man as His instrument?
>
> Exodus 19:3-8: _____
>
> Exodus 24:3-8: _____
>
> Exodus 32:15-16: _____

Up until this point, God had made covenant promises with individuals: Noah (see Genesis 9:1-17) and Abram (see Genesis 15:1-21). God cut covenant with each man and made covenant promises to their descendants. Moses, however, was the mediator of the Mosaic Covenant (see Exodus 19:3-8) and was the one God had chosen to mediate, intercede, and to reconcile the covenant promise between Himself and the Israelites. Through this covenant God promised to consecrate a people to Himself through divine Law. The core of the covenant was God's oath, 'I will be your God and you will be my people.'

God chose Moses to verbally deliver the covenant agreement to His people, to seal it, and put it in writing. And there was not another such instrument of the covenant until the man Jesus Christ. Moses was God's witness to Israel that a much greater fulfillment of the promise laid ahead, and his position as mediator predicted the position that would come through Jesus Christ.

> What does Hebrews 8:6 tell us about the ministry of Jesus in comparison to the old ministry of Moses? What does this verse tell us about the New Covenant in comparison to the Old Covenant?
>
> _____
>
> _____

> Look up the following, what does each verse tell us about the New Covenant we partake of in Jesus Christ.
>
> Luke 22:20: _____
>
> 1 Corinthians 11:23-25: _____
>
> Ephesians 1:13-14: _____
>
> Ezekiel 36:25-27: _____

Day Two: The Mediator of the Covenant

Jesus, the mediator of a ministry far superior to the one given to Moses, was the instrument God chose to deliver the New Covenant. Jesus came to verbally deliver the covenant agreement, seal it, and make a way for the Holy Spirit to put it in writing upon our hearts and minds.

Even though God's people cried out, "Everything the LORD has said we will do" (Exodus 24:3b). It was impossible for them to keep the demands of the Old Covenant. Left on our own, even with our good intensions, it is just as impossible for us to keep the commands of covenant marriage. So, God made a New Covenant, and through this New Covenant He gave us the power to fulfill the covenant's greatest commandment—to love the Lord our God with all our heart, soul, mind and strength (see Mark 12:28-31).

Beloved, you need God to love God. You need the word of God engraved upon your heart and mind in order to know the ecstasy and wonder of the divine marriage offered through the New Covenant.

What a glorious privilege we have been given through the mediation of the man Jesus Christ. What a priceless privilege to enter into a covenant agreement with Deity. A better covenant, with better promises; promises that afford us the freedom to explore the wonders of God, becoming more intimately acquainted with Him. God planned covenant marriage so we could know and experience, for ourselves, His divine love and affections. For God says, "No longer will a man teach his neighbor, or a man his brother, saying, 'Know the LORD,' because they will all know me" (Jeremiah 31:24).

> End today by meditating on Philippians 3:10a, AMP: "[For my determined purpose is] that I may know him [that I may progressively become more deeply and intimately acquainted with Him, perceiving and recognizing and understanding the wonders of his person more strongly and more clearly]" Then express your heart to God, share how much you desire to know Him more deeply and intimately, so that you may perceive, recognize, and understand Him as never before.

Day Three
The Faithful Husband

"Know therefore that the LORD your God is God; he is the faithful God, keeping his covenant of love to a thousand generations of those who love him and keep his commands" (Deuteronomy 7:9).

This week, thus far, we have attempted to receive a revelation of Christ's love by witnessing Him as a Husband. We have opened God's Word and discovered how Moses was the mediator of the Old Covenant, and how this covenant foreshadowed the New Covenant in Christ's blood. Today, as we continue to look at the heart of the Bridegroom, we will see that from the time of the Old Covenant until now, God has been faithful to all of His promises (see Psalm 145:13).

Let's begin today by asking the Holy Spirit to show us the heart of the Bridegroom for His bride, and then read Hosea 1—3

In your own words, describe the relationship between Hosea and his wife Gomer.

_____

_____

How does Hosea and Gomer's relationship parallel the relationship between God and His people?

_____

_____

Paraphrase how God expresses His heartbreak in Hosea 2:2-13?

_____

_____

What shift, or change of heart, transpires between verse 2:13 and 2:14? (Also see Hosea 11:8-9 before you respond)

_____

_____

How do we see God wooing His beloved back to Himself in Hosea 2:14-18? Check all that apply:

____ He leads his beloved into the wilderness where He can get her all alone
____ He treats her with loving kindness
____ He cares for her and restores hope to her
____ He takes her back and makes a new covenant with her
____ He removes the sinfulness of her former life

What do we witness in Hosea 2:19-23? What does this remind you of?

_____

_____

What does the Lord command Hosea to do in verse 3:1? What parallel is drawn for us in this verse?

_____

_____

How does Hosea redeem his wife? What was the cost of her payment? (v. 3:2)

_____

_____

According to 1Peter 1:18-19, how did Christ redeem His bride? What was the cost of her payment?

_____

_____

In this heart-wrenching drama found in the book of Hosea, we see the prophet coming to know and understand the heart of God when God tells him to go and marry a woman who would be unfaithful. God knew that Israel would be adulterous toward Him, just as He knew that Gomer would forsake Hosea for other lovers. In an effort to communicate His heart, and the depth of His love for His people, God commanded Hosea to take Gomer as his wife. So, Hosea married Gomer and had three children with her. Then, as God predicted, she went off with other lovers, forsaking the husband who cared for her. Due to her unfaithfulness, Hosea is now faced with the option of divorce.

According to Matthew 19:4-9, what did Jesus say was the only valid reason for divorce? Check the correct answer.

____ Irreconcilable differences

____ Marital unfaithfulness

____ When a husband and wife are no longer happy

Even God considered divorcing unfaithful Israel by saying, "…she is no longer my wife, and I am no longer her husband" (v. 2:2, NLT). However, because of the covenant promises God made to His people, this was impossible. One thing we must understand, above all else, though we are an unfaithful people, God is always faithful to all of His promises (see Psalm 145:13b).

To demonstrate His level of faithfulness, God commanded Hosea to do something even more difficult than to marry Gomer in the first place—God commanded Hosea to take her back, to redeem her and forgive her. By being obedient to God's command, Hosea exemplifies the heart of God for His people by revealing His astonishing love and merciful grace.

In his book, *All the Divine Names and Titles in the Bible*, Herbert Lockyer quotes Dr. G. Campbell Morgan in his study of Hosea by saying: "The prophet declared to the people of God that the relation existing between them and God was most perfectly symbolized in the sacred relationship of marriage; and therefore that their sin against God was that of infidelity, unfaithfulness to love. The prophet learned the truth through the tragic and awful experiences of his own domestic life. He entered into fellowship with God when his own heart was broken. Then there came to him the unutterable and most appalling sorrow that can befall the spirit of man. What the sin of Israel meant to God, Hosea learned by the tragedy of his own home and heart…. Through the infidelity of his wife, Hosea entered into understanding of the sinfulness of sin; so by God's command to him, and his obedience, thereto, he entered into understanding of how God loves in spite of sin—and loves amazingly."[23]

The name *Hosea* in Hebrew means "help or salvation."[24] The name *Jesus* comes from the Greek form of the name Joshua which means "Yahweh [the LORD] saves; Yahweh is salvation"[25]

What does Acts 4:10-12 tell us about the name of Jesus?

_____

_____

Jesus is our true salvation—the faithful Bridegroom who will never leave nor forsake those who have entered into covenant relationship with Him. No matter what we have done or not done, He will be faithful.

To the Israelites, God demonstrated His love and mercy through Hosea, revealing His salvation to a sinful people. To us, "God demonstrates his own love for us in this: While we were still sinners, Christ died for us" (Romans 5:8). In the midst of our sinful adultery, our loyal, faithful Bridegroom redeemed us, paying the price to bring us back to Himself. How then will we respond to such a gracious act of love and devotion?

Let us resolve to no longer live as the world lives (see Romans 12:2); let us no longer desire sin or its pleasures. Let us make and "fulfill our vows to the Most High" (Psalm 50:14), pledging ourselves to our eternal Bridegroom.

But before we offer our vows to the Lord, let us first examine our hearts. What warning is given in Ecclesiastes 5:4-5?

_____

_____

Like any exchange of wedding vows, we must not enter into this commitment lightly. The Bridegroom desires, with all of His heart, to exchange vows of covenant marriage with each of us; however, we must also have the same desire. The trouble is, in our humanness we are weak and unable to keep the covenant vows we make before God. However, God does not leave us without hope.

Read 2 Corinthians 12:9, Hebrews 13:5b and Ezekiel 36:25-27:

What are God's promises to us? What is our hope in keeping these vows before the Lord our God?

_____
_____
_____

Only in Christ, through the power of His Holy Spirit, can we hope to keep our vows to the Lord. Remember, we need God to love God in faithfulness and obedience. We need God in order to fulfill our vows to Him in the covenant relationship Jesus died to give us. He promises us in His word that He will never leave us nor forsake us. God has written His covenant upon our hearts. He will move us to follow Him and His ways. When we are weak, when we feel we cannot fulfill our vows to love Him with all of our heart, soul, mind and strength, our Bridegroom will give us strength. In our weakness, we can call upon Him and He will pour out His strength upon us through the Holy Spirit. We can put our hope in our faithful Husband who will help us in our weakness to be a faithful bride to Him.

If you are ready to exchange vows with the Bridegroom, and willing to depend on Him to make it happen, please read Hosea 2:19-20 aloud. As you read, hear the heart of Christ, your faithful Husband, who desires to make you His forever. Then record your vows to the Bridegroom below. Make it real. Make it personal.

_____
_____
_____
_____
_____
_____
_____
_____
_____
_____
_____
_____
_____
_____
_____

Day Four
Our Kinsman Redeemer

*"Praise be to the LORD, who this day has not left you
without a kinsmen redeemer" (Ruth 4:14).*

The book of Ruth is a true jewel in conveying the heart of Christ as our Bridegroom. From the moment we meet Boaz, the kinsman redeemer, we know him to be a man of position and power; yet, he is a man of tenderness. As you make your way through the book of Ruth, try and witness the mercies and tenderness of our Kinsman Redeemer, Christ Jesus.

Today's lesson is a long one and involves a lot of reading. Therefore, let's begin by praying for stamina, and for the heart of Christ to be revealed.

Read Ruth 1—2:

Let's set the stage; how does the story begin? Describe the circumstances in the life of Naomi and Ruth.

_____

_____

Why did Naomi decide to return to her husband's hometown?

_____

Even though Naomi urged her daughters-in-law to go home, why do you think Ruth remained loyal and refused to be discouraged?

_____

_____

Ruth begged Naomi to let her go with her, proclaiming, "Your people will be my people and your God my God" (v.16). Giving into Ruth's plea, Naomi agreed and the two women set off for Bethlehem. Worn from the burdens of life, the two women arrive in town, greeted by curiosity, and the start of the barley harvest.

In verse 2:1, we see a turning point in our story as our attention shifts to Boaz. How was Boaz introduced to us in Ruth 2:1?

_____

_____

What information are we given about Boaz in Chapter 2? What character traits do you see in him?

_____

_____

_____

What kindnesses does Boaz show to Ruth? List as many as you can:

_____   _____

_____   _____

_____

What blessing does Boaz speak over Ruth? (v. 2:12)

_____

_____

How does Ruth respond to Boaz and the kindness he has shown to her? How does Ruth view herself? What standing or position did she take? (v. 2:13)

_____

_____

What does verse 2:13 tell us about the heart of Ruth?

_____

How do you see the kindness of Boaz paralleling the kindness of Christ?

_____

_____

Based on how Boaz responds overall to Ruth, what impression do you get concerning his feelings for her? How does this equal the heart of Christ for us?

_____

_____

Ruth had absolutely nothing to offer. She was a foreign peasant girl, a Moabite who lost everything. Nonetheless, Boaz, knowing *all* about her (v. 2;11), her reputation, where she came from and all she had done, took note of her and fell in love with her. Boaz was a man of position and good standing in the community; he had wealth, land, and power. He had no reason to notice Ruth; yet, he does. He took her in his care. He was gentle and tender with her. He sheltered her, protected her, fed her and gave her water. He watched over her, poured his blessing upon her, and showed her great mercy and favor.

As hard as it may be to believe, this is exactly how our Redeemer feels about us. There is absolutely no reason for Christ to take note of us. We are a poor and needy people, we have nothing to offer; yet, He is taken captive and enthralled by us (see Psalm 45:11). In His great love He shows us mercy, kindness and favor. As undeserving as we are, He still tenderly takes us under the refuge of His care where He feeds us, protects us, and watches over us.

Read the remainder of the book of Ruth, Chapters 3 to 4.

Before we immerse ourselves in the second half of our study, look back to Ruth 2:20 for a moment. What does Naomi tell Ruth about Boaz? What does she call him?

_____

_____

The NIV tells us that Naomi called Boaz a "kinsman redeemer." The Hebrew word for redeem or redeemer is *ga'al* which means to "rescue" or "deliver." The participial form go'el, means "kinsman-redeemer."[26]

The *Expository Dictionary of Bible Words* states: "The literal and metaphorical meanings of *ga'al* and *go'el* highlight one of the major features of the divine character, that of 'kinsman-redeemer.' Boaz is the most significant and extended human example of this sociological phenomenon in ancient Israel. The office of 'kinsman-redeemer' is one that carried profound significance for the people of Israel, in that it guaranteed the preservation of a family line in the event of a premature passing of a husband who had not fathered children during his lifetime.

Significantly, the function of the 'kinsman-redeemer' was extended, in a spiritual sense, to the person of Yahweh, as one who rescued his people and preserved their status as his chosen ones, promising them an intimate and unique relationship with him forever. That role was ultimately fulfilled in the person of Christ."

Naomi understood the situation all too well, and she recognized the fact that Boaz, the one who had taken notice of Ruth, was one of their kinsman redeemers. You can just see the wheels turning in Naomi's head as she tells Ruth: "It's time that I find a permanent home for you" (v. 3:1, NLT).[27]

In Chapter Three, what does Naomi tell Ruth to do? Check all that apply:

____ Wash, put on your best cloths and wear perfume

____ Go to the threshing floor where Boaz is working

____ Do not let him see you until he has finished eating and drinking

____ Take note of the place where he lays down for the night

____ Go to him, uncover his feet and lay down

____ Listen for his instructions

Ruth did everything Naomi told her to do. Then during the night something startled Boaz and he woke up to find Ruth lying at his feet.

How did Ruth respond to Boaz when he asked: "Who are you?" (v.3:9)

_____

_____

Day Four: Our Kinsman Redeemer

What do you think is the significance of Boaz spreading the corner of his garment (NIV), covering (NAS) over Ruth?

_____
_____

Ruth, in essence, was appealing to the role of Boaz as "kinsman redeemer" on the basis of marriage. If he covered her with his garment or covering, he was agreeing to redeem her. The word *cover* according to the *Expository Dictionary of Bible Words* means to "hide" or "conceal." A secondary meaning is to "clothe."[28]

Consider the following verses; in what way does the Lord cover us?

Psalm 32:1-2: _____
Psalm 85:2: _____
Ephesians 1:7: _____

According to Proverbs 10:12, what does love cover?

_____

How does the Lord clothe those who desire His redemption? (Isaiah 61:10)

_____
_____

Returning to our story, how did Boaz respond to Ruth's request? Was he willing to redeem her? (v. 3:11) ___ YES ___ NO ___ NOT SURE

How long did Boaz wait before he put the plan of redemption into action?
   ___ Two weeks   ___ One year   ___ Until morning

Boaz, smitten with Ruth, and delighted by her request, sets the wheels of redemption into action first thing that morning. Aware that there was one man who was closer in kinship, Boaz devised a plan that would almost ensure his success, redeeming Naomi, the family's land, and Ruth.

Numbers 27:8-11 explains the succession of the "kinsman redeemer." With the understanding given to us in these verses, who do you think the closer "kinsman redeemer" might have been in relationship to Elimelech?

_____

At first, the closer "kinsman redeemer" was all too willing to redeem the property of Elimelech, but the price of the redemption became a little too high when the deal included Ruth, Mahlon's widow. All of a sudden the willing "kinsman redeemer" was not so willing.

What happened as soon as the closer relative refused to buy the land and take Ruth as his wife?

    ____ The meeting ended

    ____ Boaz immediately purchased the family's land and acquired Ruth as his wife

    ____ The people who gathered began to argue about who should purchase the estate

What blessings did the witnesses (all who gathered) proclaim over the couple?

_____

_____

So, Boaz took Ruth as his wife. He consummated the marriage; and, Ruth, who was once barren, conceived by the grace of God and gave birth to a son. Who was this child? What is the family lineage?

_____

_____

How does the story of Ruth and Boaz relate to you personally? In what ways do you witness Christ, your Kinsman Redeemer, acquiring you, giving you new life, and changing your lineage?

_____

_____

It doesn't matter who you are, where you come from, what circumstances have plagued your life, or what sins you have committed, Jesus Christ, the blessed Redeemer, has poured out His blood in order to cover all wrongs, to purchase you back and make you His own, clothing you with a garment of salvation and a robe of righteousness (see Isaiah 61:10).

End today's lesson by meditating on Ruth 4:14-15: "Praise be to the LORD, who this day has not left you without a kinsman redeemer. He will renew your life and sustain you in your old age" (NIV). What does it mean to you that the Lord has not left you without a Kinsman Redeemer—One who will renew you and sustain you all the days of your life?

_____

_____

_____

_____

Day Five
The Lover of our Souls

"You have ravished my heart, my treasure, my bride. I am overcome by one glance of your eyes… (Song of Songs 4:9, NLT).

Perhaps, unlike any other book in the Bible, we see the romantic pursuit and enduring love of Christ's heart for His bride displayed in the poem known as the Song of Songs. Hidden within its lyrical verses are the riches of a love so beautiful, so profound, so holy, and so passionate that it can only be called a sacred romance. The Song of Songs carries at its bosom the heart of Christ's longing and love for the relationship He desires to share with His beloved—His bride.

Many scholars and theologians have different opinions on the interpretation of the Song of Songs. Many pastors and Bible teachers avoid the Song of Songs in their teachings because of its sexual content. Those who dare to preach on the subject often take a more conservative approach by using its poetic verses as examples of godly marriage, and forming lessons that will help strengthen our earthly relationship with our spouse. Although, I believe this more conservative approach to the Song of Songs is valuable and applicable, I also believe that this romantic book of the Bible holds within its grasp something even more priceless—a treasure beyond anything we could ask for or imagine—union with our Bridegroom. Why else would our sovereign God inspire such a book, and place it right in the heart of His Word?

From the beginning of the Song to the end of the Song, we see parallels, examples of Christ tenderly wooing His bride as He cries out, "Arise, my darling, my beautiful one, and come away with me" (Song of Songs 2:10), to His jealous, unyielding, fiery love that burns so strongly that many waters cannot wash it away (see Song of Songs 8:6-7). There is a great deal we can learn about our Bridegroom from the Song of Songs, and the journey He desires to share with each of us as His beloved. Therefore, open your heart and join me on what promises to be a beautiful love story of unequaled and unfailing love.

Let's begin our journey by asking the Spirit of Truth to open our hearts to the possibilities of the sacred romance. Then read 1 Kings 3:5-14:

Based on these verses in 1 Kings, what kind of a man would you say Solomon was?

_____

_____

Solomon asked the Lord for wisdom. God was pleased with his request and promised to give him the very thing he asked for: "Behold, I have done according to your words. Behold, I have given you a wise and discerning heart (NASB), a wise and understanding mind (NLT), so that there has been no one like you before you, nor shall one like you arise after you" (1 Kings 3:12, NASB).

Based on 1 Kings 4:29-34, describe the extent of the wisdom Solomon received from the Lord.

_____

_____

Solomon, according to Scripture, was given wisdom, understanding, and knowledge, "too vast to be measured" (NLT). And from this great wisdom and insight the Lord gave to Solomon, he wrote the books of: Proverbs, Ecclesiastes, and the Song of Songs. Some translations even refer to the Song of Songs as the Song of Solomon.

Therefore, in our quest to *know* God, how can we forsake such wisdom? How can we turn our backs on the riches of such knowledge, insight and understanding? Solomon had an incredible relationship with God, and the Lord revealed His great favor to Solomon and inspired him to write about something very dear to His heart.

With this in mind, let's turn to the Song of Songs and read chapters 1—2 and 4.

For the purpose of our study today, we will focus on Chapters 1, 2 and 4. However, if you are not familiar with, or have never read the Song of Songs, please read the whole book. It is worth the extra effort.

> King Solomon, inspired by the Holy Spirit (see 2 Peter 1:20-21), penned this incredible poem of love shared between himself and a young Shulammite maiden. How does Solomon portray himself in the story?
>
> ___ As a tyrant   ___ As a ruler   ___ As a lover
>
> In this story, how would you describe their relationship? How does the man view his beloved? How does the woman view her lover?
>
> _____
>
> _____
>
> In what way(s) can you see the love of Christ being communicated in this poem? As Solomon wooed his beloved, how does this parallel Christ wooing his Bride?
>
> _____
>
> _____
>
> In what way(s) are you experiencing the wooing of Christ in your life?
>
> _____
>
> _____

The word *woo*, according to *Webster's Dictionary* means "to make love to, to court, to endeavor to gain."[29] A wooer is a lover. Christ is the lover of your soul, who, through His Holy Spirit, desires to gain your heart, to court you and draw you into His everlasting love.

Day Five: The Lover of our Souls

> How do you feel about experiencing Christ as a lover? Does the thought make you feel uncomfortable? Why or Why not?

I am praying that you would open your heart to this incredible revelation, as hard as it may be to receive. Do not be afraid to yearn for the intimacy of the king's chambers (see Song of Songs 1:4b). This is what Solomon's father, King David, called the secret place. The secret place is a place of exclusive passion expressed between the Lover and the beloved—a place of true worship set aside for God alone.

> What did Jesus tell us in John 4:23-24? What kind of worship does God seek?

Through the Holy Spirit, who is Spirit and Truth, God invites us into the intimacy of His chambers, into the exclusive passion of the secret place. Only by the power of the Holy Spirit can we enter. Only in the power of the Spirit can we love God the way He desires to be loved. We must learn to expand our view of worship, increasing our access to the heart of God. We must learn the power of proximity, so we can pursue Him with such genuine and burning passion that it draws us closer than we've ever been before, to the point where we begin to experience Christ as a lover.

> With this in mind, read Song of Songs 4:9-15 again. What new insight or understanding have you received?

> How do you witness Christ's passionate heart toward His bride? What do you think He is communicating to her in these verses?

I love Song of Songs 4:9-10. What does it mean to you to know you have stolen (NIV) and ravished (KJV, NLT) the heart of Christ, and that your love is delightful and pleasing to Him?

No other union on earth is like the consummation of love shared between a man and a woman. And no other connection touches us as profoundly and intensely as this sense of oneness. Physical and spiritual intimacy is the divine idea of the All-powerful Sovereign God of the Universe. The art and passion of making love is God's idea. He designed it, created it, implemented it and intended it to be shared privately between a husband and a wife—between a man and a woman joined together as one through the bonds of holy matrimony. And after creating this incredible image of total union between a man and woman becoming one, God shocks us by telling us that this is the very thing He longs for with us. From the beginning God created marriage, gender, and sexuality as a much deeper reality—as a living metaphor—of the pure and holy spiritual intimacy He desires with us, His bride.

Right now, you may be thinking: *This kind of intimacy cannot possibly be of God. He is holy and pure, and ecstasy and pleasure is of the world.* I understand why you might feel this way. I, too, felt this way when the concept of the sacred romance was first presented to me. I could not lay hold of the idea that God, our omnipotent God, wanted to have this kind of relationship with me, or anyone for that matter.

However, when looking at the sacred romance, we cannot look at it through earthly eyes. We must look at this sacred romance through a heavenly perspective. We live in a fallen world, and when we look at the worlds' idea of intimate pleasure it is perverse and permissive, exploiting the body and making physical intimacy appear ugly, and at times vulgar. This is exactly the response Satan wants each of us to embrace, because his chief goal is to keep us from the One who loves us passionately and dearly.

In order to broaden our perspective, and help us lay hold of this incredible revelation, let's look up a few words. The word *intimate* means "innermost; deeply familiar; close; and cherished."[30] The word *commune* means "to converse together intimately; to have spiritual intercourse."[31] The word *union* means "an act of joining two or more things into one; … marriage."[32] And the word *unite* means "to join; to make into one; to form a whole; …to be joined together; to grow together; to act as one."[33]

Do you recall when I said in Week Two, Day One: "To know God is to become one with Christ"? This is the desire of God's heart, that we become united with Him in relationship through Christ. United together as one bride, and united with Him in intimate communion. Our hearts and souls yearn for an experience of worship so deep, so profound, that it fills our beings with such ecstasy that we lose ourselves in complete awe of the other.

I understand this concept can be difficult to grasp, but the sacred romance, intimacy with Christ, the hunger and thirst to be united with God is grounded in Scripture.

> What did Jesus pray to His Father in John 17:20-23 and 26? Check all that apply:
> ___ Make them one with the world
> ___ Make them one with each other
> ___ Make them one with us (Father and Son)

How do the following verses express the passion and ecstasy of the sacred romance?

Psalm 42:1-2: _____

Psalm 63:1: _____

Psalm 63:3; 8: _____

Psalm 84:2: _____

Isaiah 55:1-3: _____

If you are having trouble embracing this unequaled romance, allow me to encourage you to not pull back. In many ways, the church, as a whole, is holding back, even withdrawing from her pure devotion to Christ (see 2 Corinthians 11:2-3). She is being deceived by the

Day Five: The Lover of our Souls

enemy; even being fed watered down religion as a form of Christianity. As a result, when she hears about how much Christ loves her, desires her, and longs for her, she withdraws, afraid to surrender, afraid of being made one with her Bridegroom.

As hard as it may be to believe, God is truly in love with us. Even in our weakness and brokenness, He longs for us to share divine spiritual encounters with Him—to come and drink from the inconceivable spiritual pleasures of oneness with Him.

Deep down we want and long for this relationship too. God created us this way, to desire true love and to know the spiritual pleasure of being enjoyed not only by another human, but by Him. The tragedy is we have been numbed to the revelation of God's love. The majority of believers are so disengaged from the truth of God's extravagantly lavish love for them, so trapped within the boundaries of religious Christianity, that they completely miss out on the depth of relationship Christ desires to share with them. We've been taught to settle, to put limits on our relationship with God. But Christ wants us to lay aside every preconceived notion and respond to Him the way He longs to be received—as a Lover.

If we are to ever truly grasp intimate fellowship with Christ, we must first receive a revelation into the emotional framework of His heart. We must look into the heart of Christ and allow Him to reveal the height, length, width and breadth of His love (see Ephesians 3:18-19), and to allow that revelation to turn us inside out.

Christ Jesus is looking for a devoted lover. He does not want a bride who is content to sit in the mediocrity of carnal religion. He is seeking a bride who desires an ongoing, intimate, fiery relationship with Him as a beloved Husband. The question is: Are you willing? Are you willing to surrender everything, to abandon yourself completely, so you may be given the power of the Holy Spirit to worship in spirit and truth? Are you willing to let go of complacency and reach out for the love that only Christ can give you? Are you willing to embrace the opportunity to know Christ in the joy of the sacred romance—a love affair that goes beyond the reaches of your imagination?

We come alive in the love of God, and we are never closer to Christ than when we are lost in His unfathomable love. The best moments with Christ happen in the quietness of the secret place. There is an intimacy that is closer than that of husband and wife. Embrace it!

> If you desire to go deeper in intimacy with the Bridegroom, end today by meditating on Psalm 63:1 and cry out to Him as the psalmist did, with all your heart, soul, mind and strength: "O God, you are my God, earnestly I seek you; my soul thirsts for you, my body longs for you, in a dry and weary land where there is no water…" (Psalm 63:1).

If you are not quite ready to embrace Christ as a lover, then share with Him what you think is holding you back. Ask Him to help you to see the relationship through His eyes. End today by meditating on Song of Songs 7:10, "I belong to my lover, and his desire is for me," and then ask Jesus to open your heart and help you to embrace His desire for you. Because, Dear One, if you truly desire to know God, then you must learn how to draw close to Him in the secret place.

Apply the Knowledge

In my pursuit of the Bridegroom this week, the Holy Spirit has shown me …

_____
_____
_____
_____

The verse that spoke to me the most this week is…

_____
_____

In order to make this verse a reality in my life, I…

_____
_____
_____
_____

The changes I need to make, the barriers that need to be broken down in order to know Christ Jesus more deeply and intimately as the Bridegroom are…

_____
_____
_____
_____

Lord Jesus, I desire to be your beloved, help me to develop…

_____
_____
_____
_____

The hidden treasure (see Isaiah 45:3) of His Person and personality God reveal to me this week is… This higher revelation of God's presence profoundly awakens me to…

_____
_____
_____
_____

Witnessing Christ as a Bridegroom this week has changed my perspective of God from… to…

_____
_____
_____
_____

Holy Spirit, help me to apply what I've learned to my everyday life, so…

_____
_____
_____
_____

Prayer for the Journey

Lord God, give me a revelation of Your love for me. Help me to worship You in Spirit and Truth. Teach me to love You the way You desire to be loved. Help me to know and recognize all the dimensions of Your heart and passion for me personally. Open my heart to experience greater depths of union with You through the bonds of covenant relationship. Increase my hunger and help me to…

_____
_____
_____
_____
_____
_____

Apply the Knowledge

Session Four
Gifts from the Bridegroom

Ezekiel 16:1-19; 32

"So you were adorned with gold and silver; your clothes were of fine linen and costly fabric and embroidered cloth…You became very beautiful and rose to be a queen" (Ezekiel 16:13).

God can deliver us and give us everything, yet we can still:

1.) Not _____ Him.
(Ezekiel 16:15)

2.) Take Him for _____ .
(Ezekiel 16:16-19)

3.) _____ Him. (Ezekiel 16:32)

When we _____ we give away our _____.

When we _____ we give away our _____ and _____.

When we _____ we forfeit our _____.

When we embrace _____ we give away our _____.

Week Five
Know That I AM Your Redeemer

There was nothing like the day I discovered salvation—that glorious day when I received God's grace through faith in Jesus Christ. I recall the feeling of freedom and peace as it washed over me. In that moment, with tears of gratitude, I knew I had been set free from the bondage that had weighed me down for years. I did not have all of the answers. I did not understand all of what had happened. I did not fully grasp the reality of the situation; nor did I fully comprehend all of what Jesus had done for me on the cross in paying the punishment for my sins. No, at that moment, all I knew was: *I needed Jesus.*

The price of God's redeeming grace is beyond measure. It is a treasure, a gift, so valuable we will never comprehend its worth in this lifetime. I am grateful for God's eternal redemption found in His Son, Jesus Christ. I will never forget what He has done for me, and the pit of depression from which He pulled my sorry soul. Yet, there is more to this story of redemption than we realize.

Salvation is just the beginning of a lifelong journey where God repeatedly offers His compassion, loving kindness, and tender mercies every day. With a gentle hand He leads us, if we let Him, into deeper revelations of His love and forgiveness, helping us to draw closer to Him than ever before. Psalm 103:10-11; 13 gives us this glimpse of God's tender heart, "He does not treat us as our sins deserve or repay us according to our iniquities. For as high as the heavens are above the earth, so great is his love for those who fear him. As a father has compassion on his children, so the LORD has compassion on those who fear him."

Psalm 103:10-11; 13 is a portrait of God's perfect love for us. We deserve to be treated as our sins merit; instead God offers kindness and gentleness. We deserve to be punished for our transgressions; instead God offers forgiveness and mercy. First John 4:18 says, "…perfect love casts out fear." God's perfect love helps us to come to Him when we need His forgiveness, instead of running in the other direction. Perfect love throws out the idea of condemnation (see Romans 8:1), and helps us draw near to receive God's redeeming grace.

David, the author of Psalm 103, had this revelation of God's gentle kindness that leads to repentance (see Romans 2:4). David understood God's heart and love toward him so well, that he knew how to relate to God on the foundation of God's zealous heart, rather than on his own weaknesses.

This kind of confidence in God's love, and the revelation of His passionate heart are rare in the church. We, as Christians, do not fully grasp the level of love the Lord carries in His heart for each of us. We need to come to a place, like David, where we understand, without a doubt, that our God is a redemptive God full of tender mercy, gentleness, compassion and loving kindness, so we will come to His throne of grace daily with expectation and longing.

Psalm 103:2-5; 8-13

*"Praise the LORD, O my soul, and forget not all his benefits—
who forgives all your sins and heals all your diseases,
who redeems your life from the pit and crowns you with love and compassion,
who satisfies your desires with good things…
The LORD is compassionate and gracious, slow to anger, abounding in love.
He does not treat us as our sins deserve or repay us according to our iniquities.
For as high as the heavens are above the earth, so great is his love for those who
fear him; as far as the east is from the west, so far has he removed
our transgressions from us. As a father has compassion on his children,
so the LORD has compassion on those who fear him…"*

This week we are going to:

Know that our Redeemer lives
"I know that my Redeemer lives …"
(Job 19:25).

Regard our actions before a world who does not know God
"I have chosen you out of the world"
(John 15:19b).

Consider what it takes to be an effective witness
"And you also must testify, for you have been with me…"
(John 15:27).

Practice extending God's hand of mercy
"But with you there is forgiveness…"
(Psalm 130:4).

Witness God's redemptive heart
"Because of the LORD's great love we are not consumed;
for his compassions never fail"
(Lamentations 3:22).

Day One
The Savior is Alive

"The LORD lives! Praise be to my Rock! Exalted be God, the Rock, my Savior! (2 Samuel 22:47).

Before we dive into this week's lesson on the Redeemer, we must first take into consideration an important fact—our Redeemer lives! One of the greatest misconceptions, and the reason some people do not put their faith in Jesus as the Savior of the world, is because they believe He is dead.

I have a Jewish friend. His name is Nisim. I love sitting with him and talking about the difference between Christianity and the Jewish culture. Nisim is very passionate about Jehovah God, and when he shares with me about his Jewish heritage, I am enthralled. Nevertheless, in spite of his zealous heart toward God, he does not believe that Jesus is the promised Messiah. To Nisim, Jesus was a prophet, a teacher, maybe a saint. To Nisim, Jesus was only a man who walked the earth over two thousand years ago and is no longer alive.

There are many people in this world who do not know Jesus, so let's begin today's lesson by praying for my friend Nisim, and for all those we know who do not know Jesus.

Read Luke 24:13-35:

As Cleopas and his companion walked along that dusty road from Jerusalem to Emmaus, they discussed the current events of the day. As they discussed these things, Jesus came up and walked along with them (v.15).

Who did these men say Jesus was? (v. 19)

_____

What did they say happened to Jesus? (v. 20)

_____

What had they hoped for? (v. 21)

_____

What did they say happened when the women went to the tomb? Check all that apply:

____ The women found the tomb empty

____ The women found Jesus' body

____ The women claimed they saw angels who told them "He is alive!"

After the women came and reported what they had witnessed, did the others believe their story?   ____ YES   ____ NO   Why or why not?

_____

Fill in the blanks according to Luke 24:25, NIV:

"He (Jesus) said to them, "How _____ you are, and how _____ of _____ to believe all that the prophets have spoken!"

As they continued to walk along, what did Jesus share with these two men? (v. 27)

_____

At what point did the two men finally believe Jesus was alive? (v. 30-31)

_____

Why do you think the two men did not believe Jesus was alive while He was walking with them and opening the Scriptures to them?

_____
_____

The two men (and the other eleven) did not believe the women when they went to the tomb and brought back the message from the angels. They still did not believe even when Jesus, the Word Himself (see John 1:1), came alongside of them, walked with them, and told them they were foolish to not believe the prophets and the Word of God. They did not believe until their eyes were unveiled, as Jesus broke the bread. Once they saw for themselves, they ran back to Jerusalem and proclaimed to the others, "It is true! The LORD has risen…"

What lie had been spread about Jesus according to Matthew 28:11-15?

_____

It breaks my heart when such blatant lies are readily accepted and passed on as if they are fact. The Word of God tells us something very different about the One we put our hope in, and claim as our Redeemer.

Look up the following verses:

	Who is the witness?	*What did they proclaim?*
Job 19:25:	_____	_____
Psalm 18:46a:	_____	_____
Matthew 28:5-6:	_____	_____
Acts 2:32:	_____	_____

In Revelation 1:18, Jesus said, "I am the Living One; I was dead, and behold I am alive forever and ever!" Jesus did die on the cross for our sins—but behold—He is now alive!

Day One: The Savior is Alive

According to Romans 6:8-11, what have we been given as a result of Christ's death and resurrection life?

_____
_____

Through the death of Jesus Christ, we are given the power to receive victory over sin and death. And, through His life, we are given the privilege of being alive to God, as the life of Christ reigns in us and through us.

Why is this truth significant? Why is it important to understand that Jesus died for our sins, and then was raised to life? Why is it vital that we believe Jesus lives!?

_____
_____

If you believe, like my friend Nisim, that Jesus existed at one time, but was only a teacher or prophet, then you are forsaking divine forgiveness. If you are like those two men on the road to Emmaus, before Jesus opened their eyes, hope of a redeemer has been deferred. The very foundational core of our belief as Christians is Jesus died for our sins, and rose again to give us victory over sin and death, to give us a new life in Him. No other religion in the world makes this claim.

What did the Lord proclaim about Himself through the prophet Isaiah in verses 43:11 and 44:6?

_____

Apart from the King of Israel, the First and the Last, the Lord Almighty, there is no other God—there is no other Savior. The Lord alone redeems our lives, and brings us into complete union with Himself. My dear friends, Jesus is alive! And we, who believe in His death and divine resurrection, share in His death and are made alive in Him.

How do the following verses identify this truth?
Romans 6:4-5: _____
Galatians 2:20: _____
Colossians 2:9-13: _____

How has being made alive in Christ impacted you personally? What evidence is there in your life that declares: The Savior is alive, and He is alive in me?

_____
_____

Precious one, more than anything else, the Lord's truest desire is that you be dead to sin, and alive with Him. Jesus is the Way, the Truth and the Life (see John 14:6). He is our Redeemer—the Savior of the world—and He is alive! I pray that you can claim that today with everything that is in you.

> End today by meditating on Psalm 98. These verses offer a wonderful song of praise to the Lord for His marvelous act of salvation. Therefore, let's join together and offer a new song of praise to our Redeemer. Let us shout for joy! Let us burst into jubilant song! Let's let our souls, together with all the earth, rejoice in the Lord and delight in His salvation (see Psalm 35:9).

I sincerely hope you were able to join me with songs of jubilant praise before the Lord. If, on the other hand, you are feeling spiritually dry and have lost the joy of His salvation, use the space below to cry out to the Lord as David did is Psalm 51:12: "Restore to me the joy of your salvation and grant me a willing spirit, to sustain me." You and I will never fully understand all of what our Redeemer has done for us in this lifetime, but if we open our hearts and respond to the soft whisper of His Spirit wooing us, we will once again witness the joy of His salvation and be able to proclaim from the depth of our soul, "Yes, my Redeemer Lives!"

Day One: The Savior is Alive

Day Two
The World Does Not Know Him

"The world cannot accept him, because it neither sees him nor knows him"
(John 14:17b).

Last night, as I watched a television program I do not normally watch, I witnessed two men having a dispute over Christianity. One man considered himself a devout Christian. The other claimed to be a former pastor who had turned away from the faith, because of the very attitude exhibited by the man arguing with him, and by other Christians like him. As I listened to their argument my heart sank, sick with grief. Both of these men threw Scripture at each other in an attempt to support their own viewpoint, while accusing the other of false teaching. Part of the problem was both of these men took the verses out of context in order to prevail at making their point. They used the Word of God as a weapon, instead of truth. As the battle continued, I became more and more convinced that neither of these men knew Christ, or understood His heart.

Some people who call themselves "Christians" really turn me off to Christianity. Due to their approach, if I didn't know better, or didn't have a personal relationship with God through Jesus Christ, I wouldn't want anything to do with Christianity. I believe that this is the very reason why many, who don't know Jesus, push Him, Christianity, and the church away. The world doesn't know Him, and all too often, we, the church, act like we don't know Him either.

When I listen to some of those who call themselves "Christians," my heart sinks at the critical nature and finger-pointing cynicism, as if the world is worthless and they have it all together. This type of attitude pushes people away, instead of leading them to God. Church, we need to be vessels of light and love, instruments through which God can draw people to Himself. The world is not worthless in God's eyes. He loved the world, all people, so much that He sent His only begotten Son to die for them (see John 3:16). We need to make the world take a second look, to stop and wonder what we have that they are missing out on. We need to be such instruments of love that the world hungers for what we have in Christ. As it stands, many people, especially in North America, are running from the church in mass numbers feeling unaccepted and condemned. We do not have to accept the world's behavior, or agree with their attitudes, but if we want to be part of winning a lost world to Jesus Christ, then we have got to stop with the holier-than-thou-attitude and start behaving like we *know* Jesus.

Let's begin with prayer for a lost and hurting world, and for God to make us true instruments of His light and love.

Fill in the blanks according to John 1:10, NIV:

"He (Jesus) was in the world, and though the world was made through him, the _____ _____ _____ _____ him."

The word *recognize* according to *Webster's Dictionary* means "to know again; to identify; to acknowledge; to treat as valid."[34] Even though the world was created through Him, and for Him (see Colossians 1:16b), the world did not know Him.

Look up the following verses and answer the questions:

John 1:24-26:

Who was the witness giving testimony? _____
Who did not know Christ? _____
Why didn't they know Him? _____

John 7:25-30:
Who was the witness giving testimony? _____
Who did not know Christ? _____
Why didn't they know Him? _____
How did the people respond? _____

John 8:12-20:
Who was the witness giving testimony? _____
Who did not know Christ? _____
Why didn't they know Him? _____
How did the people respond? _____

John 8:48-59:
Who was the witness giving testimony? _____
Who did not know Christ? _____
Why didn't they know Him? _____
How did the people respond? _____

The world did not know Him. The Pharisees and the teachers of the law did not know Him; and the Jewish community did not know Him. They claimed that He was demon possessed, a liar, and a false prophet testifying on His own behalf; therefore, His testimony in their eyes was invalid. They accused Him, challenged Him, and tried to kill Him. They didn't know Jesus, because they didn't know God the Father. They focused on religious rituals, instead of the truth. They clung to a false belief system based on what they were taught. Then when what they believed was challenged, they rebuked it, rebelled against it, and wanted to destroy it, because Jesus went against the very core of their religious mind set.

This is often exactly how the world reacts today when their belief system is challenged. This is why many people become upset when their worldly view is confronted. They don't want to receive the truth. They fight it, rebuke it, dispute it, make fun of it, and call those who bring the truth demon possessed, false prophets, and liars. True Christianity goes against the core of the world's belief system. It confronts the world's way of life, and dares to tell the world it is lost. Notice that I used the word *lost* and not *wrong*. One of the greatest mistakes we, as Christians, make is that we try to tell the world it is wrong; rather, we need to show the world that there is a better way. When we don't take this approach, the world yells in the face of Christianity and tells her that she is intolerant, unreasonable, unfair, and selfish.

Jesus wept as He approached the city of Jerusalem in the days before His crucifixion, because they did not know Him (see Luke 19:41), and it broke His heart. "He was in the world, and though the world was made through him, the world did not recognize him" (John 1:10). The simple truth is: The world reacts the way it does, because the world does not know God.

The comedian makes jokes about God and the church, because he doesn't know God. The non-churchgoer complains that church is boring, because he doesn't know God. Television programs have writers who create characters who mock God and make fun of Christian values, because they don't know God. Many people in the world today respond the way they do, because they do not have a personal relationship with God through Jesus Christ.

The other day, I watched a television program where the writers of the show portrayed a Christian character as pompous, judgmental, self-righteous and smug. Church, too many times, this is the world's opinion of us. Those writers wrote that scene with the perspective that all Christians act this way. Are they right? Of course not, but all too often, we, who claim to be Christians, give them this opinion because of the way we act. It's just like those two men I told you about at the beginning of today's lesson. Jesus, through His Word, told us that the world will not like us, but that doesn't mean that we should act like the world.

Read John 15:18-27 and consider the following:

Why will the world hate and turn against believers?

_____

_____

Is the world's attitude and treatment just? Why or why not?

_____

_____

What have we been given, that the world does not possess, to help us to be effective Christ-like witnesses to the world?

_____

The world does not understand; therefore, there is no point in arguing with them. They do not have the Spirit of God; consequently, they do not know God. "We have not received the spirit of the world but the Spirit who is from God, that we may understand what God has freely given us. This is what we speak, not in words taught us by human wisdom but in words taught by the Spirit, expressing spiritual truths in spiritual words. The man without the Spirit does not accept the things that come from the Spirit of God, for they are foolishness to him, and he cannot understand them, because they are spiritually discerned" (1 Corinthians 2:12-14).

When we deal with people who do not know God, we must not deal with them in anger, arguing our point by throwing Scripture in their faces, because they will not understand. If we take that approach, people will rebel and recoil. In the end, the only thing these people will be convinced of is Christianity is unbearable and critical, and that they want nothing to do with it.

So, what are we as Christians to do? Ignore the world and hope it will go away? Pray that one day the world will wake up and recognize the lies it has embraced?

What did Jesus tell His disciples they should do in Matthew 5:13-16?

_____

What did Jesus tell His disciples in Acts 1:8?

_____

We are to be witnesses of the One we know. We are to take the light God has given us by the power of the Holy Spirit and let our actions, love, and good deeds shine before man—before all those who do not know God. We are not going to win the world over with our words, which are spiritually discerned; instead we are going to win the world over with love and our acts of generosity, kindness and patience. We are not to judge or condemn the world. God the Father did not send His only Son into the world to condemn the world, but to reveal His love and to save the world through Him (see John 3:16-17). There will be a Day of Judgment when God will judge the world for its sins and unrighteousness, and the world will be without excuse (see John 15:22); but, until then, we are to bring the message of truth in love, like witnesses who know God.

> Jesus said, "...by their fruit you will recognize them" (see Matthew 7:16-20). We will know whether or not someone truly *knows* God by the fruit revealed in his/her life (Week One, Day Five). End today by meditating on Galatians 5:22-26. How are we, who have the Spirit, to live? When we live by the Spirit, what will the Spirit produce in our lives?

_____

_____

_____

_____

_____

Beloved, the world should see that we know God because we walk by the power of the Holy Spirit and that His fruit is evident in our lives. The world will not understand because it neither sees Him nor knows Him (see John 14:17), but, nevertheless, we, need to behave like disciples who have been taken out of the world with its worldly attitudes and actions. Therefore, let us challenge ourselves every day to act like the witnesses Christ has called us to be.

Day Three
Like One Who Has Witnessed

"But you will receive power when the Holy Spirit comes upon you; and you will be my witnesses in Jerusalem, and in all Judea and Samaria, and to the ends of the earth" (Acts 1:8).

This week we have been focusing on Christ as our resurrected Redeemer. Yesterday, we took a look at what it means to be an effective witness for the Lord Jesus Christ before a world who does not know God. As we continue to consider what it means to be an effective witness, we will look once again at Acts 1:8 in order to determine two vital elements that are necessary to being Christ's witnesses.

> Let's begin by asking our Redeemer to make us powerful witnesses, and then read Acts 1:8. In this verse Jesus makes two powerful statements, what are they?
>
> 1) _____
>
> 2) _____

In Acts 1:8 Jesus gives His disciples the command to be His witnesses in Jerusalem, in all Judea and Samaria, and to the ends of the earth. This would naturally be an impossible assignment; but, the good news is Jesus also tells his disciples how they will be successful in the task He has given them. First, He tells them they will receive power when the Holy Spirit comes upon them, and then He tells them they will be His witnesses. In order to be an effective witness to a world who does not know Christ, we must have two things: The Holy Spirit and a personal testimony. Without the Holy Spirit's power we will not be successful witnesses, and without a personal testimony, we have no personal experience to give evidence to.

First Vital Element: Personal Testimony

Do you know Christ as your personal Redeemer? Have you experienced the One who delivered you from captivity? In order to be an effective witness, you must first witness. You must have seen, heard, touched, and experienced the redemption that is found in Christ Jesus before you can share Jesus with the world.

In Week One, Day One, we defined the word *witness* as "testimony; one who, or that which, furnishes evidence or proof; one who has seen or has knowledge of incident; ... to be witness of or to; to give evidence; to testify."[35]

In Matthew 28:18-20 Jesus commissioned the disciples by saying, "All authority in heaven and on earth has been given to me. Therefore, go and make disciples of all nations, baptizing them in the name of the Father and of the Son and of the Holy Spirit, and teaching them to obey everything I have commanded you. And surely I am with you always, to the very end of the age." Just as He did in Acts 1:8, Jesus appointed the disciples to go and be His witnesses; to tell, show, and teach others everything they had witnessed from Him.

According to John 8:28b, where did Jesus learn this concept?

___

Before Jesus pronounced the great commission upon the disciples' lives, He first gave them the opportunity to witness Him in action, to learn from Him, to experience Him, to see, hear, and touch Him for themselves.

According to the following verses, how did the disciples witness Jesus?

John 1:14: ___
Mark 6:1-2: ___
Matthew 14:35-36: ___
1 John 1:1-3: ___

Look back over your answers and circle each time you recorded any form of the words "see, hear, and touch."

These are only a few examples of what the disciples witnessed. Each time Jesus opened His mouth, they witnessed His teaching, His encouragement, His instruction, and His testimony. Every time they looked at Him they witnessed His glory and experienced His miracles. Every time He touched someone, they witnessed His power and mercy. Every day they saw, heard, touched, and came to know the One who would one day commission them to be His witnesses.

What an incredible opportunity the disciples had. Can you imagine the power of their influence, all because they saw, heard, and touched?

How different do you think their testimony would have been void of these experiences?

___

Think about your own testimony of Jesus. How different would your testimony be if you did not witness Jesus for yourself?

___

Like the first disciples, Jesus still gives His disciples today tangible opportunities to know Him—to see His glory, witness His miracles, hear His voice, and receive His power.

Day Three: Like One Who Has Witnessed

Second Vital Element: The Holy Spirit

Again read Acts 1:8:

Record again the two powerful statements Jesus made in this verse.

1) _____

2) _____

Circle the statement that tells us how it will be possible for us to be effective witnesses.

Jesus said, "But you will receive power *when* the Holy Spirit comes on you; *and* you will be my witnesses…" *(emphasis mine)*. Notice that the power of the Holy Spirit comes first. He is the One who gives us the ability to be effective witnesses for Christ.

Read John 15:26-27:

What command did Jesus give His disciples? (v. 27)

_____

How would the disciples accomplish this mission? (v. 26)

_____

The disciples had been with Jesus from the beginning of His earthly ministry. They knew Him. They experienced Him. They could give you any fact or detail about Jesus you wanted to know; but, the power to testify came from the Holy Spirit. The disciples needed both to be effective witnesses. They needed to live it—to have a personal testimony only found through intimate experience. Then they needed the Holy Spirit to give them the authority and capability to testify.

Read Acts 2:1-41:

What happened on the day of Pentecost? Check all that apply:

____ The Holy Spirit came upon them like tongues of fire

____ A crowd gathered outside

____ Peter boldly testified about Jesus Christ

____ Three thousand accepted Peter's testimony of witness

Before Peter stood before the crowd and testified about Jesus, the Holy Spirit came upon him, and all those who had gathered together that day. Before Peter uttered one word of testimony, before 3000 were added to their numbers, the Holy Spirit fell upon all of them like tongues of fire and infused them with power, giving each one the ability to be an effective witness of Jesus Christ.

How has the Holy Spirit helped you to be an effective witness for Jesus Christ? What testimony have you given that could have only come through the power of the Holy Spirit?

From my own practice of witnessing to a world who does not know Jesus, I know for a fact that in order for me to be an effective witness I need to have both a valid testimony, and the power of the Holy Spirit speaking through me. Years ago, when I was young in the Lord, I was given many opportunities to share my testimony before large groups of people. As I spoke, the Spirit of God would come upon me, delivering my testimony with great authority. As a result of His power working through me, I watched, in amazement, many people being instantly healed, delivered and set free from all kinds of bondage. Unfortunately, I also recall other times, when I tried to witness void of the Spirit's power. The results were either disastrous or completely fruitless. I was unsuccessful in my attempt to share Jesus, because I was trying to do it in my own strength.

How do you see Isaiah 43:10 from a fresh perspective? "You are my witnesses," declares the LORD, "and my servant whom I have chosen, so that you may know and believe me and understand that I am he." In light of what we have studied these past two days, how does this verse speak to you? Do you see Isaiah 43:10 from a fresh perspective?

Day Three: Like One Who Has Witnessed

Day Four
The Need to Forgive

"Lord, how many times shall I forgive my brother when he sins against me?"
(Matthew 18:21)

It is not easy to forgive. Most of us have a very difficult time letting go of past grievances and forgiving people who have wronged us or hurt those we love. Sometimes, it is even difficult to forgive ourselves.

I know I am guilty of unforgiveness toward self. Too many times, when I made a mistake, I couldn't seem to forgive myself of the accusation. I harbored it. I carried it, again and again, before the throne of grace as if God were unwilling or incapable of forgiving me the first time. However, Christ has shown me that unforgiveness toward self is just as much of a grievous sin as not forgiving another. That's serious.

Today's lesson on forgiveness may be challenging, so allow me to encourage you to not pull back from what Scripture teaches us about forgiveness. As effective witnesses of Jesus Christ, we need to know and experience His forgiveness for the wrongs we have done, and then we need to allow Jesus to show us how to forgive those who have wronged us.

Let's begin today by praying to our merciful and gracious redeeming God, and then read Matthew 18:21-35, and answer the following.

What question did Peter ask Jesus about forgiveness?

_____

How many times did Jesus say we are to forgive someone when they sin against us?

____ Seven times

____ Seventy times seven

____ Never

In the story Jesus told, what do you think He was communicating to Peter about forgiveness?

_____

_____

How much did the servant owe the king? _____

Could the servant repay the king?   ___ YES   ___ NO   ___ NOT SURE

Did the king forgive the debt?   ___ YES   ___ NO   ___ NOT SURE

What attitude did the king have toward the servant? What emotion filled his heart?

What happened as soon as the forgiven servant left the king's presence?

Check all that apply:

    ___ The servant sought out someone who owed him money

    ___ The servant demanded the debt against him be paid in full

    ___ The servant refused to forgive the man

    ___ The servant had the man thrown into prison

How much did the man owe the servant? _____

Why do you think the servant, who was forgiven by the king, was unwilling to forgive the man who owed him?

Who told on the servant? Who did they tell?

What did the king say about the servant's behavior? How should he have treated the man? (v. 32-33)

How was the unforgiving servant treated in verse 34?

What do you think is the parallel to being tortured in prison until the debt is paid in full?

God has forgiven us of much, far more than we could ever hope to repay. Yet, so many times, we cannot find it in our hearts to forgive another who has wronged us—even if the sin against us is a little one.

Not too long ago, my husband and I were sitting at a car dealership finalizing a purchase transaction. As we sat there, the salesman, who was also the owner, told us about another man who cheated him. Angry, the salesman went on and on about what this man had done, and how he had hurt him. "How can I forgive this man?" The salesman questioned. "If I forgive him, it is like I am saying what he did was okay. And it's not okay."

A friend of mine suffered a heinous injustice when his 18-year-old daughter was drugged and raped by a young man at a party. He was furious, so enraged by the boy's actions that he wanted to hunt him down and kill him. Thankfully my friend sought the Lord instead of carrying out his threat. As a result, Christ helped Jim find forgiveness in his heart to where he began to pray for this young man. He even asked God to forgive this boy and to help him find redeeming grace. Now that's a God thing! By the power of God's mercy, my friend was able to find it in his heart to exonerate that boy when at first it seemed impossible.

The ability to forgive comes from God. If we are going to be able to forgive another, then we must first receive God's mercy for ourselves; and then, we must pray for that same divine mercy to be manifested in our hearts. Just as Jim allowed Christ to work in his heart, we, too, must allow Christ to empower us to forgive.

Forgiveness will not right the wrong. It will not undo the injustice of the situation, but when we forgive from our hearts, it sets us free from the anguish. Unforgiveness is like a cancer that consumes the mind, heart, and soul and will eventually manifest itself in the body through anger, bitterness, hatred, and resentment—even depression. Unforgiveness can even cause violent means of response like murder. When we do not forgive the injustice of others, even forgive ourselves for the mistakes we make, we are thrown into a pit, a prison that will only bring us torment. And just as Jesus implied in Matthew 18:34, we will not get out of prison until we forgive from our heart.

Read Luke 23:32-34:

What injustice did Jesus suffer?

_____

In spite of this injustice, what did Jesus cry out to His Father for?

_____

May these verses remind us that in order to find the strength to forgive others, even ourselves, we must look to the cross. Jesus was tortured, beaten beyond recognition, and executed mercilessly; yet, in spite of all He suffered, Jesus cried out for those who victimized Him. We must look at the injury and persecution done to us as Jesus did. We must lay hold of the heart of the Father. God the Father watched His Son being condemned and mistreated by cruel and sinful men; nevertheless, He made a way for those same men to find mercy through the very injustice done to His Son. When we look at what Jesus went through, knowing that He cried out for forgiveness, how can we not cry out for that same mercy? When we look at our situation through the eyes of God, and put our circumstances in perspective by holding it up against the light of such a gracious heart, how can we hold a grudge?

Does seeing your situation through God's eyes help you come to a place of forgiveness? Is there someone you are having a difficult time forgiving? If so, cry out to God and ask Him to help you forgive this person, no matter how painful the sin is against you.

_____
_____

How does forgiving others help you know and understand God's redeeming heart better?

_____
_____

Forgiveness has its Benefits

Read Luke 6:37-38:

What comparison does Jesus make in these verses? Why is it both important and beneficial to forgive?

_____
_____

How we judge, we will be judged. If we don't forgive, our sins will not be forgiven. Whether we want to believe it or not, how we treat others will come back to us—good or bad.

It is not our place to pass judgment, to condemn, or even hold a grudge. Our job is to desire forgiveness, and give God the room to do His job.

Fill in the blanks according to Romans 12:17; 19, NIV:
"Do not _____ anyone evil for evil."
"Do not take _____, my friends, but leave room for God's wrath, for it is written: 'It is mine to avenge; _____ _____ _____ ,'" says the LORD."

On the contrary, what does Romans 12:20-21 tell us to do?

_____

I understand that when someone has wronged us, hurt us deeply, even hurt someone we love, it is hard not to take matters into our own hands and try to bring about vindication. It is human nature to want to lash out, to be angry, resentful, and full of unforgiveness. We want the person who hurt us, or hurt our loved one, to suffer. But the truth of the matter is: Being unforgiving and vengeful only increases our pain.

Day Four: The Need to Forgive

Remember, not taking vengeful actions, or forgiving someone for any harm he/she caused, doesn't indicate what he/she did is okay. Forgiving someone from your heart makes you okay. God knows what you've been through. He knows all the pain you've suffered, and He does want to vindicate you. However, in order to receive justification, freedom, and healing, you need to release these things into His hands.

If you treat the person who has wronged you with generosity, you leave room for God to deal with him/her in His way. By showing forgiveness God will esteem you, and effectively deal with the person who has wronged you. Rest from your actions and attitudes to get even—rather, rest in God and give him the room to act on your behalf.

What if the person who wronged us is a brother or sister in Christ? What does Colossians 3:12-15 say about forgiveness?

_____

What will be the benefit for forgiving as God forgave us? Check all that apply:

____ Peace will rule in our hearts

____ Love will knit us together in Christ

____ We will live in fellowship with God and each other

According to the *Expository Dictionary of Bible Words*, one translation of the word *forgive* in the Hebrew is *aployo* which means to "let go; release; send; forgive."[36] For our own sake, we must "let go" of the offense, "send" it far away from our hearts, "forgive" as the Lord forgave us, and then "release" it into the hands of God.

Forgiveness is not for the benefit of the person who wronged us, forgiveness is for us—our benefit. Without forgiveness, our heart, mind, and soul will be tortured in the prison of resentment and bitterness. Unforgiveness will destroy our lives. We must not let that happen. We must seek forgiveness as God sought forgiveness by extending us His hand of redemptive grace.

Not too long ago, I was placed in a position where I needed to forgive a debt against me. A dear friend had wounded me deeply. It took me several days, but I sat down with her face-to-face and expressed the hurt and resentment I was carrying; but, I also told her I forgave her and wanted to restore the relationship. She responded favorably. She shared with me that she knew something was wrong between us, but because I had waited to openly share with her, she didn't realize the depth of the offense. As a result of our candidness, we both came away with a wonderful sense of peace and freedom.

"Just recently I heard about a woman who was charged for her husband's murder. After a whirlwind court battle, she was found guilty and was separated from her children. After three years in prison, it came out that her best friend had murdered her husband. Despite the immense hardship this tragedy caused her and her family, by the grace of God, Debbie forgave her husband's murderer and was able to pick up the pieces of her shattered life and move forward in hope with her children.

"Trish grew up an abused child. She was terrified of her dad, and that fear carried over into her relationships with other men. Unable to control her emotions, anger and resentment took over her life. For several years Trish struggled with her out-of-control feelings; until, one day, she made up her mind to no longer allow the pain of her past to rule over her. Determined, Trish cried out to God for help. It took a little time, but day-by-day Trish found the strength to forgive her father, and find the joy and peace of mind she was looking for."[37]

Beloved, you don't have to restore the relationship with the person who harmed you, but you do need to forgive. Forgiveness is the only answer. Forgiveness is the only way you will find freedom. Forgiveness gives you the opportunity to heal, so the pain of your emotions will not have as much power over you. Beloved, I know it's hard, but let go of the injustice done against you. Give room for God's judgment to vindicate you. God doesn't treat us as our sins deserve; therefore, shouldn't we find the room in our hearts to not treat our fellow man as his sins deserve? Let go. Cry out, "Paid in full!" Allow Christ to throw open those prison doors of torment and set you free.

> If there is someone you need to forgive, please do not end today without settling the matter in your heart. Use the space below to pen your letter of forgiveness before God. If the Lord leads you to go and verbally express your forgiveness to this person, please do not hesitate. The benefits you will receive will be worth it.

Day Five
Know Where to Run

"...he rescued me because he delighted in me" (Psalm 18:19).

Hopefully this week we have been seeing the Redeemer through fresh eyes. We began the week proclaiming: "My Redeemer lives, and because He lives, I'm alive!" In Day Two, we examined our actions before a world who does not know Him. In Day Three, we considered the two vital elements necessary to be an effective witness of God's redeeming love. Then yesterday, we looked at our need to not only find forgiveness through our Redeemer, but we discovered the benefits of forgiving others as He forgave us. Today, we are going to take another turn on our redemption road, as we consider the sustaining mercy of our Redeemer.

We are grateful, aren't we, for the saving grace of our Lord and Savior, but our redemption does not end with salvation. There are times, every day, if you're like me, where we need a safe place to run. A place where we know we are loved and can continue to find forgiveness and grace for our daily needs, sins, and mistakes. We need a place where we know we can find peace in the arms of a God who loves us and takes great delight in us, even in our weakness.

Let's begin today by asking the Redeemer to reveal His compassionate love to our hearts, and then read Psalm 103:1-18.

My heart is overcome. As I read these verses in Psalm 103, I hear the Lord speak to me. Earlier this morning I needed a safe place to run. I needed a hiding place where I could find comfort and forgiveness—a place where I could be reminded of His compassionate love and delight for me.

> Do you know God takes great delight in you? Are you utterly convinced that God is merciful, forgiving, kind, tender, gentle and loving? Do you believe He forgives you, heals you, redeems your life from the pit, and crowns you with His glorious love and compassion? Do you know, in the depth of your soul, that when you are faced with either disaster or grievous sin, He is the first place you can run? Share your heart.

_____
_____
_____
_____

I ask this, because there are many believers who have read, countless times, in their Bible these wonderful attributes of God; yet, these same believers run from God and try to hide behind a cloud of misconception, convinced that He will be harsh and angry, even unwilling to forgive their sins.

When I was a young believer, before I grasped the heart of God through the redemption found in His Son, I, too, carried this same inappropriate fear of God. But remember what we discussed in Week One, Day Four, maintaining an *appropriate* fear of the Lord is the crucial key to receiving many things. Appropriate fear of the Lord is the beginning of knowledge (Proverbs 1:7), and teaches a man wisdom (Proverbs 15:33). An *appropriate* fear of the Lord reveals God's holiness and will establish a strong foundation upon which to build a relationship with Him. Through *appropriate* fear, God will show us compassion (see Psalm 103:13). But I was not operating in this appropriate fear; as a result, I was consumed by dread and anxiety, unable to go to God in my need and sin.

As I read my Bible, the wrath of God displayed in the Old Testament terrified me. As a result, I was petrified to make a mistake of any kind, big or small. I walked a very tight rope in my walk with Jesus, convinced that if I messed up, even just a little, God would bring upon me His wrath and judgment. I knew in my head God was compassionate, slow to anger, and abounding in love—I read it—but it was not a reality in my life until I accepted the truth that God loved me and delighted in me.

Over time, as Jesus continued to reveal His compassionate love for me, I learned that when I did make a mistake, He did not treat me with contempt or even harsh words. He treated me with gentleness and kindness, not only because of His redemptive mercy, but because He delighted in me and wanted to restore me.

Read Palm 18:16-19:

What understanding did David have about God and His willingness to rescue him?

_____

_____

Let me be very clear. God does not take delight in our sin. God did not delight in David's sin, but David knew God's tender mercy, forgiveness and grace, whether he blew it big time, or life simply got too hard. David knew beyond any doubt that God loved him, took great delight in him, and was willing to rescue him again and again.

A miracle takes place within our souls when we come to understand God's heart toward us and that He delights in us. Once we grasp the fact that God carries great love for us, and delights in us personally, we find the confidence to run to Him in our time of need.

Fill in the blanks according to Psalm 16:3, NIV:

"As for the saints who are in the land, they are the glorious ones in whom is _____ my _____."

What does God do for the one in whom He delights?

Psalm 22:8: _____

Psalm 37:23-24: _____

Zephaniah 3:17: _____

Day Five: Know Where to Run

The word *delight* according to *Webster's Dictionary* means "to give great pleasure to; to charm; to take delight in; the source of pleasure; great satisfaction; joy."[38] Synonyms for *delight* are "enjoyment, pleasure, happiness, glee, gladness, and enchantment."

With this definition in mind, ponder Lamentations 3:22-23, "The LORD's loving-kindnesses (NASB) indeed never cease, for His compassions (NASB, NIV KJV), mercies (NLT), never fail. They are new every morning; great is your faithfulness."

As you ponder Lamentations 3:22-23, what penetrates your heart? What emotions arise in your soul as you receive the revelation that the loving-kindness of the Lord will never stop, end, or die away; and that His mercies never fall short, compromise, or cease to exist?

_____

_____

How often is the Lord's mercy and loving-kindness offered to us?

____ Once a year   ____ Only when we deserve it   ____ Every day

If you have sinned, compromised in your walk with Jesus, or messed up in any way, you can run to the Lord. His loving-kindness and mercies are fresh every day. If you are willing to openly confess your sins and truly repent, His redemptive grace will cover you.

If you are in a place right now where you are separated from God, turn toward Him and remember all His benefits. Run into His arms and ask for His mercy. He will not treat you as your sins deserve. He will not condemn or reject you. Allow His abounding love and compassion to be gracious to you. Let Him satisfy your soul with good things, for God loves you and takes great delight in you.

When we step out of the will of God by allowing sin and compromise to reign in our lives, we can feel the pain of disgrace. Sometimes we want to hide and hope, in time, no one will remember. When we try to hide our sin instead of confessing it, we put up a barrier between us and God. When we try to hide our offenses, we are kept from knowing God's mercy.

Other times, we want to prove to God we are sorry. We think we have to do something to merit grace and earn God's forgiveness. We begin to pray more, study harder, and diligently serve more, believing we are doing some kind of penance. This is a deception and only prolongs our restoration. If we want to find redemption and grace, we cannot hide our sins. We need to turn away from all wrongdoing and run to our Redeemer who can cleanse, heal, and restore us.

As that young believer afraid of God's wrath, I was fearful with each mistake, sin, and poor choice I made. I thought God would treat me as my sins deserve. Yet, God brought great victory into my life by persistently revealing His love for me in vast gentleness. Each time I blew it, He responded with kindness and redemptive grace. Each time I sinned and confessed, He responded with patience. Each time I made a poor choice and repented, He responded with mercy. And each time He responded to me in this way

I melted. As a result, my heart began to soften, and I learned, over time, that it was okay to make mistakes. This new understanding did not give me permission to sin (see Romans 6:1-2), rather it set me free because when I did make a mistake I knew I could run to God for help and mercy.

As we saw earlier, David, too, learned this same lesson about God's redemptive grace. David made many mistakes, and some huge ones; yet, God called David a man after His own heart (see 1 Samuel 13:14). David had received the revelation that he was the delight of God's heart (Psalm 18:19). When David sinned and then cried out to God, David knew that because of God's holiness He would deal with the sin, but he also knew that God would not treat him as his sins deserved.

Consider Psalm 51. What did David ask for from the Lord?

Psalm 51:1-2: _____

Psalm 51:7: _____

Psalm 51:10: _____

Psalm 51:12: _____

What hope did David base his request on? What attributes and attitudes of God was David relying on? Check all that apply:

___ God's unfailing love   ___ God's desire to make him clean again

___ God's compassion   ___ God's desire to restore the relationship

___ God's mercy   ___ God's desire for a humble and repentant heart

David wrote Psalm 51 in response to the sin of committing adultery with Bathsheba, and having her husband killed in battle because he wanted her for himself (see 2 Samuel 11). The Lord sent Nathan, the prophet, to David who confronted him about his sin (see 2 Samuel 12). Now, David could have run away, denied it, or even blown it off without care, but he didn't. When Nathan revealed the sin David committed, David cried out: "I have sinned against the LORD" (2 Samuel 12:13).

David immediately confessed his sin. His response before God was based on the loving kindness, mercy, and compassion he had come to know in God. Instead of running away, David ran straight to God and poured out his repentant heart through Psalm 51. This strengthened David's love and pulled the cord of relationship tighter.

Can you relate? If so, give an example of a time when you sinned, yet ran straight into the arms of God knowing that God would deal with the sin, yet would restore you.

_____

_____

If you do not resist the Lord, if you are willing to submit to His rebuke when He sends word that you have sinned, He will reveal Himself tenderly to you. Not only to rebuild and strengthen the relationship, but to restore your dependency on Him.

According to Romans 2:4, what is the purpose of God's kindness toward us when we sin?

___ To make us feel bad

___ To pardon the offence

___ To lead us to repentance

I can relate to David's scenario all too well; but, thankfully I also knew the Lord's kindness which lends to repentance. At one point, in my walk with Jesus, I was greatly deceived by the enemy of my soul which led me into a grievous sin against the Lord. I saw the warning signs and sensed the prompting of the Holy Spirit, but I only multiplied my sin by dismissing them and justifying my actions. It's not that I didn't want to see the truth; I was blinded by the enticement of the enemy. I took the bait—hook, line, and sinker—following the lie straight into the enemy's trap. This went on for several months, as my sin mounted I fell deeper into the pit.

Finally, there came a point when the Holy Spirit had no other option but to hit me over the head with the truth in order to expose the lie, and the sin I was engulfed in. As the light of His truth shone into the darkness, I felt all the blood drain from my head. I felt sick with remorse, and mortified that I had made such a terrible mistake. Now, at this point, I could have allowed myself to be destroyed by the sin. I could have run in the other direction in fear of what God might do to me, but I didn't. At that moment, my only thought was: *I have to get to Jesus.*

I ran to my bedroom, closed the door, and threw myself on the floor and began to cry out to God. I was a mess as I repented and called out for His mercy. Within minutes, I felt His strong presence surround me. Peace and comfort flooded my heart, and I knew He had forgiven me. Once again, He turned my crimson sins white as snow.

The days that followed were extremely powerful as His Spirit communicated to my heart and soul the power of His redemptive grace, and the fortification of His love for me. Nothing was going to keep us apart. No matter what I had done or believed, He would not leave me, nor forsake me (see Hebrews 13:5). His one and all-consuming agenda was to bring me back into His loving embrace, and reassure me that nothing had changed between us. In a split second, He had redeemed me, cleansed me from my sins, and revealed His inexhaustible love for me.

End today by rewriting Psalm 103:2-5; 8-13. As you do, insert your name, or the proper pronoun, in place of "you, your, us, those." Make it personal. Then when you are finished, read the verses you have recorded out loud. Let the truth of this message take root in your heart.

Apply the Knowledge

In my pursuit of the Redeemer this week, the Holy Spirit has shown me …

_____
_____
_____
_____

The verse that spoke to me the most this week is…

_____
_____

In order to make this verse a reality in my life, I…

_____
_____
_____
_____

The changes I need to make in order to make God's redemptive grace more of a reality in my life are…

_____
_____
_____
_____

Lord Jesus, I desire to be a more effective witness to a world who does not know You, help me to…

_____
_____
_____
_____

The hidden treasure (see Isaiah 45:3) of His Person and personality God revealed to me this week is… This higher revelation of God's presence profoundly awakens me to…

_____
_____
_____
_____

Witnessing God as Redeemer this week has changed my perspective of God from… to…

_____
_____
_____
_____

Holy Spirit, help me to apply what I've learned to my everyday life, so…

_____
_____
_____
_____

Prayer for the Journey

Lord God, You are not only the Redeemer of the world—You are my Redeemer. I want Your life and love to be evident in me. I desire to be an effective witness, one who reveals the essence of who You are to a world that is lost, and does not understand Your great love. Help me forgive those who have offended me, so I may be a vessel You can…

_____
_____
_____
_____
_____
_____
_____

Apply the Knowledge

Session Five
I Will Reestablish my Covenant
Ezekiel 16:59-63; 17:22-24; 30-32

*"I will establish my covenant with you, and you will **know that I am the LORD**"*
(Ezekiel 16:62).

1.) The Redeemer just doesn't _____ _____ .

2.) Through the _____ Branch, the Redeemer _____ His _____ to reestablish His covenant.

3.) The story of redemption is very _____ .

4.) The story of the Redeemer is a _____ of _____ .

Week Six
Know That I AM Your Shepherd

David was a man of passion, a man of strong desire, and a man after God's own heart. He was a man who knew God—a witness who passionately pursued the heart of God. He was not perfect in His quest, but he was determined. And his strong zealous, adoring heart toward the God he came to know intimately reveals itself all throughout the Psalms. One Psalm in particular that has captured both the heart and imagination of many is Psalm 23. What was this great king of Israel thinking when he wrote Psalm 23 that begins with the proclamation: "The LORD is my shepherd"?

Prior to his kingly reign, David began his life as a simple shepherd boy on the hills of Bethlehem. David knew, firsthand, the responsibilities and hardships of being a shepherd. He understood the difficulty and joy of tending to his father's sheep (see 1 Samuel 16:11; 17:15; 17:34-35). By putting together both his relentless pursuit to know and understand the heart of God, and his experience as a shepherd, David saw in the God of Israel something special—a personal Shepherd. He saw a Shepherd who loved him and cared for him. A Shepherd who offered him personal attention and guidance—who gently tended to all of his needs, while protecting him from those who threatened him. *Jehovah-Rohi*—the LORD is my Shepherd truly meant something extraordinary to David.

The term *shepherd* occurs approximately 80 times in the Bible, and has several meanings, all of which are suggestive of the many-sidedness of Jehovah's shepherd office. It is translated as—*feeder, keeper* (Genesis 4:2); *companion* (Proverbs 28:7); *friend* (Judges 14:20); *pastor* (Jeremiah 17:16); *herdsman* (Genesis 13:7); *shepherd* (Psalm 23:1). Thus the LORD is the Feeder to provide, Keeper to protect, Companion to cheer, Friend to help, Pastor to comfort, Herdsman to gather, and Shepherd to lead."[39]

This week we will attempt to witness the many roles of our Shepherd. We will see Him as the One who watches over His sheep as protector, provider, and complete sustainer of life. We will see Him as the mighty Shepherd who guards His flock from danger, and the tender, gentle Shepherd who loves and guides His lambs. And finally, we will witness the Lord Jesus as the Good Shepherd who saves the lives of His sheep by giving up His life.

May the Lord bless you this week in your pursuit of Him.

Psalm 23

*"The LORD is my shepherd, I shall not be in want.
He makes me lie down in green pastures, he leads me beside quiet waters,
he restores my soul.
He guides me in paths of righteousness for his name's sake.
Even though I walk through the valley of the shadow of death,
I will fear no evil for you are with me;
Your rod and your staff, they comfort me.
You prepare a table before me in the presence of my enemies.
You anoint my head with oil; my cup overflows.
Surely goodness and love will follow me all the days of my life,
And I will dwell I the house of the LORD forever."*

This week we are going to:

Be fed by the bread of His presence
Then Jesus declared, "I am the bread of life"
(John 6:35).

Find rest for our souls
"Come to me, all you who are weary and burdened, and I will give you rest"
(Matthew 11:28).

Be led by His Staff
"…he will guide you into all truth"
(John 16:13).

Dwell in the refuge of His protection
"If you make the Most High your dwelling—no harm will befall you"
(Psalm 91:9-10).

Witness the love of the Good Shepherd
"I will bring them together like sheep in a pen,
like a flock in its pasture…"
(Micah 2:12).

Day One
Fed by the Shepherd's Hand

*"I am the LORD your God, who brought you up out of Egypt.
Open wide your mouth and I will fill it" (Psalm 81:10).*

I hope you've come hungry today and ready to partake of the Lord. Begin today's lesson by praying for God to fill all of your needs, and then read Psalm 23.

As we begin our week of witnessing the Shepherd and His tender loving care, we will start at the beginning of Psalm 23: "The LORD is my shepherd; I shall not be in want" (v. 1). In order to grasp the true meaning and fullness of Psalm 23, we must first understand verse one. In order for all of the other verses to take root and bring forth a harvest, each of us must, first and foremost, understand that the LORD is my shepherd, and I shall not be in want—all of my needs will be met, no matter what season of life I am in.

This is not to say that you and I will never want anything at all, or that it is even wrong to want, but what the verse implies is that because the Lord is our personal shepherd, we will not be in want because all of our needs will be met.

Read the following paragraph out loud and allow the words to really take root in your heart: God is my Shepherd; therefore, He cares for me by making me lie down in green pastures, and leading me beside the still waters. He restores my soul. He guides me and protects me. And when I walk through the valley of the shadow of death, even there my needs will be met for He is with me. His rod and His staff bring me comfort—whether I am in the green pastures of abundance, or the darkness of the valley, I will not be in want. Whether I am in the green pastures of abundance, or the darkness of the valley, I will not be in want. Even in the presence of my enemies, He fills all my needs. He anoints my head with oil and my cup overflows, because the LORD is my Shepherd. He is my strength, my comfort, my sustainer, my protector, my fulfillment in all of life.

Is He not worthy of all praise!

With this perspective of Psalm 23:1 in mind, "The Lord is my Shepherd, I shall not be in want," let's take a couple of days and consider verses 2-4.

Record Psalm 23:2-3a below:

What do you think is the purpose of the green pastures? Why do you think it is necessary for the Lord to lead you there?

Why do you think He leads His people beside the still waters, like a shepherd watering his flock?

_____
_____

One of the first and most important lessons the Lord taught me was to come to Him every day. By doing this, it gave Him the opportunity to feed my soul and care for my inner needs, so that my soul could find rest through His word and His holy presence. Over the years, as I have drawn closer to the Lord, I have learned to appreciate more and more verses like Mark 6:31 which says, "Come with me by yourselves to a quiet place and get some rest." Without that quiet place, coming before Him daily to rest in the shadow of His presence, being fed by His love and the meat of His Word, I would most assuredly be like a sheep that has gone astray.

The Shepherd leads us to lush green pastures and beside quiet waters, because He desires to meet our spiritual needs. He takes us aside, when we are willing to make the journey, so He can feed our souls and give us a drink from His living water.

One thing we may not realize, or find interesting, is that the best and greenest pastures and springs of water are found in the valleys and foot hills. A shepherd knows this and will intentionally lead his sheep through the valley, even though it is often a more dangerous route, because wild animals can hide in the dark places. Nevertheless, he will take the risk because he knows he will find everything he needs to care for his flock. Before I came to realize this about shepherding, I always thought of the valley as a bad place—a place full of loneliness, pain, even despair. It was the mountain-top experiences I lived for; those glorious moments where I could experience God's manifest glory.

It's logical, if you think about it. Lush green grass does not grow on mountain tops. Often, because of the high altitude, it is too cold for anything to grow there. But if we desire to lie down in green pastures, then we will need to allow our Shepherd to lead us through the wilderness valley.

Read Exodus 16:

What were the Israelites complaining about? (v.3)

_____

What did the Lord provide for them every morning? (v. 4) What was it called? (v. 31) Where did it come from?

_____

What did it look like and taste like?

_____
_____

Why was the Lord testing them through His provision?

How often were the Israelites to gather the bread? (v. 4, 21a)

How much were they to gather? (vs. 16-18)

What did Moses instruct them to do with the leftovers in verse 19?

What happened when the people did not listen to this instruction and tried to keep some of the bread until the next morning? (v. 20)

It is vital we understand the importance of coming to God every day to be filled and fed by His manna from heaven. We need to learn to follow His instructions by coming to Him, through His Word and Spirit, to gather all we need for that day.

I must confess there have been mornings I do not even make it out of the tent. Other mornings, when I do go out to gather, I forget to bring a basket. On those days, when I do not take the time to partake of His manna, I am more easily attacked by the enemy and provoked by the world. I fall into the temptation of sin far more easily; and I seem irritated by things that don't normally influence me when I am full of His manna.

I know the importance of coming to the Lord every day to partake, and I long to be in His presence dining on the bread He provides; but, there are some mornings when I am simply too tired, even unwilling to make the sacrifice. Then there are the mornings when my spirit struggles to make the connection. I am distracted by the other things that are running through my mind, and I can't seem to focus on Jesus.

Do you ever feel this way? Do you want and long to experience the presence of God in your everyday life, yet, somehow you feel as if you have completely missed out? If so, do not despair, God's mercies are fresh and new every day—and so is His manna. He has not forsaken you, therefore, pick up your basket and ask the Lord to teach you how to gather the fresh manna that falls daily from heaven. And when you do, when you come with longing and a willing desire to be with Him—not only to eat, but to worship—heaven will open up and you receive those sweet flakes of white manna. As you convey your love and devotion to God, He will pour out His life giving manna over you, and your soul will eat and be satisfied.

Read Isaiah 55:1-3:

How do these verses in Isaiah invite and implore you to come and partake of His provision? What is the benefit in following the Lord's command?

_____
_____

In Luke 11:3, Jesus taught His disciples to ask the Father each day for their daily bread. Remember the manna does not keep overnight. We cannot store up the manna. The manna was sent from heaven every day to fill a physical need, as well as make a Spiritual implication. We need to eat every day, three times a day, to sustain our physical bodies; and, we need to come *every day* to have our souls fed. Our souls can grow weary and hungry if we do not take the time to fill them in the presence of the Lord. Many of us are spiritually starving to death and we don't even know it. We can sense something is wrong. We feel depressed, oppressed and frustrated, but we can't seem to figure out why. In many cases, it is because we're not taking the time to come to God, allowing Him to give us what we long for and need. If we do not come daily to commune with God through His Spirit in prayer and through His Word, we will spiritually starve in the wilderness of life.

Read John 6:32-35:

Who gives us the true bread? Where does it come from?

_____

What did Jesus call himself in verse 35?

_____

What did Jesus say of the person who comes to eat and drink of Him?

_____
_____

Jesus is the true bread of life. He is the manna from heaven. He is our only source of soul satisfaction. The Lord provides all we need—every day. He invites us to come and eat what is good, to have our souls filled with the richest of Him, so that we may live (see Isaiah 55:2-3). The provision is before us, but so is the test. The Lord rains down from heaven His life giving manna, but will we follow His instructions and gather all we need?

Now, let's allow our Shepherd to lead us beside the waters of life.

Read Exodus 17:1-7:

What did the people complain about this time? (v. 2)

_____

Day One: Fed by the Shepherd's Hand

How did the Lord provide? Where did it come from? (v. 6)

_____

What does 1 Corinthians 10:3-4 tell us about what they (the Israelites) ate and drank?

_____

Who was the rock they drank from? (v. 4)

_____

What does John 4:10-14 tell us about the Living Water?

_____

_____

Who is the Living Water?

_____

What is the reward for those who come and drink?

_____

_____

What did the Psalmist long for in Psalm 42:1-2? What is the spiritual significance?

_____

_____

In the long journey through the wilderness the Israelites received *spiritual meat* and *spiritual drink*, precious gifts from God. Jesus was this *spiritual drink*. He is the Water of Life—drink of Him (see Revelation 22:17). Jesus was the *spiritual meat*. He is the bread of life—hunger for His presence and then eat of Him. Oh, the life of a soul that comes regularly to the feet of Jesus to partake of His life-giving manna, and to drink from His life-giving water. God has made known to us the path of life; and there is fullness of joy in His presence and eternal pleasure at His right hand (see Psalm 16:11). Therefore, come every day and open wide your mouth so the Lord may fill it (see Psalm 81:10).

Beloved, do you know Jesus as our Shepherd, or are you in want? When He beckons you to come and lie down in green pastures do you come, or do you come up with excuses? Do you afford Him the opportunity to lead you beside the quiet streams of His love, or are you too busy? Jesus is calling to you, "Come and be filled; then you will *know that I AM God.*"

End today by meditating on Exodus 16:12: "In the evening you will have meat to eat, and in the morning you will be filled with bread. Then you will *know that I am* the Lord your God" *(emphasis mine)*. Share any hindrances or struggles you may have in coming to the Lord daily. Then share with Jesus your longing to be obedient to His command, to come every day and gather all that you need.

___

___

___

___

___

Day Two
Rest for Your Soul

"Let the beloved of the LORD rest secure in him, for he shields him all day long, and the one the LORD loves rests between his shoulders" (Deuteronomy 33:12).

Yesterday we followed our Shepherd into green pastures and beside the quiet waters, so we could partake of the Bread of Life and drink from His living water. Today we will look at the next portion of Psalm 23. "Even though I walk through the valley of the shadow of death, I will fear no evil for you are with me; your rod and your staff, they comfort me" (v 4). In this life, we will walk through some deep valleys, and some difficult days; however, Psalm 23 also tells us we can still find comfort from the Shepherd's rod and staff.

Like gardening, I know very little about shepherding. However, as I read other books and study from those who do know something on the subject, I am learning more and more about the role of a shepherd, how he handles his sheep, and the tools he uses to aid him in his work. This new understanding has drawn some wonderful parallels for me, giving me new insight into the work and care of the Good Shepherd, the Lord Jesus.

For example, I learned that the rod and the staff are two different things with different purposes. The shepherd's *staff* is a long, smooth, slender stick, about 8 feet in length and often has a crook or hook at one end. A shepherd will choose his staff carefully, and will cut and shape the staff to best suit his own personal use. The staff is a unique tool used for the care, management and benefit of a shepherd's flock. In a shepherd's hands, the staff is a symbol of concern, compassion, and comfort, as he uses his staff to guide his sheep gently along a new path or along a dangerous, challenging route.

The rod, on the other hand, is much shorter; approximately 2 feet long, and is strapped to the shepherd's belt. Contrary to the staff, the rod conveys the concept of authority, power, discipline, and defense against danger.

Yet, even with these vast differences between the rod and the staff, David declared in Psalm 23:4, "...for your *rod* and your *staff*, they comfort me" (*Emphasis mine*). Based on what we just learned about the shepherd's staff, it is easy to see why the staff would bring us comfort. But the rod, although a tool of authority, power and discipline, should also bring us comfort.

For example, a shepherd used the rod to examine and count the sheep. In Ezekiel 20:37 the LORD said, "I will take note of you as you pass *under my rod*, and I will bring you into the bond of the covenant" *(Emphasis mine)*. This passing *under the rod* meant not only coming under the shepherd's control and authority, but it also meant that each sheep was subject to his most attentive, personal examination. A sheep that passed *under the rod* was one that had been counted and inspected to make sure it was healthy.

When we come under our Shepherd's rod, we not only come under His intimate care, but also His authority and control. When we pass *under the rod* we come under the yoke of His authority and direction, hence, His Word. This is where we find rest for our souls.

With this lesson on shepherding in mind, let's begin by praying for the Shepherd to help us pass *under the rod*, and then read Matthew 11:28-30.

Who was Jesus talking to in these verses? (For context, look at Matthew 11:20-26.)

___

What is the invitation Jesus made to them in verse 28? What do you think Jesus is communicating to His listeners in this verse?

___

In verse 29, what does Jesus instruct His listeners to take and put on?

___

If they were obedient to the Shepherd's command, what would be the benefit? What would they find?

___

How does the Shepherd describe His yoke in verse 30?
___ Demanding
___ Cumbersome
___ Easy

What do you think Jesus meant by the statement: "My burden is light"?

___

Today, we live in a society that believes we should be self-sufficient. We need to be in control and answer to our own authority. The truth of the matter is, when we try to run things it only leads to worry and anxiety, weariness and heavy burdens. But Jesus said, "Come to me, all of you who are weary and carry heavy burdens, and I will give you rest" (v. 28, NLT). In this context of Scripture, Jesus is talking to people who do not know Him, or who have moved away from Him, and are trying to do things their way and in their own strength. In the same way, when we do not know Jesus as our Savior, or when we move away from Him due to disobedience, we struggle as we try to wear the yoke the world tries to put on us. Whenever we think we can manage our own circumstances, be our own boss, or find strength from anyone or anything other than the Lord, we come out from under His yoke. Nevertheless, Jesus continues to invite us: "Come to me…I will give you rest. Take my yoke upon you…you will find rest for your soul. For my yoke fits perfectly, and the burden I give you is light" (NLT).

The word *yoke* according to *Webster's Dictionary* means "wooden framework fastened over necks of two oxen, etc. to hold them together; …bond or tie; emblem of submission, servitude, bondage; …to put on a yoke; to couple or join; unite in marriage; to attach … to be joined."[40]

When we put on the yoke of the Lord, we are being joined to Him, united in a common effort; tied together, bonded forever. Again we are given the imagery of being one with God—joined—united—fastened—tied together—moving together as one. When we put on the yoke of God's authority, we put on a symbol of submission, obedience, and surrender; and, we agree to accept His terms and conditions of the covenant relationship in complete servitude and bondage. We need not worry though, because Jesus said His yoke is easy and His burden is light. When we join with Him, moving as one with Him, He gives us the easy part. Under His control and authority we find rest because He is doing all the work. Our part is to submit, to be obedient to His direction, and He does all the rest. Amen!

I realize we often don't like coming under the authority and control of someone else, because we think we are giving up something. But when we come under the yoke of the Lord, coming under His authority and control, we actually gain a great deal. Let me show you what I mean.

The word *control* means "to have under command; to regulate; to check; to restrain; to direct."[41] Synonyms for the word authority are "power, ability; influence." The concept is still unpleasant, I know, but stay with me and look up Colossians 2:9-10.

> What does Colossians 2:9-10 say about Christ and the relationship you have with Him? Check all that apply:
>
> ____ Christ is the fullness of the Deity in bodily form
>
> ____ Christ is the head of every power and authority
>
> ____ In Christ you have been given His fullness

Our problem with giving up our lives and coming under the Lord's authority and control is because our view of Jesus is far too small. According to Colossians 2:9-10, all the fullness of the Deity lives in bodily form, and, we, who are joined (yoked) with Christ, are given fullness in Christ, who is the head of every power and authority.

Day Two: Rest for Your Soul

Dear One, grasp this: When you and I come under the yoke of Christ's authority, passing under His rod, allowing Him to have complete control, we gain His power and authority. Remember when Jesus said to the Father in John 17:10, "All I have is yours, and all you have is mine." He was expressing the terms and conditions of the covenant relationship. When we surrender, putting on that emblem of submission, becoming completely His, offering Him all we are, then everything He has, all of His power and authority, become ours through the Holy Spirit. Glory to God!

"Therefore," Jesus says, "do not worry about your life…" (Matthew 6:25). Pass under the rod of my Word. Put on the yoke of My authority, and you will find peace and rest for your soul."

> According to Colossians 3:15, when do we experience peace?
> ___ When we do things our way
> ___ When we worry and fret over our circumstances
> ___ When we allow Christ to rule in our hearts

Beloved, with His yoke upon you, when you do walk through those deep valleys and dark days, when you experience tragedy and difficult circumstances, you will not fear. Under the Shepherd's rod, you will not drown in worry and anxiety, because you will know that you are not operating in your own power, but in His power and control.

> Conclude today by meditating on Psalm 62:1, 5: "My soul finds rest in God alone; my salvation comes from him. Find rest, O my soul, in God alone; my hope comes from him." How has God encouraged you to find rest in Him alone? How have you found rest and comfort from the Shepherd's rod?
>
> _____
> _____
> _____
> _____
> _____
>
> If your heart, soul and mind is not currently finding rest and peace, read Philippians 4:4-7. Then pray in worship, with thanksgiving, and ask Jesus to help you to come under His rod, to put on His yoke of authority, so you may experience His peace and rest.
>
> _____
> _____
> _____
> _____
> _____

Day Three
The Staff That Leads and Guides

"He guides me in paths of righteousness for his name's sake" (Psalm 23:3).

Today, as we attempt to understand more about our Shepherd, we will continue our examination of Psalm 23, again reflecting on the shepherd's rod and staff. If you recall, we learned that both the shepherd's staff and rod have many uses (I only named a few). Yesterday, we primarily focused on the rod of the shepherd's authority. Today, as we consider the shepherd's tools, we will focus on the staff.

> Let's begin today by praying for the Shepherd to lead and guide us in His ways, then let's consider the following verses and record what each one says about the guidance and leadership of the Lord.
>
> Psalm 25:4-5: _____
> Psalm 73:23-24: _____
> Proverbs 4:11: _____
> Isaiah 49:10: _____
> Isaiah 58:11: _____

Our Shepherd leads and guides us continually. He guides us into all truth. He leads us along straight and righteous paths, and leads us with compassion beside streams of water. He teaches us His ways. He gives us counsel, and guides us in the way of wisdom.

> Based on what we have learned, thus far, about the staff in the shepherd's hand, the comfort that it brings to the sheep and the guidance it gives along the path—what conclusion can we make about the staff of our Shepherd? Who or what is the staff?
>
> _____
> _____
>
> What did Jesus call, and/or say about the Holy Spirit in the following verses?
> John 14:16-17a: _____
> John 14:26: _____
> John 16:13: _____

In John 16:7, the *King James Bible* calls the Holy Spirit the Comforter. The NIV and NLT translations call Him the Counselor; while the NAS refers to the Holy Spirit as the Helper. *The Amplified Bible* takes it even further by saying: "However, I am telling you nothing but the truth when I say it is profitable (good, expedient, advantageous) for you that I go away. Because if I do not go away, the Comforter, (Counselor, Helper, Advocate, Intercessor, Strengthener, Standby) will not come to you [into close fellowship with you]; but if I go away, I will send Him to you [to be in close fellowship with you]" (John 16:7).

The Holy Spirit is the Staff of our Shepherd. Let's take a minute and compare this concept from a spiritual standpoint. As we consider the many uses of a shepherd's staff, we will see that each use can be categorized into three primary purposes. First, a shepherd uses his staff to draw the sheep into fellowship with each other. Secondly, the shepherd uses his staff to draw the sheep to himself, and, finally, he uses his staff to guide the sheep. Let's look at each of these three primary uses and parallel them to the work of the Holy Spirit.

1. He draws the sheep into fellowship:

According to the following verses, how does the Holy Spirit lead us into fellowship and unity with each other?

1 Corinthians 12:4-7; 12-13: _____

Ephesians 2:22: _____

Ephesians 4:3-4: _____

Fellowship is companionship, a partnership, close association. In fellowship with each other, through the Holy Spirit, we join together in close union, becoming one with each other, one body, unified, like one flock moving in one direction with its Shepherd.

According to Colossians 3:12-15, how are we to come together? List the characteristics we are to show each other:

_____   _____
_____   _____
_____   _____
_____   _____

Galatians 5:22-23 lists the fruit of the Spirit. Compare the fruit of the Spirit to the list you compiled from Colossians 3:12-15. Check the traits that overlap.

___ Love   ___ Joy   ___ Peace
___ Patience   ___ Kindness   ___ Gentleness
___ Goodness   ___ Faithfulness   ___ Self-control

The very traits we need in order to come together in unity are given to us through the power of the Holy Spirit—the Shepherd's Staff. It is not our own strength or ability, but the supernatural ability of the Holy Spirit to guide us into fellowship with each other, unifying us into one body, a dwelling place for God (see Ephesians 2:21-22).

2. He draws the sheep to the Shepherd:

Consider the following verses, how does the Holy Spirit lead us into fellowship with our Shepherd?

John 14:17-18; 20: _____

John 15:26: _____

John 16:14-15: _____

Through the Holy Spirit, our relationship with the Shepherd becomes real and personal; forming a connection so intimate that He shares mysteries and confides in us the secrets of His covenant (see Psalm 25:14). And through the Spirit there comes a knowing, deep within us, that we are in touch with Christ—that we are one with Him, that we belong to Him, and that we are under His attentive care. Just as a shepherd draws a sheep to himself for personal inspection by using the hook of his staff, the Holy Spirit of God woos our hearts and draws us to Christ for intimate fellowship and spiritual union. And through this individualized devotion there comes a marvelous awareness of His comfort, love, and tender correction.

3). He guides the sheep:

Consider the following verses, how does the Spirit lead and guide us?

John 14:26: _____

John 16:8-11: _____

John 16:13: _____

The Spirit of Truth will guide us into all truth. He is a Guide we can trust—our constant Companion who will personally give us direction at every phase and situation in life. He will guide us away from sin and away from what is harmful and false. He will lead us in paths of righteousness for His name's sake (see Psalm 23:3), persistently, moment by moment, need by need, revealing God's will for our lives.

As we come to *know* our Shepherd, we recognize that we can trust Him to help us to be unified with Him and with each other, and that He will lead us and guide us only into what is pure and right—the center of His perfect will.

Let's end today by meditating on Galatians 5:25. Fill in the blanks according to the NIV: "Since we live by the Spirit, let us _____ _____ with the Spirit." Pray and ask the Holy Spirit to make Galatians 5:25 a constant reality in your everyday walk with the Shepherd.

_____

_____

_____

_____

Day Four
The Shepherd Protects and Guards
"I will protect him for he acknowledges my name" (Psalm 91:14b).

"See, the Sovereign LORD comes with power and his arm rules for him. See, his reward is with him, and his recompense accompanies him. He tends his flock like a shepherd: He gathers the lambs in his arms and carries them close to his heart; he gently leads those that have gone astray" (Isaiah 40:10-11). In these verses, the witness Isaiah paints a pleasing image of our wonderful Shepherd. He is strong and powerful, able to protect us in our weakness and guard us from every danger and trouble. Yet, He is tender and gentle as He carries the lambs in His arms, close to His heart.

Let's begin today by praying for the Shepherd to lead and guide us in His ways, then let's consider the following verses and record what each one says about the guidance and leadership of the Lord.

Psalm 25:4-5: _____

Psalm 73:23-24: _____

Proverbs 4:11: _____

Isaiah 49:10: _____

Isaiah 58:11: _____

In Samuel 17:34-35, we see a wonderful example of the kind of protection our Shepherd offers us through the actions of David as he protected his father's sheep by fighting off the lion and the bear. It was as if David was saying, "Nothing is going to harm my father's sheep. You're going to have to go through me in order to get to my sheep." Jesus says the same thing as He protects us. Nothing is going to get to His sheep without first going through Him.

Let's begin today by asking the Shepherd to hold us close to His heart and protect us from all evil, and then please read Psalm 91.

In Week Two, Day Three we considered Psalm 91:1-4 as we learned about the refuge of the Father's wings, learning to rest in the shadow of the Almighty. Today, as we continue to examine God's shepherd heart, in Psalm 91 we'll discover His great desire to guard and protect us as we take refuge in Him.

List the different types of danger stated in Psalm 91:1:6:

_____   _____

_____   _____

_____

Where do we find refuge from these dangers?

_____

Summarize verses 9-10:

_____

_____

What victories can we claim if we make the Lord our dwelling place? (v. 10-13)

_____   _____

_____   _____

_____   _____

According to verses 14-16, what does the Lord proclaim He will do for those who love Him and acknowledge His name? Check all that apply

____ Rescue him   ____ Deliver him

____ Protect him   ____ Honor him

____ Answer him   ____ Satisfy him

____ Be with him in trouble ____ Show him His salvation

As a lowly sheep, what does the Lord's proclamation mean to you?

_____

_____

Sheep are stubborn creatures, seemly brainless, except they are brilliant at getting lost. They are afraid of just about everything, and they easily fall prey to wolves and other wild animals. Their heavy wool and skinny legs make them top heavy, making it easy for their prey to catch them. Sheep are a calamity waiting to happen.

Though we may not like to admit it, we, too, are like sheep. We are fearful to the point of acting stupidly. We make wrong choices, because we are afraid of failure. We dive into harmful relationships because we are afraid of being alone. We, even as believers, often wander and stray in every direction, except in the direction of the Lord. Yet, even in our weakness, God's shepherd heart is drawn toward us. Daily He yearns to be our constant guard and protection against anything and everything that sets itself up to destroy us. However, if we are to find protection, a solid refuge, and guard against dangers, pestilence, and harmful prey, we must remain in the shadow of our Shepherd, walking close to Him as a sheep being guided by his master.

This does not mean nothing bad will ever happen or we will be liberated from making wrong choices; but, when we abide in the shelter of the Most High, we will find that our souls, hearts and minds are guarded and protected in the shelter of His presence.

According to *Webster's Dictionary*, the word *guard* means "to protect from danger; to accompany for protection; to watch by way of caution or defense; to keep watch."[42] And for the word *protect* we find: "to defend; to guard; defending from injury or harm."[43]

Based on what we considered in Psalm 91, and the definitions we just read for *guard* and *protect*, how do we see the Shepherd at work in the following verses?

Psalm 31:20: _____

_____

Psalm 32:7-8: _____

_____

Psalm 33:18-19: _____

_____

Psalm 121:3-8: _____

_____

What comfort do you receive from knowing that the Lord—your Shepherd—is always on the job?

_____

_____

I find great reassurance, in the fact, that my Shepherd is ever watchful, ever present. When I abide in Him, He is my constant companion who protects me from trouble and guards me from things that are harmful.

What does the Lord guard? Match each verse with its reference.

_____ 1 Samuel 2:9:   a.) All your ways
_____ Psalm 25:20:   b.) The feet of His saints
_____ Psalm 91:11:   c.) The path before you and behind you
_____ Isaiah 52:12:   d.) Your life

What should we regularly ask the Lord to help us guard or guard against? Match each verse with its reference.

____ Psalm 141:3:   a.) False teachers
____ Proverbs 4:23:   b.) What is entrusted to us
____ Acts 20:29-31:   c.) Our mouth
____ Luke 12:15   d.) Our heart
____ 2 Timothy 1:14:   e.) Greediness
____ 2 Peter 3:17:   f.) Being led astray

According to Philippians 4:6-7, what does the peace of God guard when we bring our requests to Him?

_____

The Lord—the Lord alone—indeed is our compassionate Shepherd. He is near, night and day, guarding His flock with ever watchful eyes, protecting them against danger and pestilence. He guides them with His staff in the ways of truth and righteousness. He leads them beside the still waters, and feeds them with the bread of His presence. Under His care and authority, they find rest for their souls. In Him they find peace of mind, security, and satisfaction for every need and care of life.

With all we have learned this week about the Shepherd, do you, like David, see something special in God? Has He become your personal Shepherd? Are you ready to proclaim: "The LORD is *my* Shepherd, I shall not want!"? Does *Yahweh-Rohi*—the LORD is *my* Shepherd truly mean something extraordinary to you?

End today's lesson by meditating on Psalm 23. Then pen your own version of Psalm 23 based on your personal experience and relationship with God as *your* Shepherd.

_____
_____
_____
_____
_____
_____
_____
_____
_____
_____

Day Four: The Shepherd Protects and Guards

Day Five
The Good Shepherd

"I am the good shepherd; I know my sheep and my sheep know me"
(John 10:14).

What a week this has been as we have come to a greater understanding of the heart of God through the passion and tender care of a shepherd. What a lowly job it is to be a shepherd. It is hard work, and often lonely. Despite the difficulties and hardships, however, there is no other place a true shepherd would rather be than with his sheep. A true shepherd is utterly dedicated to his lambs. He knows them thoroughly, and his sheep know him.

Up until now, we have been looking at the care, guidance, and protection of the Shepherd for His flock. Today, we are going to shift our focus to witness the Shepherd Himself, and the sacrifice He made for the flock He loves.

Let's begin today by asking the Shepherd for deeper understanding, so we may know Him even better. Then, please read John 10:1-18.

This parable has three parts, list the three parallels Jesus used to communicate His role:

1: _____
2: _____
3: _____

All three parts of this parable talk about the relationship between the Shepherd and His sheep. To try and capture what Jesus is communicating, we'll look at each section individually.

I am the true Shepherd:

According to verse 2, who is the true shepherd?

____ The one who climbs over the fence

____ The one who calls the sheep by name

____ The one who enters through the gate

Why is it important to understand that the true shepherd only enters through the gate? What did Jesus call the one who entered some other way? (v. 1)

_____
_____

Once inside the sheep pen, what does the shepherd do? Check all that apply:

____ He calls to his sheep by name

____ He leads them out

____ He guides them with His voice

In John 10:1-5, Jesus not only gives His audience a mental picture of the true Shepherd, but He also gives them a warning.

What do the sheep do when they hear a stranger's voice? Why?

_____

_____

What warning should we take away from verse 5? What is the spiritual implication?

_____

_____

What examples do 2 Peter 2:1-3a give about strangers (false teachers) that should cause us to run away?

_____

_____

Look again at John 10:5. How important is it that we know the Shepherd's voice? Also reflect on 1 Samuel 15:22 and Revelation 3:20 as you consider your response.

_____

_____

_____

When the sheep were kept in a pen at night, many flocks were gathered together while a watchman stood guard. In the morning, each shepherd would enter the sheep pen through the gate and call to his flock. The sheep would recognize their shepherd, and only those sheep belonging to that shepherd would come. Only those who truly belong to Jesus will know His voice. Only His flock will follow Him because they recognize His voice. "My sheep," Jesus said, "listen (NIV), recognize (NLT), and hear (NAS) my voice." Only those who know Jesus will obey Him and partake of Him.

Day Five: The Good Shepherd

I am the Gate:

Going back to our main text in John 10, what did Jesus say about those who enter through Him? (v. 9)

According to verse 10a, what does the thief come to do? What are the spiritual consequences and implication?

According to John 10:10b, if the sheep enter through the Gate and follow the Shepherd, what did Jesus promise? What are the spiritual rewards?

As we examine these verses in John 10:7-10, we get a sharper picture—not only of the Shepherd—but the crowd that He might have been addressing.

According to John 10:19, who was Jesus speaking to? How did the people respond to His message?

"I tell you the truth, I am the gate for the sheep" (v. 7). You can almost hear the pain in His voice as Jesus desperately tried to get His audience to understand that He, and He alone, was the way to salvation.

What does 2 Peter 3:9 tell us about the desire of the Lord's heart for those who do not know Him?

The greatest desire of the Shepherd's heart is that we all enter through the Gate and know the true Shepherd. However, the thief will try and do everything he can to steal, kill and destroy.

What does 1 Peter 5:8 tell us about the one who does not want us to know the Good Shepherd and His way to salvation?

The enemy of our souls prowls around looking for someone to devour. Like a hungry lion (or wolf) looking for a tender sheep to kill, he is out to annihilate. The enemy's chief goal is to keep us spiritually lost. In this way, the thief steals the chance for salvation offered through God's grace, and keeps those who do not know the true Shepherd away from the abundant life found only in Christ. The good news: Jesus came to seek and save the lost (see Luke 19:10). He is the way, the truth, and the life (see John 14:6). Amen!

Stop and take a few minutes to pray for someone you know who is lost. Pray they will enter through the Gate and come to know the true Shepherd and the sound of His voice.

I am the Good Shepherd:

What does the Good Shepherd do for His sheep? (v. 11)

"By this we come to know (progressively to recognize, to perceive, to understand) the [essential] love; that He laid down His [own] life for us" (1 John 3:16, AMP). Could the passion of anyone's heart be greater? I don't think we can begin to fathom the sacrifice that was made on our behalf.

Read Isaiah 53:5-6:

Record the sacrifice Jesus made for His sheep and why?

Isaiah 53:5-6 reminds us that we are all like sheep that have gone astray. Without the sacrifice of our Good Shepherd, we would all be directionally impaired, powerless to live a life of freedom and abundance. The enemy and the world persistently try to lead us astray. They constantly try to pull us off course with wrong desires, self-centered motives, and sinful natures. But Jesus, the Good Shepherd, laid down His life for His sheep in order to bring back those who are lost and wandering.

"I myself will tend my sheep and have them lie down,' declares the Sovereign LORD. 'I will search for the lost and bring back the strays. I will bind up the injured and strengthen the weak, but the sleek and the strong I will destroy. I will shepherd the flock with justice" (Ezekiel 34:15-16). What a glorious portrait of relationship! A Shepherd, so in love with His own He would willingly make the ultimate sacrifice to lay down His life for them, so they could know Him and be with Him forever.

What parallel did Jesus draw in John 10:14-15 between Him knowing His sheep and His sheep knowing Him? Based on this parallel, how intimate is the familiarity and closeness between the Shepherd and His sheep?

Oneness with God—this is His ultimate goal. And He will do anything to accomplish it!

Day Five: The Good Shepherd

As we start to conclude this magnificent week of witnessing the tender care and merciful love of our Shepherd, read Revelation 7:14-17 aloud. Then compare these verses with Psalm 23. What similarities are revealed between these two portions of Scripture?

Revelation 7:14-17	Psalm 23

I am in awe right now, overcome with emotion, at the connection between Revelation 7:14-17 and Psalm 23. The Lamb at the center of the throne is our Shepherd, both in this life and the life to come. He is, and will always be, our eternal Shepherd—and we will not be in want. For all eternity He will lead us beside the quiet, living waters. He will feed us with the bread of His presence. Never again will we hunger or thirst. Never again will we be plagued by pestilence and danger. We will live in safety. We will find rest for our souls, because the Lamb at the center of the throne—our Shepherd—will watch over us forever.

Is there any other response to what we have witnessed this week than to offer Him our worship?

End today by meditating on Psalm 95:6-7: "Come, let us bow down in worship, let us kneel before the LORD our Maker; for he is our God and we are the people of his pasture, the flock under his care." Let us reflect on Jesus—the One who is both the Lamb of God and the Good Shepherd—let us come before Him and offer Him our genuine worship and praise.

Apply the Knowledge

In my pursuit of the Shepherd this week, the Holy Spirit has shown me …

_____
_____
_____
_____

The verse that spoke to me the most this week is…

_____
_____

In order to make this verse a reality in my life, I…

_____
_____
_____
_____
_____

The changes I need to make in order to submit to the various roles of the Shepherd are…

_____
_____
_____
_____
_____

Lord Jesus, I desire to keep in step with your Spirit (see Galatians 5:25). Help me to be steadfast on the pathways of life, so I may…

_____
_____
_____
_____

The hidden treasure (see Isaiah 45:3) of His Person and personality God revealed to me this week is… This higher revelation of God's presence profoundly awakens me to…

_____
_____
_____
_____

Witnessing God as a Shepherd this week has changed my perspective of God from… to…

_____
_____
_____
_____

Holy Spirit, help me to apply what I've learned to my everyday life, so…

_____
_____
_____
_____

Prayer for the Journey

Lord God, You are *my* Shepherd. I long to know You and the tender care of Your hand in my life—the way a sheep knows the tender love and care of its shepherd. Lord, I want to know and understand Your heart the way David did. I want to know for myself the joy of embracing You as *my* personal Shepherd. You gave up everything just to have the privilege of owning me, protecting me, comforting me, guiding me, nourishing me, and offering me companionship. Because You are *my* Shepherd, I shall not be…

_____
_____
_____
_____
_____
_____

Session Six
You are My Sheep
Ezekiel 34:1-31

*"I will take note of you as you pass under my rod, and I will bring you into the bond of the covenant.
Then you will **know that I am the LORD**" (Ezekiel 7-38b).*

1.) The Shepherd does not take the _____ of His sheep _____ .

Two primary charges came against the shepherds of Israel:

a.) The shepherd's motives were only to

_____ _____

_____ .

b.) The shepherds were _____ _____ the _____ best interest.

(Ezekiel 34:1-10)

2.) The LORD is your Shepherd; you will _____ _____ _____ _____ . (Ezekiel 34:11-16)

3.) The Shepherd will _____ _____ _____ . (Ezekiel 34:11-16)

4.) In the heart of the Shepherd, we see the _____ . (Ezekiel 34:17-31)

5.) Everything God does points us to _____ _____ . (Ezekiel 34:25-31)

6.) We cannot serve two _____ . We are all _____ to something.

Week Seven

Know That I AM Your Healer

The Healer—this is how I was introduced to Jesus. I was an adult when I came to know Christ. I had been reared in the church, but I did not have a personal relationship with God. Just prior to receiving Christ as my Lord and Savior, I had been suffering in the pit of depression for almost a year. It crippled my mind, heart, spirit and soul and destroyed every part of me. I felt like everything had been taken from me. I tried to find help; but, I couldn't find anyone who would or could help me, so I became suicidal. It was here, at the lowest point of my life, that I cried out to a God I didn't know. Nevertheless, because of His compassion and unfailing love, when Jesus heard my desperate cry, He reached into the depths of my despair and pulled me from that pit, placing my feet on solid ground. Suddenly, Jesus became very tangible to me. From that time on, Jesus has revealed Himself as the Healer of my heart, mind, soul, and spirit. He has touched and transformed my life with wholeness.[44]

Hearing other testimonies about the Lord's healing power, and His touch on people's lives, is priceless to me. My heart is moved every time I hear another precious soul share about the power of Christ's love through His healing hand upon his or her life.

For many of us, "the Healer" is how we first met Jesus. Jesus will meet us, right where we are, in the pit of our need and helplessness, and introduce Himself by healing us. So many people in the New Testament were introduced to Jesus for the first time as Healer. There were the ones who needed physical healing, such as the blind men (Mt. 9:27-34), the leper (Mt. 8:1-4), the woman who had been bleeding for twelve years (Mt. 9:20-22, Mk 5:25-34), and the lame (Luke 5:17-26). Then, there were the ones who needed spiritual or emotional healing, such as the woman at the well (John 4:4-26), the demon possessed (Luke 4:31-37), and the sinful woman (Luke 7:36-50). These are only a few examples of the many people Jesus healed during His earthly ministry.

As a new believer, I remember how these stories of healing touched my heart. I remember weeping over the stories as our ladies' Bible study group made their way through the gospel of Mark. I could relate to these people of the Bible. Perhaps I had not been physically blind, but I had been spiritually blind. Perhaps I had not been bleeding for twelve years, but I knew what it felt like to be touched by Jesus and instantly healed.

Nonetheless, in all of these healings, including mine, I have come to realize that there is something else at stake. When Jesus comes to heal us, He not only comes to heal us from our infirmities, He comes to heal our soul. The goal is wholeness, spiritual maturity, and complete transformation, the very things that will reveal God's glory to the world.

This week, it is my prayer that the Holy Spirit will lead us into complete healing—whatever that is, whatever the need, whatever the circumstance—so we may come to know Jesus more profoundly.

Isaiah 61:1-3

*The Spirit of the Sovereign LORD is on me,
because the LORD has anointed me to preach good news to the poor.
He has sent me to bind up the brokenhearted, to proclaim freedom
for the captives and release from darkness for the prisoners,
to proclaim the year of the LORD's favor—
to comfort all who mourn, and provide for those who grieve in Zion—
to bestow on them a crown of beauty instead of ashes,
the oil of gladness instead mourning,
and a garment of praise instead of a spirit of despair.
They will be called oaks of righteousness,
a planting of the LORD for the display of his splendor.*

This week we are going to:

Witness the Lord's healing hand
"I am the LORD, who heals you"
(Exodus 15:26b).

Realize that faith makes a difference
"According to your faith will it be done to you"
(Matthew 9:29).

Anticipate finding joy in our suffering
"Consider it pure joy, my brothers, whenever you face trials"
(James 1:2).

Remember we are never alone in our suffering
"Because he himself suffered when he was tempted, he is able to
help those who are being tempted"
(Hebrews 2:18).

Yearn to know Christ in His suffering
"We share in his sufferings in order
that we may also share in his glory"
(Romans 8:17).

Day One
The Hand of the Healer

"Great crowds came to him, bringing the lame, the blind, the crippled, the mute and many others, and laid them at his feet; and he healed them" (Matthew 15:30).

How can we know the Healer if we never have a need for healing? As I begin writing this week's lesson on the Healer, I am in need of physical healing. Due to my recent contact with poison ivy, certain parts of my body are infected with an irritating, red and itchy rash that doesn't want to go away. My mother is in the hospital battling cancer. She is desperate for physical healing and believes God with all her heart that He will heal her.

My middle child, Jessica, recently encountered the Healer this past summer during a youth conference in Orlando, Florida. Since she was 12 years old, she has suffered from panic attacks and many phobias; one in particular caused her to be fanatical about washing her hands. While we, our church youth group (which I helped to chaperon), were at the conference, Jessica cried out in prayer for healing. It was an earnest prayer filled with tears and longing. She needed the Healer, and she got the Healer. During the conference a miracle took place, and my daughter was instantly delivered from her fears and panic attacks. Today Jessica is a different person. She is confident. She stands up for what she believes in—even against those who try to convince her that doing things the world's way is okay. She is passionate about Jesus, and one of the boldest young people I know. Jessica met the Healer.

Begin today with prayer. Let's ask for any healing needs we currently have, and then let's witness the Healer in the pages of His Word.

Please read Mark 5:24-34:

Who needed healing? What was the healing need? How long had she been suffering?

How did she try to get help? Did it make a difference?

Even though the woman had been treated unsuccessfully by many doctors, she still reached out to Jesus. Why? Record her thoughts from verse 28 below:

What happened when she touched Jesus? (v. 29)

In every version I have of the Bible, verse 29 begins with the word "immediately;" except the KJV which uses the word "straightaway." Whatever your version says, I am convinced it implies that there was absolutely no hesitation in her healing. Immediately—not next week—not a year from now, or even 5 minutes later—immediately she was healed and freed from her suffering.

> Have you ever experienced or witnessed an immediate healing as a result of reaching out to Jesus? If so, share your story.
>
> _____
> _____
> _____
>
> In verse 30, Jesus knew instantly that someone had touched him. What question did He ask? Why do you think He asked this question?
>
> _____
> _____
>
> Who did the disciples say touched Jesus? (v. 31) What logic did they use to come to this conclusion?
>
> _____
> _____
>
> Why do you think Jesus did not accept their answer?
>
> _____
>
> Mark 5:32 says that Jesus "kept" looking to see who had touched Him? Describe how you think Jesus might have been searching? How long do you think this search went on? Why do you think Jesus was determined to find out who she was?
>
> _____
> _____
> _____

Then, finally, in verse 33, the woman, knowing what had happened to her, came trembling and fell at His feet and told Him what she had done.

> What was Jesus' response to her? Record His words in verse 34:
>
> _____
> _____

Day One: The Hand of the Healer

Jesus did not search for the woman because He wanted to let everyone in the crowd know she had come to Him for healing. He did not insist on finding out who she was so she could thank him for His mercy and help. No, Jesus wanted to set her free—completely (see John 8:36; Galatians 5:1). He wanted to confirm to her that her faith in Him not only released her from her affliction, but from her shame. She didn't have to hide anymore.

Think about it. Can you imagine the shame this woman must have felt for 12 years? Can you imagine the suffering and turmoil she must have gone through during that time? Scripture doesn't tell us what kind of bleeding the woman suffered, but I think we can safely assume it was a menstrual-type bleeding, rather than internal bleeding. In her culture, when a woman was bleeding during her monthly cycle, she was considered unclean (see Leviticus 12:1-8; 18:19). In the culture's eyes, this woman, to some degree, was like a leper. Most likely when people passed by they ignored her, even shunned her. She was alone. No one could help her; not even the doctors. So when she heard Jesus was in town, she had to get to Him, even if she felt uncomfortable to approach Him.

This woman felt humiliated. If she was not embarrassed by her condition and the disgrace that it brought her, then why did she come to Jesus in secret? Every other account of healing that I have read about in Scripture, the people came to Jesus and asked for healing. Some, like Bartimaeus, the blind beggar by the side of the road, shouted his need for healing at the top of his lungs (see Mark 10:46-52; Luke 18:35-43). He was not ashamed to let Jesus, nor the world, know that he was in need of healing.

Read each of the following accounts and answer the questions:

Mark 1:32-34:

How many people witnessed Jesus as the Healer?

_____

List the different kinds of healing Jesus performed.

_____
_____

Matthew 4:23-25:

How many people witnessed Jesus as the Healer?

_____

Record the different kinds of healing Jesus performed.

_____
_____

Mathew 15:30-31:

How many people witnessed Jesus as the Healer?

_____

Record the different kinds of healing Jesus performed.

_____

_____

Do you see any of these people being shy about their need or suffering?
___ YES   ___ NO

How would you describe the people's desire to get to Jesus and be healed, or have someone close to them healed? Check all that you think apply:

___ shy   ___ deliberate   ___ unwavering

___ desperate   ___ demanding   ___ persistent

___ determined   ___ ho-hum   ___ timid

Other: _____

What explanation would you give for the people's persistence in wanting to get to Jesus?

_____

_____

Have you ever been tenacious in your approach to receive healing from Jesus? Explain your approach. Did you ask others to join you in your request? How did Jesus answer your prayer, or are you still waiting to receive His healing?

_____

_____

_____

We do not need to be shy or embarrassed to ask for help and healing. We have a Healer, with a great multitude of witnesses, who is able to heal any sickness or disease, any affliction or suffering. Whether it is physical, emotional, or spiritual He is able to set us free and release us from the clutches of suffering.

If you are still waiting to receive the healing you asked for, do not give up. First, make sure there is no sin involved. Ask the Holy Spirit to examine your heart and reveal to you anything that might be keeping you from receiving God's healing. If He reveals something, confess your sin and turn away from it.

What does Psalm 66:18 tell us about sin and unanswered prayer?

_____

Day One: The Hand of the Healer

Summarize James 5:14-16:

What happened in Matthew 9:2-7 as a result of the man's sins being forgiven?

On the other hand, recognize that not all afflictions are the result of sin.

What question did the disciples ask Jesus in John 9:1-3?

What did Jesus say was the reason for this man's blindness? (v. 3)

Most of the time I have found, through my own need and suffering, that if God does not answer right away, or the way I thought He would, it is because He has something else in mind (see Isaiah 55:8-9). Just because God seems to be silent does not mean He is uncaring, unwilling, or inactive. We may not always understand, but when God is silent, it usually means He is about to reveal another part of Himself and is preparing you to see another part of His character. God desires to reveal Himself to you through your circumstances, and then use you and your circumstances to help others who are suffering. Wait upon the Lord and watch for the miracle. God may not give you exactly what you ask for, but you can rest assured that He will give you what you need in order to bring wholeness into your life.

End today by meditating on Romans 8:28-39. How do these verses bring you comfort and hope in the midst of your present circumstances?

Day Two
When Jesus Saw Their Faith

"Then he touched their eyes and said, 'According to your faith will it be done to you'" (Matthew 9:29).

Faith—as believers we hear this word all the time. Scripture says, "Without faith it is impossible to please God" (Hebrews 11:6). Jesus told His disciples, "…if you have faith as small as a mustard seed, you can move a mountain" (see Matthew 17:20). Faith is reliance upon God; a submissive trust, believing God will do what He says He will do in spite of what we see going on around us. By faith we are healed (see Mark 10:52), saved (Eph. 2:8-9; Luke 7:50); encouraged (Romans 1:12), made righteous (Romans 1:17), justified (Galatians 3:24); and protected, able to extinguish all the fiery darts of the enemy (Ephesians 6:16). Today we will look at some verses that focus on faith. As we examine these verses, we will see that faith is the power behind the hand of God.

Let's begin by praying for our faith to increase, and then read Luke 7:1-10 and answer the following:

Who was in need of healing? What was his need?

___

Who was sent to Jesus to inform Him about the need for healing? (v.3) Why do you think the centurion sent the people he did to Jesus?

___

How did the messengers approach Jesus about the need for the servant's healing? What did they tell Jesus about the servant? (v. 4-5)

___

Why did the centurion send word to Jesus, and not go himself to seek the Lord's help? Check the correct response:

___ The centurion was too busy to go

___ The centurion didn't want to leave his ill servant

___ The centurion felt unworthy

How does the centurion's attitude and approach for healing differ from the woman who had been bleeding for twelve years?

___

Day Two: When Jesus Saw Their Faith

What happened just before Jesus and His followers reached the centurion's home? Check all that apply:

____ The centurion's friends ran out to meet Jesus

____ The friends stopped Jesus from coming into the centurion's home

____ The friends delivered another message from the centurion

What was the message the friends gave to Jesus? Fill in the blanks according to Luke 7:7b-8 (NIV).

"But _____ the _____, and my servant _____ _____. For I myself am a man _____ _____, with soldiers under me. I _____ this one, 'Go,' and he goes; and that one, 'Come,' and he comes. I _____ to my servant, 'Do this,' and he does it."

"When Jesus heard this…" (v. 9), what emotion did Jesus express? What did He tell the people who were following Him?

_____

_____

When the messengers returned to the house, what did they find? What had happened to the servant? (v. 10)

_____

A centurion was a Roman military commander who was in charge of a division of 100 men. And this particular centurion had a servant whom he highly valued (v.2). We are told in verse 2 that the man was very sick and dying. Matthew 8:6 (another version of this story) tells us the servant was paralyzed and suffering terribly. One thing was for certain—the man was in need of healing—he needed Jesus.

The man's commanding officer, though feeling unworthy (not shy or ashamed), sent word to Jesus, asking Him to come and heal his servant. I find it interesting that the Roman centurion officer sent Jewish elders to Jesus to tell Him about his servant, and to give Jesus the added information that this servant loved the Jewish people, and even helped build the synagogue. The centurion's choice makes me wonder if he was trying to influence Jesus in any way. Since he was a Roman soldier, did he conclude that Jesus would not come otherwise? Did he think Jesus would come more quickly if He knew that the man in need loved the Jews? I don't believe the centurion had ulterior motives, but I do think he seriously valued his servant and truly wanted Jesus to come to his aid. Nevertheless, Jesus did come. Not because this man loved the Jews, but because Jesus loved this man.

When Jesus arrived on the scene, however, the centurion sent more messengers (friends) to tell Jesus not to come into his home, again, because he felt unworthy. This breaks my heart. How many times do we do this very thing? We need Jesus; yet, do not allow Him to fully come into our lives because of feelings of unworthiness. I am getting a little off the main point here, but I want to make another point. In our human sinful nature we are unworthy of the Lord, but He doesn't look at us and call us "worthless." Jesus wants to come into our homes (our lives) and heal us. We must learn to invite Jesus in and not just cry out to Him from a distance. Jesus was headed straight for the centurion's home, but He was stopped from going in. He was prohibited access. We must never allow that to happen. Let's invite Jesus in and make Him feel welcome!

> Do you ever feel unworthy of Jesus? Have you stopped Him from completely entering your home, even though you're in need of Him? Share your heart?
>
> _____
> _____

To the centurion's credit—Jesus said, "I tell you, I haven't seen faith like this in all the land of Israel" (v. 9, NLT). Jesus was amazed (NIV, NLT), He marveled (NAS) at the faith He saw in this man. The centurion understood the power and influence of authority. He, himself, was under authority, and had command and position over his regiment. The man understood supremacy, power, rule, and the capacity to give commands, and have those orders carried out. Because of his understanding he knew that Jesus did not even have to touch the man, but simply speak and his servant would be healed. The centurion's demonstration of faith not only brought on a miracle of healing, but a word of commendation from Jesus. He recognized that Jesus had the authority to give orders to heal, just as he could give orders to his men and have his orders carried out.

> Look up the following verses. What happened when the Lord spoke?
>
> Genesis 1:3: _____
> Genesis 1:6-8: _____
> Genesis 1:11: _____
> Genesis 1:14-15: _____
> Genesis 1:20-21: _____
> Genesis 1:24: _____
> Genesis 1:26-27: _____

God said...and it was so. "For He spoke, and it came to be; he commanded, and it stood firm (Psalm 33:8). All the Lord needs to do is speak into your circumstances. He only needs to whisper one word into your life and it is done.

> What healing word do you need Jesus to speak over you? Send Him a message and invite Him to come and speak over you, then have confidence, like the centurion, that He will deliver you.
>
> _____
> _____
> _____

Day Two: When Jesus Saw Their Faith

It is vital that we have the faith that believes Jesus is able.

Paraphrase what Jesus told His disciples in Matthew 21:21-22:
_____
_____

Another story of faith is found in Matthew 9:27-31 where two blind men came to Jesus and asked for healing. Jesus questioned them, "Do you believe that I am able to do this?" (v. 28). They responded in faith, "Yes. Lord." (v.28). Then, based on their faith, Jesus touched them and said, "According to your faith will it be done to you" (v. 29). The New Living Translation records Jesus' words in Matthew 27:29 as: "Because of your faith, it will happen." (NLT)

Look up the following verses. Record what happened as a result of having faith:
Matthew 9:2: _____
Mark 5:34: _____
Luke 7:50: _____
Luke 17:19: _____
Luke 18:42-43: _____

What stands out to you the most about having faith?
_____

When we have faith we are: saved, forgiven of our sins, healed, made well, I'd even say "made whole," and we receive sight, both physical and spiritual.

Now, look up the following verses and describe the result from a lack of faith?
Matthew 8:26: _____
Matthew 13:58: _____
Mark 4:40: _____
Mark 6:5-6: _____
Luke 12:28-29: _____
James 1:6: _____

What stands out to you the most about having a lack of faith?
_____

"If you do not stand firm in your faith, you will not stand at all" (Isaiah 7:9b). Without faith we are consumed by fear and doubt. Without faith we worry and fret, even over the simplest things in our lives. Without faith we paralyze the hand of God. Did you catch the phrase: "Because of their unbelief, *he couldn't* do any mighty miracles among them"? (Mark 6:5, NLT) It wasn't that Jesus wouldn't do the miracles, or that He was powerless to perform the miracles, but He *couldn't* do the miracles. Without faith Jesus could not heal them. Not that their lack of faith made Him any less God, but their lack of faith tied His hands. The moment we forget that God is all-powerful, we stop the power of God in our lives.

Read Matthew 17:14-20:

Why couldn't the disciples drive out the demon and heal the boy?

_____

What did Jesus tell them would be the measure of their strength if they had faith? (v. 20)

_____

Where did Peter say faith comes from? Fill in the blanks according Acts 3:16 (NIV).

"By faith in the name of Jesus, this man whom you see and know was made strong. It is Jesus' name and the _____ _____ _____ _____ _____ _____ that has given this complete healing to him…"

Faith comes from God through the Holy Spirit (see Galatians 5:22-23), but we must make the decision to exercise trust and reliance on God. When we do not exercise the faith we have been given, we will not be able to overcome the demons (circumstances) in our lives. When we decide to accept doubt and unbelief, instead of trusting God, we will continually see a lack of power in our lives. Jesus said, "…if you have faith…nothing will be impossible for you" (see Matthew 17:20).

No matter where you are right now, whether steadfast in your faith, or struggling to hold on, diligently pray for more faith. End today by meditating on Luke 17:5: "The apostles said to the Lord, 'Increase our faith!'" Now use the space below to implore the Lord, as the apostles did, to increase your faith. Then make the choice to submit to God through faith.

_____
_____
_____
_____
_____
_____

Day Two: When Jesus Saw Their Faith

Day Three
Finding Joy in Suffering

*"Dear brothers and sisters, whenever trouble comes your way,
let it be an opportunity for joy" (James 1:2, NLT).*

Thus far, we have witnessed the hand of Jesus as He healed the multitudes from any and all afflictions. We witnessed a woman who was freed, not only from her illness, but from her shame. Then we witnessed the great faith of a man who understood faith from the standpoint of authority. And we learned that without faith we will not witness the miracles God desires to do in our lives. But what about those times when we exercise great faith and we still do not receive the healing we pray to experience? What then?

Life is full of anguish; and even though we have a Healer who is willing, ready and able to restore us, sometimes our transformation is not found in the healing, but in the pain. Sometimes Jesus says, "My grace is sufficient for you, for my power is made perfect in weakness" (2 Corinthians 12:9). So often, God gives us faith not to give us what we want, but to carry us through the trial. Beloved, if we desire to *know* Jesus, then we cannot focus on the healing miracles. In order to truly know the Healer, we must recognize that there is great purpose in suffering; and, in order to know Christ in intimacy we must also fellowship with Him in suffering.

It's wonderful to experience a miraculous healing from God. We want the miracles He can provide, we want to be freed from the pain, but God doesn't want us to pursue His miracles—He wants us to pursue Him. God doesn't want us to only know His healing, He wants us to know the Healer.

For the remainder of this week, we will center our attention on suffering. Don't panic—through these lessons we will realize we are not alone, and that great joy can be found even in the midst of our pain.

> Let's begin today by praying for the Holy Spirit to help us understand why we suffer. Then let's ask Christ to help us accept His finishing work in our lives, as He perfects us through trials and hardships.
>
> Fill in the blanks according to James 1:2, NIV:
>
> "Consider it _____ _____, my brothers, whenever you face trials of many kinds…"

I don't know about you, but when I think about going through trials, the last thing I want to do is celebrate. Nonetheless, the Bible clearly tells us to consider hardship and trials an "opportunity for joy" (NLT), and to "count it all joy" (KJV). The word *joy* according to *Webster's Dictionary* means "gladness…rejoicing."[45] Synonyms are "bliss, delight, pleasure." Finding pleasure in trials? Finding delight, even bliss and gladness in hardship? Rejoicing over my circumstances? How is this possible? Sorrow, grief, mourning, burden and pain would be better adjectives to express the ache my soul feels when it is drowning in the depths of a trial.

When you are suffering in the midst of a trial or difficult situation, how do you normally react? What do you focus on when you are going through hardship?

As we seek to find joy in our trials, let's consider how James, Peter, and Paul handled hardship, and how they found joy in the midst of great suffering.

Read James 1:2-4:

What does James say is the reason for trouble (NLT), trials (NIV), and temptations (KJV)?

What results when our faith is tested? (v.3)

What is the goal? (v.4)

Jump down to James 1:12. What is the reward for enduring tests and trials?

Where do you see James placing his focus in times of trial and suffering? Check the correct response:

____ On the loss
____ On eternal completion and reward
____ On the effect the trial is having on the people

Consider James 1:4, 12 in the margin. What motivation are we given for finding hardship, trials, and trouble pure joy?

Read 1 Peter 1:3-9:

What is Peter's description of joy in suffering? What did Peter consider a joy? Does Peter's version of joy in suffering differ from James? If so, how?

"But let endurance *and* steadfastness and patience have full play and do a thorough work, so that you may be [people] perfectly and fully developed [with no defects], lacking in nothing" (James 1:4, AMP). "Blessed is the man who preserves under trial; for once he has been approved, he will receive the crown of life which the Lord has promised to those who love Him" (v.12).

Day Three: Finding Joy in Suffering

Even though Peter and the people were suffering grief in all kinds of trials, where was their focus? Check the correct response:

____ On the setbacks the trials were causing

____ On their pain and suffering

____ On their eternal inheritance and reward

What did Peter tell the people were the purposes for their suffering? (v. 7)

_____

_____

What would be their reward for enduring? (v. 8-9)

_____

Faith is vital in our journey with Jesus. We need faith to be healed *and* to be made whole. Through suffering in all kinds of trials and hardships, our faith is given an opportunity to grow and be strengthened. As our faith grows we become mature and complete (NIV), fully developed (NLT), perfect and entire (KJV).

In order to help us grasp the joy of the situation a little better, let's look up a few words. According to *Webster's Dictionary* the word *complete* means "entire; finished; perfect; with no part lacking; to bring to a state of entirety; to make perfect; to fulfill; to accomplish"[46] For *perfect* we find "complete; faultless; …excellent; of the highest quality."[47] And for *mature* we find "fully developed; …to ripen; to perfect"[48]

We endure now so when Christ returns we will be complete, finished, whole, lacking nothing, ripened to perfection. Our joy is found in the process of our eternal completion. And in this process, our focus must remain on Christ and the eternal work that is taking place. The key to experiencing joy in suffering is found in where we place our focus. If we keep our eyes on Jesus and eternity, instead of our present circumstances, we will find joy and the ability to rejoice in times of suffering. Therefore, let's look ahead to our completion with great joy, so we may receive the crown of life (see James 1:12).

According to Jude 1:24, who else will be rejoicing with great joy at our completion?

_____

Christ will present us to Himself with exceeding joy (KJV), a radiant church, complete, mature, fully developed, without stain, holy and blameless (see Ephesians 5:27), finished to perfection, a lovely bride of the highest quality. Therefore, as we suffer and go through trials of many kinds, "let us fix our eyes on Jesus, the author and perfector of our faith, who for the joy set before Him endured the cross, scorning its shame, and sat down at the right hand of the throne of God" (Hebrews 12:2). We have a great deal to look forward to, and what we suffer in this life is not for nothing—it is the hope of eternal reward in Christ Jesus.

Now, let's turn our attention to Paul's attitude on suffering and how he and his companion found joy in the midst of their trials.

Read Acts 16:16-34:

List the trials and suffering Paul and Silas endured:

_____   _____

_____   _____

_____   _____

In the midst of their circumstances and suffering, where did they place their focus?

____ On their pain and suffering

____ On plans to break out of the prison

____ On God

How did Paul and Silas keep their focus? Who else heard them? (v. 25)

_____

What happened as a result of their focus? Check all that apply:

____ An earthquake shook the foundation of the prison

____ The prison doors flew open and the chains fell off

____ The jailer dropped to his knees and asked for salvation

____ The jailer took Paul and Silas to his house to feed and care for them

____ The whole house received God's saving grace

We may not realize what is happening at the time, but when we focus on God through worship, God can shake the very foundation of our circumstances. Our worship can throw the doors to our prison cells wide open and unlock the chains of bondage that have us bound. When we focus on God through worship, during our time of trials and suffering, others notice. They look at us and wonder: *Why are they joyful when they are in so much pain?* When we worship, no matter the circumstances, pain, suffering, trial or hardship others will want what we have. They won't understand it, but they will want it because they will see something different in us. As a result, our focused worship offered to God in the midst of suffering can bring about salvation for others.

Worship changes our perspective. It takes our heavy heart and makes it light. When we offer our hearts in true worship, the Holy Spirit will make our worship a strong offering to God. Then, through worship, God will lift us up in fellowship with Him, so we can see our circumstances and suffering from His perspective. When we see our suffering through God's eyes, our spirit and soul find the strength to endure the hardship and trial.

Our victory and joy comes when our eyes are focused on Jesus and our hearts are flooded with worship. Try it the next time you are sitting in the pit of despair. Muster up all you have to give, even if it is a little bit, and bring your offering to God. As you begin to worship, the Holy Spirit will take over and increase your ability to love God through the pain with incredible amounts of praise. Through the power of the Holy Spirit you will find the strength to endure, as your heart and soul come alive with hope and joy.

> End today by meditating on Romans 8:18 "I consider that our present sufferings are not worth comparing with the glory that will be revealed in us." As we look forward to our eternal reward in Christ, and the joy of being His perfected bride, let us find joy today in our circumstances by focusing on Christ Jesus through worship.

Day Four
Not Alone in Our Suffering

"Praise…the God of all comfort, who comforts us in all our troubles…
(2 Corinthians 1:3-4).

Thankfully, no one I know has experienced every tragedy there is to suffer. There are times, however, when what we experience makes us wonder how we will ever survive. I know suffering is not easy—it never will be. Yet, as we fix our eyes on Jesus, "the author and perfector of our faith" (Hebrews 12:2), we will find joy in the process of becoming mature and complete, a perfected bride who will one day stand before her Groom filled with unending jubilation. As we make our way through today's lesson, I pray we will be encouraged to discover we are never alone in our suffering. Jesus, our Healer, is with us; and there is great purpose in all that we go through.

Let's begin today by praying for the God of all comfort to comfort us in our time of need, and to show us that we are never alone in our suffering.

Read Hebrews 2:18 and 4:15-16:

What touches your heart the most about these verses?

One of the reasons Christ Jesus knows us so well, and possesses such great understanding about all that we go through, is because He is no stranger to suffering. He knows, firsthand, every heartache, pain and sorrow we endure in this life, because He Himself endured these things. He truly was a man of all sorrows.

Read Isaiah 53:

In each of the following verses, describe what Jesus suffered. Then go back over your responses and place a star next to any suffering you can relate to personally.

v. 2b: _____

v. 3: _____

v. 4: _____

v. 5: _____

v. 7: _____

v. 8: _____

v. 9: _____

v. 10: _____

v. 12b: _____

If I had my way life would be perfect. It would be a pleasant journey with no pain or sorrow. Inevitably, however, something always comes along and smashes the plans that I meticulously put together. Stuff happens, and when it does it often creates havoc by disrupting my well laid agenda. When bad things happen, and I am in the midst of suffering, I think about all Jesus endured, so that I don't become weary and give up (see Hebrews 12:3). I will never suffer as greatly as Jesus did, but Scripture promises that, in this life, I will drink from His cup (see Matthew 20:22).

We all will go through a lot in our lifetime: hardship, heartache, sorrow, pain, grief, trials, more suffering than we would like to think about, but we must always remember that we are never alone in our suffering. So, when we are going through something that is extremely difficult we need to look to Jesus, so we can find strength in our time of need.

Look again at Isaiah 53, what was Jesus' reward for enduring?

v. 10: _____

v. 11: _____

v. 12a: _____

According to Hebrews 12:2, what was Jesus' reward for enduring?

_____

_____

During His time of suffering, Christ Jesus focused on God and the eternal promises that His Father had given Him. Jesus knew His Father would raise Him from the dead, seat Him at His right hand, give him authority over all things, and present Him with a purified bride to reign with Him forever.

> How does dwelling on your eternal destiny in Christ give you hope in time of suffering?
>
> _____
> _____
> _____

Also, as we suffer, we can keep in mind that we do not have to wait until eternity to see good come from our afflictions. Jesus will take what we suffer now and use it to help others who are suffering. If we let Him, He will take the ashes of our pain, and turn them into a glorious crown of beauty for His glory (see Isaiah 61:3).

> Read 2 Corinthians 1:3-11:
>
> Fill in the blanks according to 2 Corinthians 1:3, NIV:
>
> Praise be to the God and Father of our Lord Jesus Christ, the Father of _____ and the God of _____ _____.
>
> According to verse 4, what will the Father of compassion give us in our time of suffering? What is the purpose of what we receive from God?
>
> _____
> _____
>
> How does verse 7 confirm that we are not alone in our suffering?
>
> _____
> _____
>
> What have you suffered that God used to comfort someone else? Explain how God comforted you, and then used your time of suffering to comfort another.
>
> _____
> _____
> _____

I am living proof God can and will redeem a harmful past in order to give hope to someone else. At the beginning of this week on the Healer, I briefly shared about a season when my soul was drowning in depression. At the time, I didn't see or understand why depression had consumed my life, nor did I see the beauty God would bring from the ashes of my pain. Yet, at my lowest point, when I was seriously considering suicide, the

Healer reached into my well and healed me, giving me a miraculous and powerful testimony—a testimony of hope, of love and deliverance, of healing power and his unfathomable grace. Over the years, God has taken my testimony and shared it with others, offering hope to the hopeless. Never, in my wildest dreams, would I have guessed God would use what I had gone through as a light in dark places. Yet, from my painful past, God created a ministry dedicated to helping others find hope, healing, and freedom for their souls.

You and I won't be fully healed from our suffering until we allow God to reveal His glory through our pain. Great joy is found in serving others. Therefore, permit God to turn your wailing into dancing and remove your sackcloth and clothe you with joy. (see Psalm 30:11). The Healer wants to infuse your pain with power, and then help you to comfort and encourage others who are suffering.

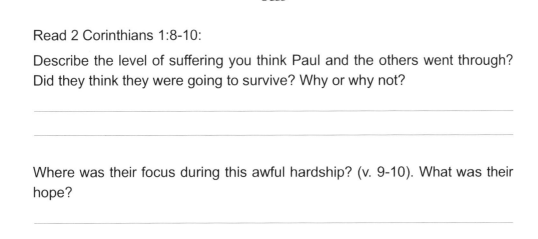

Read 2 Corinthians 1:8-10:

Describe the level of suffering you think Paul and the others went through? Did they think they were going to survive? Why or why not?

_____

_____

Where was their focus during this awful hardship? (v. 9-10). What was their hope?

_____

Recently, I watched a Billy Graham telecast about the shooting that took place at Virginia Tech. As I watched the trauma, I was amazed at the sense of loss and despair; yet, at the same time, there were many people who professed Christ and found peace and hope in Him.

I believe that it is during the hardest times of our lives that we experience Christ more—more of His comfort, more of His peace, more of His presence. Not that we do not experience the presence of God at other times, but there is something profound that takes place when we cry out to Him in our suffering that seems to move the heart of God, drawing Him closer in our time of need.

In 2003, my husband and I went through a season where our lives were turned upside down. It was, without a doubt, the most difficult time of our marriage as we struggled through a loss of health and finances. When my husband collapsed, he became so ill that I wasn't sure if he would ever be able to work again. Yet, it was also the most wonderful time, because of the increase of the presence of God in our lives.

Like never before, as I worshiped my way through this time, I had a deeper awareness of Jesus. And from this increased awareness of His manifest presence, I was given an increase of faith and joy. Call it mercy. Call it grace. Call it whatever brings you encouragement—it was all God.

In the midst of our dark trials, the Healer will come and make Himself known. In knowing Christ and resting in His goodness, our souls can find rest and a peace that transcends all understanding. Not the kind of peace that comes only when life is easy and circumstances are good (see John 14:27), but the kind of peace that brings quietness of heart and mind even in the midst of trouble. It's that sense of calm and gentle reassurance that no matter what happens He is with us and is working everything out for our good.

As we discovered yesterday, the eternal goal is wholeness, complete spiritual maturity, so we may be presented to Christ as a perfected bride. In order to obtain this goal, however, He will often take us to the depths of suffering. From there, He will reveal Himself as Healer and meet our need. Whether, it is the miraculous healing we seek, or the grace to sustain the trial.

Fill in the blanks according to 2 Corinthians 12:9, NIV:

"My _____ is sufficient for you, for my power is made perfect in _____."

So many people in this world suffer. Past and present, they have and are, suffering from every kind of affliction and disease—knowing great depths of sorrow, heartbreak, loneliness and pain. In the midst of this suffering Christ is ever present, working in us the end result, and bringing joy and comfort in the process. He is turning our lives into a drink offering, so that others may know the compassion of the Father in their time of need; even to the point of bringing them the hope of eternal salvation. We may never know how God is using us. We may not like it, or even understand why we are in the center of such a terrible time, but if we keep our focus on Jesus and the hope of eternal glory with Him, knowing that He understands our weakness, we can rest assured that we will be able to endure for the greater good.

God always has a purpose in everything He does, or allows to come into our lives. Whether it is success or suffering, God will use it for His glory and purposes, if we allow Him. It is never for nothing. During these times, God will bring beauty from the ashes as He shapes our character and reveals Himself. Don't think of these hard times as always something negative. There is great worth in times of hardship and struggle, and these times help us to *know* God.

End today by receiving the comfort of God through Psalm 10:17; Psalm 22:24; and Psalm 34:17-18. Allow His healing balm to soothe your soul. Allow His Word to ease your hurt, and increase your understanding that Jesus is with you in your time of suffering.

_____
_____
_____
_____
_____

Day Five
I Want to Know Him

"But rejoice that you participate in the sufferings of Christ, so that you may be overjoyed when his glory is revealed (1 Peter 4:13).

Today, as we continue to know the Healer through times of suffering, we will consider the ardent cry of a man who truly desired to know Christ in both intimacy and suffering.

Let's begin by praying to truly know Christ, and what it means to fellowship with Him in both intimacy and suffering.

Read Philippians 3:1-12:

What did Paul claim about himself prior to knowing Christ? What was his background? (vs. 4-6) List as many claims as you can:

_____   _____
_____   _____
_____   _____
_____   _____

What statement does Paul make in verse 7? What does he now consider as loss?

_____

What declaration did Paul make in verse 8? What did it mean to him to know Christ? Record Paul's expressive words, according to your translation.

_____

_____

In what three areas of relationship did Paul pray to know Christ?
1. _____
2. _____
3. _____

Paul was a Pharisee, a pure Hebrew Jew, circumcised on the eighth day, a people of Israel, and a member of the tribe of Benjamin. Paul, in his own eyes was righteous, loyal to the house of David, zealous for God in his persecution of the church, and faithful in keeping with the law. He described himself as perfect, righteous, and faultless. Before knowing Christ, Paul considered himself to have everything: religious power, good standing, and righteousness before God and the people. Yet, after meeting Christ on the road to Damascus one particular day (see Acts 9:1-19), he sings a different tune: "I consider everything a loss compared to the surpassing greatness (NIV), priceless gain (NLT), surpassing value (NASB), of knowing Christ Jesus my Lord." I love the depth of the *Amplified Bible* as it records Philippians 3:8: "I count everything as loss compared to the possession of the priceless privilege (the overwhelming preciousness, the surpassing worth, and supreme advantage) of knowing Christ Jesus my Lord."

The things that Paul once thought of as successes and assets were now the very things and attitudes that he came to realize were stumbling blocks to him, and actually had kept him separated from God. Paul continually endeavored to "press on" (v.12), to know Christ. Paul wanted to know His voice, His love, His personal touch, His heart, emotions, longings and desires. He wanted to know Christ in the richness of a close personal relationship. When Paul said in Philippians 3:10 that he wanted to *know* Christ; he was using the Greek word *ginosko*, meaning "to know intimately."[49] And this intimate relationship was more important to him than anything else. Paul considered *knowing* Christ his ultimate asset.

> How would you describe the value of knowing Christ? What do you now consider "as loss" in comparison to knowing Christ in a personal and intimate relationship?
>
> _____
>
> _____
>
> _____

Something I find interesting, and, at times, even hard to comprehend, is the fact that as Paul fellowshipped with Christ in a personal relationship of love and devotion, a union worth more to him than anything else, he could have stopped there and focused on the pleasure of their relationship, but he didn't.

> What does Paul proclaim in Philippians 3:10-11?
>
> _____
>
> _____

Paul considered *all* things as loss compared to the surpassing greatness of this one thing—knowing Christ. Every hardship, every failure, every success, and every act of service in ministry he counted as nothing compared to knowing Christ. Success was not Paul's goal, and failure was not his handicap. Paul's focus was on Christ, and the extreme privilege of knowing Him in intimacy, power, and suffering.

Something became very clear to me as I studied Paul and his attitude of considering all things as loss—knowing Christ became Paul's calling in life. Knowing Christ became his greatest purpose. The ministry, acts of service, preaching, evangelism—these were not his calling—they were the byproducts of his pursuit to know Christ. Paul witnessed, firsthand, the beauty and ecstasy of an intimate connection with Christ, and He experienced the agony of sharing in His suffering. From these experiences Paul came to know Christ. He then took what he shared with Christ and told the world.

In a similar way, I am not called to be a writer. I am called to know Christ through a personal relationship. The books, Bible studies, poems, and inspirational stories—everything that I write—is the outcome of the relationship, the fruit of knowing Christ as I press into Him in intimacy and suffering.

Our focus, the one thing that should consume our hearts, souls, and minds is the extreme privilege of knowing Christ. From there, through the depth of our relationship with Him, He manifests Himself to the world.

> Consider the following verses. What did it mean to Paul, and the other apostles, to fellowship with Christ in suffering? What was their mind-set as they drank from His cup?
>
> Acts 5:40-42: _____
>
> Romans 5:3-5: _____
>
> 2 Timothy 1:8: _____

They rejoiced in suffering for the sake of His name, because it verified that they knew Christ and shared in His fellowship. They rejoiced because they understood the outcome, the end result of their suffering. They rejoiced in the hope they had in Christ, the hope that would not disappoint them. They rejoiced because of the love they received from God through a personal relationship. They rejoiced because they knew that through their connection with Christ, He would manifest Himself through them in power. And because of these revelations, they invited and encouraged others to join them, to share in suffering for the gospel.

The Bible tells us that because we belong to Christ, because we share in His fellowship, we will share in His suffering. It sounds unpleasant, and not something any of us would readily jump at; unless, we, like Paul and the other apostles, receive the same revelations.

> Read 1 Peter 4:12-16:
>
> What did Peter instruction the believers to do when they faced suffering? (v. 13 and 16) Check the correct response:
>
> ____ Mourn and complain
>
> ____ Be strong and stand firm
>
> ____ Rejoice and praise God
>
> Why is participating in the suffering of Christ a reason for rejoicing and a time for praise?
>
> _____
>
> _____
>
> _____

Day Five: I Want to Know Him

According to verse 14, why should we rejoice when we are insulted (NIV), reviled (NAS), or reproached (KJV) for the name of Christ? Check the correct response:

____ Because it will make us feel better

____ Because we will gain God's approval

____ Because the Spirit of God rests on us

In my previous Bible study, *Transformed by Desire*, I made an interesting discovery. As I researched the topic of purification, and looked up the meaning for the word *bless*, I learned something I wasn't expecting. The word *bless* means "to consecrate; glorify; sanctify; set apart."[50]

When we are insulted because we are Christians, it is because we are consecrated, set apart, made holy and sanctified for the glory of God. We who belong to Christ need to understand that in order to truly know Him, we will not only enjoy the pleasure and beauty of His presence, we will also fellowship in His suffering, so we may also share in the power of His resurrection. When we fellowship in His suffering, we receive from God the power and manifestation of His Spirit of glory. The very power of God will rest on us, giving us the strength to endure, to overcome, to reveal Christ, and to rejoice. Therefore, may we boast all the more of our weakness, so that Christ's power may rest on us (see 2 Corinthians 12:9b).

Do we truly comprehend the cost involved in knowing Christ? What it really means to know Him in both joy and suffering? Do we know what it means to know Him in His death, so we may also know Him in the ecstasy of His resurrection? You and I need both experiences to be whole in Christ, to be mature, complete, not lacking anything, so that the power of God may be visible in us.

As I read about Paul, the man he was, and the man Christ transformed him into, I am in awe. I don't fully understand how He did it, but through the power of love Christ motivated that man to pray for suffering beyond what he could hope to bear. Paul himself said, "For Christ's love compels us" (2 Corinthians 5:14). Christ took a man full of himself, his own righteousness and accomplishments, and humbled him into a man who pursued Christ with everything He had. Paul left behind everything he valued, and once thought important, for a life of suffering and danger, of insult and revile. Why?

Paul witnessed Jesus! He understood Christ's heart. He experienced Christ's love. As a result, he desired to go to the extreme with Jesus. Paul's heartfelt cry was to *know* Christ, both in intimacy and suffering, sharing in His death, so that he could also share in His glorious life and power.

No matter what we go through in this life. Whether, hardship, trials and trouble, or glorious gain and success, we must count it all as loss, because nothing compares with the surpassing privilege of knowing Christ Jesus our Lord. There is no greater worth in life, nothing as valuable as knowing Him. Therefore, in all things, we must forget what is behind and "press on," like Paul, toward the ultimate prize—the joy of *knowing* God.

End today by meditating on the following poem:

The Cost of Knowing Jesus

I truly do not comprehend the cost,
The cost of knowing Christ.
I come to church on Sunday,
All but willing to sacrifice.

I sit among believers,
Quite comfortable in the pew.
I lift my songs of worship,
And offer thanks in praise so few.

Quite satisfied to look polite,
As not to disclose the pain.
I listen to the sermon,
Yet, heed nothing of gain.

I look upon the One called Jesus,
To grab a remnant of remain.
My heart truly longing,
Yet, I try my best to refrain.

Oh, what is this thing called fellowship?
To know Jesus in suffering and pain?
To walk the road less traveled;
To find the path of sorrow a gain?

Others tell me it is possible;
To discover in such a place as this,
To know the joy, to know the best,
To know glorious heightened bliss.

Open my eyes, dear Jesus,
And cause our relationship to grow.
Transform my heart, empower my way,
As You did with those long ago.

I want to know You as Paul did,
John and Peter, too.
What is this cost You speak of?
Show me, Lord, please do.

Apply the Knowledge

In my pursuit of the Healer this week, the Holy Spirit has shown me …

The verse that spoke to me the most this week is…

In order to make this verse a reality in my life, I…

Jesus, I don't want to only know the miracles of your healing, I want to *know* the Healer. The changes I need to make in order to *know* You more profoundly as my Healer are… Help me to…

The hidden treasure (see Isaiah 45:3) of His Person and personality God revealed to me this week is… This higher revelation of God's presence profoundly awakens me to…

Witnessing God as Healer this week has changed my perspective of God from… to…

Holy Spirit, help me to apply what I've learned to my everyday life, so…

Prayer for the Journey

Lord, I desire to know You the way Paul did. Yet, I do not know what I ask; therefore, I ask first for Your mercy. Paul had a great desire to know You in the extreme pleasure of intimacy. He also had the desire to know You in Your death, so that he could also know You in the power of your resurrection. I, too, pray to know You this way. I want to know You in the joy of intimate encounters, and to fellowship with You in suffering, so that I may experience…

Apply the Knowledge

Session Seven
Rebuilder of Desolate Souls
Ezekiel 34:1-31

*"Then the nations around you that remain will **know that I the LORD** have rebuilt what was destroyed and have replanted what was desolate. I the LORD have spoken, and I will do it'" (Ezekiel 36:36).*

1.) Everything God does points to _____ _____ .

2.) Through covenant promise, God's healing hand will _____ every wrong and _____ everything right.

3.) The Healer will _____ us of our sins, _____ and _____ what was ruined, and _____ what was destroyed.

   a.) Healing begins when we can _____ there is a _____ .

   b.) The Healer wants to bring _____ and _____ to our weary souls.

   c.) Restoration means _____ _____ .

   d.) When a city is fortified it is _____ , secure, sheltered and protected.

Week Eight

Knowing the Name of God

I am not a big fan of autographs. I do have some signed books that mean something to me if the person who signed them is also a friend. I do not like to sign autographs, but I will if someone asks me. I simply don't see what the big deal is. It's a name on a piece of paper. Now, if that name appears at the bottom of a check, then that's a different story, then that piece of paper holds value.

A name, even if it is tied to a famous celebrity, carries no power, value, or importance. It is just a name made up of vowels and consonants; and, whether it is written down or spoken out loud, there is no real everlasting significance to that name.

There is a Name, however, that carries strong presence and demands attention—a Name that when spoken the earth shakes and the mountains melt like wax. It is a Name that demands esteem and honor—a Name that evokes great authority and sends the demons running. It is a Name that is above every other name.

If we want to know God, and what He says about Himself, then it is necessary to search for the revelation found in His Name, and the Titles God reveals to us. This week, it is my humble mission to point out some of the Names and Titles of God. As I do, I pray continually for the Holy Spirit to unveil each Name and Title to us in a fresh new way. I pray He will lift the veil and give us a type of privileged access, so we may be given greater insight into the character, passion and heart of God's Holy Name.

I am looking forward to studying the Name of God with you this week. Due to the fact that we only have a week to accomplish such a great task, we will not have the liberty to fully encompass every Name or Title by which God reveals Himself. Therefore, I encourage you to invest some time in continuing this gracious pursuit.

As we examine His magnificent Name together, I pray our faith and confidence in Him will increase. May we be continually encouraged by His wonderful, marvelous, matchless Name—the Name that will stand firm for all eternity.

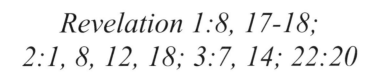

Revelation 1:8, 17-18;
2:1, 8, 12, 18; 3:7, 14; 22:20

*"I am the Alpha and the Omega…
who is, and who was, and who is to come, the Almighty.
I am the Living One; I was dead, and behold I am alive for ever and ever!
…who holds the seven stars in his right hand and walks among the seven golden lampstands. …who is the First and the Last…
…who has the sharp-double edged sword…the Son of God,
whose eyes are like blazing fire and whose feet are like burnished bronze.
…who is holy and true…the Amen,
the faithful and true witness, the ruler of God's creation.
He who testifies to these things says, 'Yes, I am coming soon'"*

This week we will focus on:

The beauty of His Name
"This is my name forever, the name by which I am to be remembered"
(Exodus 3:15).

The power of His Name
"No one is like you, O LORD; you are great,
and your name is mighty in power"
(Jeremiah 10:6).

The sustaining sufficiency of His Name
"I AM WHO I AM"
(Exodus 3:14).

The characteristics revealed in His Name
"The LORD is my rock, my fortress and
my deliverer…my shield…my stronghold"
(Psalm 18:2).

The privilege of professing His Name
"Give thanks to the LORD, call on his name…"
(1 Chronicles 16:8).

Day One
His Name is Jesus

'"What is your name, so that we may honor you when your word comes true?'
He replied, 'Why do you ask my name? It is beyond understanding (NIV),
seeing it is wonderful (NASB), it is secret (KJV) (Judges 13:17-18).

God, in His infinite wisdom, has revealed to us the name of His Son—Jesus. And from the first mention of His name, when it poured from the lips of an angel informing Mary that she would give birth to a son, the name Jesus has been a blessing to those who put their faith in it.

Throughout the centuries, no other name has been sweeter or more wonderful to the Christian believer than the name of Jesus. To those who put their hope and faith in His name, there is deliverance. To those who call on His name, there is unstoppable power. To those who seek the name of Jesus, there is no greater love and peace. Yet, the name of Jesus is beyond our comprehension. We cannot even begin to understand its meaning, appreciate its splendor, or value its integrity.

Jesus, a name that found its origin in the heavenly realms, according to Herbert Lockyer, is "in a sense His only name, all others being titles."[51] According to Lockyer, when we read or proclaim Jesus as the Prince of Peace (Isaiah 9:6), Judge (Acts 10:42), Morning Star (Revelation 22:16); King of kings (Revelation 19:16); High Priest (Hebrews 3:1); Bread of Life (John 6:35); or Master (Matthew 23:8, 10), we are not engaging His name, but proclaiming the titles that reveal the characteristics that are synonymous with the name of Jesus.

I am overwhelmed already. Let's stop and take some time to pray in the precious Name of Jesus, so we may be given wisdom and revelation to know and understand what we have been given through His marvelous Name.

According to Matthew 1:21, what name did the angel tell Joseph to give to the son Mary had conceived through the Holy Spirit? _____

One of the things I love best about the Jewish culture is that their names mean something. When I first met my friend Nisim he proudly told me his name means "miracles." In the Jewish culture, when a name is given to a child, it represents something special to one or both of the parents.

What name did Abraham give to his son in Genesis 21:3? What does the name mean? (Also see your Bible footnotes.)

_____

What names did Leah give to her sons in Genesis 29:31-35? What is the meaning of each name? What was Leah communicating through their names?

Name	Meaning	Communication

Oh, how I wonder what God the Father was thinking when He gave His only begotten Son the name Jesus? Before we begin our research for the meaning of the name Jesus, take a little time to ponder what you think the name meant to His Father. What do you think God the Father was trying to communicate to the world?

The name Jesus is truly beyond us, beyond our understanding, and we may never fully appreciate its meaning in this life; nevertheless, God has given us glimpses into the depth and wonder of His Son's name.

"This first syllable *Je* corresponds to *Jeho*, or *Jah*—Jehovah. This name of God speaks of the divine authority that Jesus came as the great I AM. *Je* tells us of His eternal Godhead, of His covenant relations, and of His mighty power and superior love. The second syllable *sus* is associated with the name *Oshea*, *Hosea*, or *Houshaia*, meaning "help," signifying "Jehovah our savior," or "Deliver," or "the help of Jehovah." In Greek, Jesus is a form of the name Joshua, which itself is a contraction of *Jehoshua*. Thus, in the second part of Je-*sus*, we are assured of pardon and peace, of deliverance from sin and hell."[52]

Divinity and salvation, sovereignty and mercy, covenant promise and its fulfillment all rolled into one name—the precious name of Jesus. This beloved name was so valued and cherished by those who knew Him, that no other name or title was proclaimed more in the gospels then the simple yet complex name of Jesus. This delightful truth is evident in the fact that out of the 700 times the name Jesus appears in the New Testament, over 600 references are found in the four gospels alone.

Matthew proclaimed the name of Jesus 170 times. Mark referred to Jesus approximately 100 times. Luke used the name Jesus almost 100 times, and the Apostle John, the disciple whom Jesus loved, used His name about 250 times.

What stands out to you the most regarding this evidence in the use of Jesus' name?

One thing that stands out to me is that those who knew Him best called Him Jesus. This familiar use of the name Jesus by His disciples affirms the value His name had in their hearts and minds. To them, His name declared something extraordinary: *who* He is and *what* He is.

> When you pray or talk to Jesus, by what name or title do you most often use or refer to? Why is that name or title special to you?

> End today by meditating on Matthew 16:13-15. "When Jesus came to the region of Caesarea Philippi, he asked his disciples, "Who do people say the Son of Man is?' they replied, 'Some say John the Baptist; others say Elijah; and still others, Jeremiah or one of the prophets.' 'But what about you?' he asked. 'Who do you say I am?'" Put yourself in the disciple's shoes. Who and what is Jesus to you? What does His name mean to you personally?

Day Two
No Other Name

"'On that day there will be one LORD, and his name the only name"
(Zechariah 14:9).

Do you ever call upon the name of Jesus just to tell Him you love Him? I do. Sometimes, I call upon Him just to hear Him answer me. You may think my approach is a waste of prayer, but I don't believe Jesus thinks so. When I call out to Him this way, He seems to delight in my childlike quest. Without hesitation His Spirit embraces me like a down-comforter, and I become acutely aware of His love and presence.

> At what times do you call upon the name of Jesus?

There is no other name like Jesus. No other name by which men are saved (see Acts 4:12). No other name by which we are healed. There is no other name by which we can find refuge and strength, or delight in more.

Today we are going to consider the authority found in the name of Jesus. Let's begin by calling upon His name, so we may ask Him to help us comprehend the power that is found in His name alone.

There is something incredible about the name of Jesus. It is without equal. It is beyond compare. The name of Jesus is unparalleled, incomparable, perfect and inimitable—it is the one and only. Everything you could possibly want or need is found in that Name. The name of Jesus is a strong tower, a refuge, a place of shelter from the storms of life. In His name we find peace, joy, freedom, and victory over sin and the enemy. Nothing has the power to save us, heal us, deliver us, or give us pleasure like the name of Jesus.

What did Jesus tell His disciples about asking in His name?

John 14:13-14: _____

John 16:23: _____

Look up the following verses. Record the testimony of those who found power and authority in the name of Jesus.

Acts 3:3-7: _____

Acts 4:10: _____

Acts 4:12: _____

Acts 16:18: _____

Romans 10:9-13: _____

According to the following verses, what do we find when we ask, seek, and trust in the name of Jesus? Match the reference with the correct answer:

Psalm 9:9-10:	refuge and safety
Psalm 20:6-7:	great power
Psalm 124:8:	protection
Proverbs 18:10:	deliverance
Jeremiah 10:6:	help

When you call on the name of Jesus, which blessing do you desire the most?

_____

According to Colossians 3:17, what are we to do in all things?

_____

Of the power and authority found in the name of Jesus, which one means the most to you and why?

_____

Day Two: No Other Name

The power of His name brings comfort, security, deliverance, and help. According to Philippians 2:9-11, what other authority has been given in the name of Jesus?

___

In all you do, in all of your circumstances, do it all in the name of Jesus. Jesus—the name by which we find salvation for our souls (see Romans 10:13). Jesus—the name Paul proclaimed is the name above every other name (see Philippians 2:9). Jesus—all power in heaven and on earth is given in that beloved name and that name alone (see Philippians 2:9-11).

At the end of the age, what will be significant to those who had revered, honored, and called upon the powerful name of Jesus?

Revelation 3:8-9: ___
Revelation 11:18: ___
Revelation 22:4: ___

Divine power, majesty and authority are affirmed in the name of Jesus, and anyone who dares to proclaim His name, honor His name, revere His name, and call upon His name will be greatly rewarded, and will forever be marked by the most celebrated of all names.

What do the following verses tell us about the dwelling place of God?

2 Chronicles 7:16: ___
1 Corinthians 3:16: ___
2 Corinthians 6:16: ___

We, as true believers in Jesus Christ, are empowered with the Name that is above every name, because we contain the Spirit of the living God. God dwells in us and with us. Therefore, we can call upon the name of Jesus and receive power. We can appeal to His name and find mercy. We can rest in His name and discover peace. We can stand on His name and find strength. We can proclaim His name and declare victory. There is no other name, in heaven and on earth, with that kind of power and authority.

End today by meditating on Jeremiah 15:16, "…for I bear your name O LORD God Almighty." How does knowing that you bear the divine and powerful name of Jesus help you to overcome your circumstances? Praise Him! Because you bear His Name, you have power and authority—everything you will ever need.

___
___
___
___

Day Three
He is the I AM

"Then the LORD came down in the cloud and stood there with him and proclaimed his name, the LORD" (Exodus 34:5).

This week, thus far, we have focused on the name that is above every name—the name of Jesus. In Day One, hopefully, we came to a better understanding of His glorious name as we broke it down in order to appreciate its meaning. Then, in Day Two, we considered the authority and power found in His name alone. Today we are going to strive to come to an even richer understanding of *HaShem*, meaning "the Name," as we open God's Word to deem His omnipotent name, YHWH.

Let's begin with prayer…. As I write this opening request for prayer, I am overcome with the need to get on my face. As I come before the Lord in my lowly state, I am consumed with trepidation and wonder. I hope you are, too. As you pray prior to beginning today's lesson, take this opportunity to humble yourself before God. If you are physically able, join me and get on your face before Him.

>When you are ready, turn with me to Exodus 3:13-15.
>
>When Moses met God for the first time, he asked God a question more profound than he ever realized. What was the question?
>
>_____
>
>What answer did God give to Moses? Record the exact translation.
>
>_____
>
>What did the Lord declare about His name in verse 15b? Check all that apply:
>
>____ This is my name forever
>
>____ This is the name by which I am to be remembered
>
>____ My name is to be remembered generation to generation

The New Living Translation records God's name as: "I AM THE ONE WHO ALWAYS IS." What do you think was going through Moses' mind as the God of Abraham, Isaac and Jacob spoke His name? Remember this was their initial meeting. Up until now, Moses had only heard about God. Perhaps the words from Job 42:5 filled Moses' heart before Job ever had the chance to speak them, "My ears had heard of you but now my eyes have seen you."

>What thoughts run through your mind as you hear and ponder the name of God?
>
>_____
>
>_____

I don't think Moses had any great understanding or revelation about God's name at first. It may have even sounded odd to him, mysterious, baffling, or alarming. But, eventually, *HaShem* "the Name" became an all-sufficient name where Moses, and the Israelites, found victory, freedom, promise, and sustaining power.

When I think about the name of God and what it means to me, I am stunned by divine presence and overtaken by His preeminence. Just the thought of His name gets me excited. It wasn't always like this, however. There was a time when, like Moses, I didn't understand the name of God, and therefore didn't appreciate it or the power His name possessed. I didn't see God as my abundance in life, mostly because I didn't know Him. It took going through some hard blows of life to awaken my soul to the reality that God, and God alone, would be my complete satisfaction. Now, I AM WHO I AM, means everything to me.

To the Jewish people, the name YHWH is linked with the Hebrew verb "to be" which means the "self-existent one" or the "one who causes to be." Through His Name God illuminated His covenant promise and reminded His people that His all-powerful presence would remain with them forever. To the Jewish people YHWH (yah-WEH) was the most sacred name.

The Hebrew name for God, "YHWH, is formed by four Hebrew consonants, and appears more than 6,800 times in the Old Testament. It appears in every book but Esther, Ecclesiastes, and the Song of Songs."[53] In most English translations of the Bible, the Hebrew Yahweh is translated as LORD (all caps), except the KJV.

Though scholars translate YHWH as "yah-WEH," the true pronunciation is lost, mainly because God's name was so revered by the Israelites that they refused to speak it out loud. This refusal to speak the name of God originated around 200BC when Pharisee Law demanded that the people not speak God's name for fear of profaning it. To this day, the Jewish community reveres God's holy Name so much that it still remains unuttered.

During the Middle Ages YHWH was rendered *Jehovah* when the four consonants YHWH were converted to JHWH. Then some of the vowels, taken from the Hebrew word Adonai (meaning Lord, Master), were inserted into JHWH producing the name *Jehovah*.

In the King James Version, "JAH, meaning the Independent One, is a shortened form of the name *Jehovah*. This name signifies, *He is*, and can correspond to I AM; such as Jehovah corresponds to the fuller expression I AM THAT I AM."[54] For example, Psalm 68:4 (KJV) declares, "Sing unto God, sing praises to his name: Extol him that rideth upon the heavens by his name JAH, and rejoice before him." Notice that Psalm 68:4 instructs us to extol (praise, worship, exalt) the name of JAH. Do you realize that every time you shout or sing "Hallelujah" you're fulfilling this instruction? "Hallelujah" means "Praise ye Jah?"

God wants us to know Him and proclaim Him as the "I AM." His greatest desire is for us to enter into the covenant relationship founded upon His name, and to know Him as our All-in-all.

In the book of John, for example, Jesus proclaimed over and over, "I AM!" "*I am* the bread of life" (v. 6:35). "*I am* the light of the world" (v. 8:12). "*I am* the gate." (v. 10:7). "*I am* the good shepherd" (v. 10:11). "*I am* the resurrection and the life" (v.11:25). "*I am* the true vine" (v. 15:5). "*I am* the way, the truth and the life" (v. 14:6). "…*I am* he" (v. 18:8).

Reflect on the following verses and record how JAH (meaning He is) proclaims I AM?

Genesis 15:1: _____

Isaiah 43:15: _____

Jeremiah 3:14: _____

Matthew 28:20: _____

Revelation 1:8; 17: _____

Revelation 1:18: _____

He is your shield and every great reward. *He is* your faithful Husband and loyal God. *He is* the First and the Last, the Living One who is with you always. *He is* your King, your Creator, your Holy One, your Jehovah.

Hear the heart of JAH. Allow His words to penetrate your soul: "Let me be everything to you: your Guide, your Teacher, your Strength, your Comforter and Encourager. Let me be your provider in all things, whether it is love and affection or physical needs. Let me be the source of your joy and delight, and the safe place of refuge you run to.

"Know that I AM your Father who loves and cares for you. Know that I AM your Divine Bridegroom who adores you and waits with great anticipation for the celebration and joy we will share for all eternity. Know that I AM your Healer who makes you whole. Know that I AM your Shepherd who will sustain you, guard and protect you. Know that I AM your Warrior who will fight for you. Know that I AM your Coming King who will ride on the clouds to bring you home. Know that I AM everything you will ever need. I AM WHO I AM."

When God opened my heart to Isaiah 43:10, I began to see the importance of knowing, believing, and understanding that He is. The whole premise of this Bible study is founded on this one principle. We can no longer be content and complacent in our relationship with God. We must, like Moses, go beyond our initial reaction into a deeper, more profound understanding of Who He is and how He desires to reveal Himself.

End today by meditating on our central verse for this study, Isaiah 43:10, "You are my witnesses,' declares the LORD, 'My servant whom I have chosen that you may know and believe me, and understand that I AM he." In light of what we have studied these past two days, how does this verse speak to you? How do you see Isaiah 43:10 from a fresh perspective?

_____

_____

_____

_____

_____

_____

Whether your prefer YHWH or JAH, what does His Holy name mean to you? How has calling on His omnipotent name changed your life?

_____

_____

_____

_____

_____

_____

_____

_____

_____

_____

_____

Day Three: He is the I AM

Day Four
What's in a Name?

"The name of the LORD is a strong tower; the righteous run to it and are safe"
(Proverbs 18:10).

In the Scriptures, when God encountered people, He often revealed His name. In doing so, He made known a part of His character. Other times, as people encountered God, they proclaimed His name because they had experienced its worth.

Let's begin with prayer, so we may come to know and understand the value of His name.

Then look up the following verses and record the name by which God is revealed and treasured, and its significance.

Genesis 16:7-14: _____

Genesis 22:1-18: _____

Genesis 28:10-18: _____

Exodus 17:14-16: _____

Do you know God as *El Roi*, the God who sees you and knows your suffering? Are you convinced He is *Jehovah Jireh*, the God who provides all your needs? Has He become your banner, your victory in every battle of life? Is your house called *Bethel?* Have you yielded your vessel, your soul, to the consuming presence of the Lord?

We will not consider the richness found in all of the priceless names and titles of God; but, as we focus on the character found in His name, we will do a lot of digging. Roll up your sleeves, Beloved, and let's be found faithful in our pursuit.

Read Psalm 18:1-3:

Place a check mark next to the characteristics the psalmist proclaimed of God.

___ deliverer	___ rock	___ fortress
___ refuge	___ protection	___ salvation
___ stronghold	___ shield	___ strength

What did David do in order to experience these characteristics of God? (v.3a)

_____

Some of my favorite characteristics of God's name are the ones that bring comfort, security and reassurance. I rest on these characteristics. When life gets too hard they are my place of shelter and strength.

How about you? Which characteristics of God's name do you rest upon when circumstances are overwhelming?

_____
_____

Although all of the characteristics found in God's name are precious, for the purposes of today's lesson, we will consider God as our rock, fortress, refuge, shield and stronghold.

Fill in the blank according to Psalm 144:1, NIV:

"Praise be to the LORD my _____"

Meditate on this characteristic of God's name. What does this characteristic mean to you?

_____
_____

At what times in your life have you stood upon the Rock?

_____
_____

"My God is my Rock" (Psalm 18:2). To me, *Yahweh Tsuri*—The Lord my Rock means stability. One of the things I love about Jesus is that He is consistent. He is not up when life is going well, and down when circumstances are hard. He is the one true, stable force in my life.

We, as humans, tend to be moved by our circumstances. We react emotionally to our current situation and present surroundings. Not the Lord—He is our unmovable Rock. Frankly, I can't think of a better name to describe God's permanency and faithful commitment in our lives. He is a God who can be counted on in all situations.

Look up the following verses and record the promises we can count on from God our Rock.

Psalm 62:1-2: _____

Isaiah 26:3-4: _____

Matthew 7:24-27: _____

Perfect peace, rest, salvation, unshakable faith, a place of refuge—these are the promises that belong to those who put their faith in *Yahweh Tsuri*. Let these blessings sink into your heart. Apply these promises to your life. Hardship in life will come. Tragedy will come. The mountains of circumstance will shake beneath your feet, but your faithful Rock will never be shaken (see Isaiah 54:10). His faithful and compassionate love will stand. His covenant promises will endure forever. In Him you have constant, steadfast, unshakeable stability.

Fill in the blanks from Psalm 91:1-2, NIV:

"He who dwells in the shelter of the Most High will rest in the shadow of the Almighty. I will say of the LORD, 'He is my _____ and my _____, my God, in whom I trust."

Meditate on these characteristics of God's name. What do they mean to you?
_____

At what times in your life have you taken refuge in God and found Him to be your safe fortress?
_____

To me, *Machseh*—Refuge, and *Metsuda*—Fortress means shelter from the storms of life. They are a sanctuary when the world is harsh, or I am hurting. The fortress of God's mighty arms is a safe place where I can unload my heavy burdens and be completely real with Him. His refuge is a place I can run to and let it all come spilling out, even when it gets downright ugly.

I remember one time in particular, I had gone through an awful season. At that time, I didn't understand why God had allowed such terrible circumstances to happen. Yet, I ran to Him and threw myself face down on the floor. With clinched fists, I pounded on that floor and shouted, "I trusted you! Why did you let this happen? I don't understand. Help me to understand." In His own way, over time, God did clarify the necessity for such a challenging experience; but, the point here is, at that moment, when all seemed hopeless and devastating, God was my refuge, my fortress of safety. As I shouted at Him and pounded my fists on the floor, I became increasingly aware of His presence as He took hold of me and drew me close. Even though I couldn't have been uglier, He was my shelter and comforter.

Who or what do you turn to when you are afraid or in trouble? Where do you turn when you are hit hard by circumstances or experiences that leave you wounded? Where is your place of safety? If you are turning to anyone or anything else other than God, it will prove to be a weak alternative to the refuge of His loving fortress.

From the verses below, record the hope we have in our Refuge and Fortress.
Psalm 9:9: _____
Psalm 31:2-3: _____
Psalm 46:1: _____
Psalm 62:8: _____

Come to Him when you are hurting and pour out your heart shamelessly. He is your refuge in times of trouble. He is your fortress when you're oppressed. He is there, always willing and ready to listen and help in times of hardship and despair.

This leads us to our next characteristic found in God's name.

Fill in the blanks according to Psalm 3:3, NIV:

"But you are a _____ _____ _____, O LORD; you bestow glory on me and lift up my head."

Psalm 27:1b, NIV:

"The LORD is the _____ of my life—of whom shall I be afraid?"

Meditate on these characteristics of God. What do they mean to you?
_____

At what times in your life has God been your Shield and your Stronghold?
_____
_____

When we think of a shield, we have visions of a warrior standing tall in battle with his sword in one hand, while holding fast to his shield with the other. A *shield* is a weapon of protection and defense, a safeguard or barrier between the warrior and his enemy. A *stronghold* denotes strength. And when it is applied to God, the principal association is linked to the idea of a strong place of refuge. It means a physical dwelling place of security. God wants us to be in His dwelling place—His stronghold.

The enemy also desires to place us in a stronghold, but his stronghold wants to destroy us spiritually and physically. When we are in the stronghold of God, the iron grip of His presence, He holds us tightly so nothing can harm us. Even though the enemy, hardship, disaster, sorrow, and illness try to take us out of the fight, our God will be our place of safety that shields us from anything and everything that may come against us in this life.

When I think of the Lord as *Magen*—shield, and *Maoz*—stronghold, meaning "strength," I think of the power and security of His manifest presence.

Consider Psalm 27:4-5 in light of this meaning: "One thing I ask of the LORD, this is what I seek that I may dwell in the house of the LORD all the days of my life, to gaze upon the beauty of the LORD and to seek him in his temple. For in the day of trouble he will keep me safe in his dwelling; he will hide me in the shelter of his tabernacle."

Psalm 27 assures us that when we take refuge in God's sanctuary, He protects us; He hides us, like a shield, in the shelter of His presence.

According to the following verse, how is God's presence among us like a shield and stronghold?

Joshua 1:5; 9: _____

Psalm 46:1-5: _____

Isaiah 43:2-5a: _____

Day Four: What's in a Name?

Be strong and courageous; do not be discouraged or terrified, God will be with you. When you walk through raging waters and pass through the fire, they will not harm you because He will protect you. He will be your ever-present help. And when everything around you is shaking and your life is turned upside down, God will be your shield, your strong place of security.

God promises that He will be with you as your Rock, Fortress and Refuge, Shield and Stronghold, if you let Him. If you want to experience the promises of God that are found in the characteristics of His name, you must run to Him. This means you make God your only option—not your last resort, or even your first resort—your only resort. It means aligning your life with God. Running to Him means submitting to His desires, being filled with His Spirit, and trusting Him to take care of you, knowing He will act only in your best interest (see Romans 8:28).

Do not allow feelings of unworthiness, anger (even anger toward God), bitterness, self-reliance, guilt, or hopelessness stop you from running to God. Your troubles are not too difficult and complex that God cannot reveal His presence and the characteristics of His name to you. Just as He appeared to Hagar in the desert, He can manifest Himself to you too. Therefore, call on the name of the Lord and invoke the promises of God.

> End today by meditating once again on Psalm 18:1-3. Praise Him for being your Rock, Fortress, Refuge, Shield and Stronghold. If there is anything that is keeping you from knowing God as your Rock, Fortress, Refuge, Shield and Stronghold, openly share your heart with Him, even if it gets ugly. Beloved, you are in a safe place.

Day Five
Call on the Name of the Lord

"Those who know your name will trust in you, for you, LORD, have never forsaken those who seek you" (Psalm 9:10).

Have you noticed a common thread woven through our lessons this week? Have you witnessed the necessity, power and importance of calling on the name of the Lord? God has the only name that can be relied upon; therefore, in today's lesson we are going to take a look at the privilege and price of invoking His holy name.

Begin with prayer, and then look up the following verses. Record what they have in common:

Genesis 12:8: _____

Genesis 13:4: _____

Genesis 21:33: _____

Genesis 26:25: _____

In Genesis 4:26, what privilege did men begin to acknowledge?

_____

Enosh, the grandson of Adam and the son of Seth, lived 905 years. The Bible tells us in his time, "…men began to call on the name of the LORD" (v. 26). When I first read this verse, it seemed strange to me that this would be the point that men would begin to invite God into their midst. We know God spoke with both Cain and Abel; but, it wasn't until the time of Enosh that men began to *call upon the name of the Lord*. Why? One possible reason is because of sin. There was a distinct contrast between the line of Seth and the line of Cain. Enosh, the son of Seth, walked in obedience to the Lord, where Cain and his offspring were notorious for their sin. Cain was banished from God's presence because he made the same mistake his parents did by not taking responsibility for his sin when he murdered his brother Abel (see Genesis 4:1-16).

We do not need to be perfect to call upon the name of the Lord. If that were the case, I, for one, would never be given such a privilege. Jesus is the only name by which men can be saved, when we call upon the name of the Lord for salvation we are often at our lowest point of depravity. Calling upon the name of the Lord is a freedom we are given, no matter where we are in life, when we seek God's grace and liberation from sin. However, if we, like Enosh, desire to continually call upon the name of the Lord in our daily lives, invoking its power, we must walk in obedience to the Lord.

As we journey with Jesus, even as obedient witnesses, we will make mistakes; however, when we do err, we must take responsibility for the sin in confession and repentance. Sin is a big deal if it is not dealt with. When we don't take ownership of our sins, we are separated from God in fellowship and lose the joy of calling upon His name until we do turn back to Him with godly sorrow.

Fill in the blanks of Jonah 3:8, 10, NIV:

"Let everyone call urgently on God. Let them _____ _____ their _____ _____ and their violence…. When God saw what they did and how they _____ from their evil ways, he had compassion and did not bring upon them the destruction he had threatened" (Jonah 3:8, 10).

There is great reward for those who turn away from their sinful nature. God reveals mercy to those who willingly call to Him through confession and repentance. First John 1:9 tells us: "If we confess our sins, he is faithful and just and will forgive us our sins and purify us from all unrighteousness."

Fill in the blanks according to Zephaniah 3:9, NIV:

"Then I will _____ the lips of the peoples, that all of them may _____ on the _____ of the _____."

God alone saves us from our sins, and God alone gives us the honor of calling upon His name. What we must remember is His name is holy, so in order to use His name and receive all its benefits, we need to allow the Lord to purify us.

Look up the following verses. What are the benefits of beseeching God's holy name?

Psalm 50:15: _____

Psalm 116:12-13: _____

Psalm 145:18: _____

Jeremiah 33:3: _____

What does 2 Timothy 2:22 instruct us to do?

_____

_____

According to 2 Timothy 2:22, what do those who call on the name of the Lord possess? Check the correct response:

___ a pure heart   ___ evil desires   ___ a perfect life

Remember, we don't have to be perfect; but, we do need to turn away from evil desires. If we want to call upon the name of the Lord, we must allow God to cleanse us by His redeeming grace and purify our hearts and lips daily so we may utter His name in purity. If we desire the privileged access to the name that is above every name, we must be willing to pursue righteousness, faith, peace and love. Then, when we call upon the name of the Lord, He will hear and respond. He will deliver us in the day of trouble. He will answer us, and offer us wisdom into the things we do not know or understand. He will give us the opportunity to know Him and experience His goodness.

Beloved, God wants to bless you with the priceless advantage and remarkable freedom of calling upon Him, but are you prepared to pay the price? There is great reward in calling upon the name of the Lord, but there is also great sacrifice. Synonyms for the word *sacrifice* are "give up; forgo; forfeit; let go; surrender." Therefore, are you ready to *give up* your old life and sinful nature in order to receive His mercy and salvation? Will you *forgo* the evil desires of your youth in order to come before His throne with confidence, knowing He will hear you when you call? Will you *forfeit* your will and plans in order to receive His benefits for your life? Are you willing to *let go* of everything that hinders you, in order to have the esteemed honor of calling out in times of trouble? Will you *surrender* completely, so He may purify and sanctify you through and through?

Ask God to examine your heart. Is there anything that is hindering your ability to call upon His holy Name? If the Holy Spirit reveals any area of unrighteousness, please use the space below to ask for God's forgiveness and purifying grace, because *Jehovah mekoddishkem*—The LORD who Sanctifies you—desires to answer your call.

_____

_____

_____

_____

Now, with the pure heart you have been given by God's grace and mercy, call upon His Name with purified lips and pray to Him for the circumstances in your life. If you are carrying a heavy burden, call upon His name. If your heart is full of love and praise, call upon His name. If you are lonely and need a friend, call upon His name. If you are feeling blessed, call upon His name and rejoice with Him.

The following is a list of some of the names and titles of God. Use it as a guide to call upon His name in your area of need or praise.

El Shaddai—All-Sufficient One (Almighty)—with Him all things are possible.

El Elyon—The Most High God—whose strength, mercy, and sovereignty cannot be equaled.

El Olam—The Everlasting God—whose eternal plans will not fail.

Elohim—Creator—whose creative power reveals His invisible qualities, eternal power, and divine nature.

Jehovah Jireh—The LORD is my Provider—He is able to supply all your needs.

Jehovah Shalom—The LORD is Peace—He is your source of all peace and comfort.

Jehovah Tsebaoth—The LORD of Hosts—whose supremacy reigns over every universal power.

Jehovah Rophe—The LORD who Heals—whose healing hand can make you whole.

Jehovah Shammah—The LORD is There—He is always with you.

Jehovah Tsidkenu—The LORD our Righteousness—whose love interceded on your behalf to restore you and bring you into fellowship with Himself.

If you desire to know, believe, and understand that *He is (JAH)* in a more profound way, learn to pray in the names of God. Whatever your need or blessing, call upon His name. He is listening.

Apply the Knowledge

In my pursuit of the *HaShem* this week, the Holy Spirit has shown me …

_____
_____
_____
_____

The verse that spoke to me the most this week is…

_____
_____

In order to make this verse a reality in my life, I…

_____
_____
_____
_____

The changes I need to make in order to invoke the name of the Lord in my daily life are…

_____
_____
_____
_____

Lord God, I desire to *know* your name and the privilege I am given in calling upon your name, help me to…

_____
_____
_____
_____

The hidden treasure (see Isaiah 45:3) of His Person and personality God revealed to me this week is… This higher revelation of God's presence profoundly awakens me to…

Witnessing the names of God this week has changed my perspective of God from… to…

Holy Spirit, help me to apply what I've learned to my everyday life, so…

Prayer for the Journey

Jehovah God, I desire to be awakened to the truth, power, and authority that are offered in Your name alone. Give me insight and revelation so I may understand who You are through the knowledge and preeminence of Your name. Increase my awareness of Your divinity and salvation, sovereignty and mercy, found only in Your name. Purify me so…

Apply the Knowledge

Session Eight
My Holy Name
Ezekiel 39:7

*"I will make known my holy name among my people Israel, I will no longer let my holy name be profaned, and the nations will **know that I the LORD am** the Holy One in Israel"*
(Ezekiel 39:7).

1.) The first time God revealed His name in Scripture was in _____ _____ _____.
(Genesis 1:1)

   a.) This name in Hebrew is _____.

   Elohim is the plural form of El, which is God, and encompasses the Trinity (Father, Son and Holy Spirit) and describes God in the unity of His divine personality and power

2.) Through creation reminders of God's _____ and _____ are everywhere. (Romans 1:20)

3.) All creation speaks _____ .

(Psalm 97:6; Psalm 19:1-4)

4.) Elohim, Creator of heaven and earth, _____

_____ _____ ____ _____ people.

Week Nine
Know That I AM Your Warrior

What comes to mind when you think of Christ as a warrior? Does knowing Jesus as a warrior bring you comfort, or would you rather not know this side of Him at all? Does your mind fill with trepidation, or do you find hope that this mighty Warrior is always at your side? Many of us find a great deal of assurance and security when we think of Jesus as a loving bridegroom or tender shepherd, but there is much more to Jesus than what we can comprehend. If we are going to *know* God, then we are going to have to examine some characteristics about Him that may make us feel uncomfortable—even afraid.

I am excited about this week; I hope you are, too. The warrior side of Jesus can be exhilarating, if we learn to broaden our perspective to view Him in a fresh way. Our perspective of Jesus is vital if we are to see Him as a magnificent warrior, mighty in battle. For this reason, we will begin this week by searching both God's Word and creation for the divine privilege of beholding the glory of this great Warrior. The Bible tells us that from the beginning, God's invisible qualities—His eternal power and divine nature—are clearly seen and understood from what has been made (see Romans 1:20). And Psalm 19:1-4 tells us that through creation no person will be stripped of the glorious opportunity to know and witness God in the splendor of His work.

At I type these things, I have to smile as I think about our up-and-coming lessons on the Warrior in light of what we just learned about God in our previous video from Week Eight. It was no accident that God gave us Ezekiel 39:7, coupled with a focus on His Name, Elohim, as a transition into our coming week. Oh yes, the Creator has indeed set the stage for the mighty Warrior He intends to reveal to us. I hope you are ready to be challenged in your journey with Jesus—let's begin.

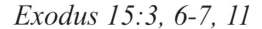

Exodus 15:3, 6-7, 11

"The LORD is a warrior; the LORD is his name.
Your right hand, O LORD, was majestic in power.
Your right hand, O LORD, shattered the enemy.
In the greatness of your majesty you threw down those who opposed you.
You unleashed your burning anger; it consumed them like stubble.
Who among the gods is like you, O LORD?
Who is like you—majestic in holiness, awesome in glory, working wonders?"

This week we will endeavor to:

Seek the image of God through His creation
"…now my eyes have seen you"
(Job 42:5).

Behold Him as Isaiah, Ezekiel, Daniel and John did
"…the heavens were opened and I saw visions of God"
(Ezekiel 1:1).

Witness heaven's Champion
"…there before me was a white horse,
whose rider is called Faithful and True"
(Revelation 19:11).

Understand that Jesus is more than a gentle Shepherd
"…the LORD is with me like a mighty warrior"
(Jeremiah 20:11).

Come under the banner of the One who can save us
"But I, when I am lifted up from the earth,
will draw all men to myself"
(John 12:32).

Day One
Image of God

"For since the creation of the world God's invisible qualities—his eternal power and divine nature—have been clearly seen, being understood from what has been made, so that men are without excuse" (Romans 1:20).

Who are we that God would give us the freedom to see His splendor every day we live upon this earth? That we would be given the privilege to lift our eyes to the heavens and see the delectation of His glory stretched across the sky like a tent. Within the boundaries of His creation, God has given us breathtaking opportunities to experience and witness His majesty and magnificence. Through creation, the Maker of heaven and earth has given us clues, intentionally laying before us His divine nature, invisible qualities, and eternal powers. Through creation, the invisible becomes visible, and we are given a foretaste of God's supremacy, personality, and existence.

I must admit to you, when the Lord began to lead me in this portion of our study on Christ as the Warrior, at first, I thought it would be all about spiritual warfare, Ephesians 6 kind of stuff. I imagined Christ as our magnificent warrior, victorious in battle, executing incomparable strength against the enemy. I never dreamed we would take the first two days to discuss the image of God. However, once God began to reveal His intention and direction, it made perfect sense. We receive a revelation of God's omnipotence by receiving a revelation of His awesome presence. How we see Christ is extremely important; and the perspective we have of Him will determine our success in walking in daily victory.

Therefore, let's begin by asking the Spirit of Truth to open our spiritual eyes, so we may witness His majesty, beauty, and power in the world around us from a fresh perspective.

> Read Revelation 1:12-18 and mark the images of Christ that we are given in this portion of Scripture. Check all that apply:
> ____ He had the appearance of a man
> ____ He was surrounded by the seven spirits of God (golden lampstands)
> ____ He was dressed in a long robe with a golden sash across His chest
> ____ His head and hair were white like snow and wool
> ____ His eyes were blazing like fire
> ____ His feet were like bronze glowing in a furnace
> ____ His voice was like mighty rushing waters
> ____ His face shone like the sun

Isn't it amazing how the writer of Revelation gives us something familiar to try and explain something that is unfamiliar? John took pieces of creation to try his best to describe the splendor and greatness that stood before him. The very image that simply made his body melt into a heap on the floor could not possibly be formed into words, unless God in His infinite mercy gave us something tangible to draw from. Therefore, like the Apostle John, we, too, are going to draw upon the reference of creation. May God grant us the ability to see the unmistakable union between Scripture and the works of His hand, so we may visualize the wonders of His magnificence and majesty.

Read Job 40:

As Job stood before God after a long and devastating trial of loss and suffering, God confronted him with the overall question: "Who is like me?"

Beginning with verse 15, what comparative reference does God draw from in order to answer the overall question He presented to Job?

___

In this description, what earthly images are given to Job in order to compare the greatness of God? List a few:

___ ___
___ ___
___

One possible translation for a *behemoth* is "elephant." The *New Living Translation* says "Hippopotamus." I think the elephant makes more sense, because God said the tail swayed like a cedar, possibly referring to the trunk. God made reference to the powerful muscles of his belly; the great strength of his loins, and He compared his bones to rods of iron. Then God asked, "Can anyone capture him? Can they catch him off guard and seize him?" (v.24).

How do you see this earthly image as a parallel to Christ as the Warrior?

___

Read Job 41:

What earthly image does God draw from here?

___

List a few of the earthly parallels Job is given:

___ ___
___ ___
___

The possible reference for *leviathan* is "crocodile." In these verses, God draws a parallel between the strength of the crocodile to that of His own. I love verse 8: "If you lay a hand on him, you will remember the struggle and never do it again!" It is like God is saying, "No one messes with a crocodile, and no one is strong enough to mess with me!" Amen!

In these verses God speaks of His great strength and graceful form—through the parallel of a crocodile, God draws attention to His own image and invincibility.

Day One: Image of God

How does this earthly representation give you an image of the Warrior?

_____

_____

Compare the following verses with a few of the descriptions of the leviathan found in Job 41. Connect the reference to the description. (May have more than one possible answer.)

Revelation 1:14   smoke pours from his nostrils

2 Samuel 22:9   eyes like the rays of dawn

Song of Songs 5:14   strong limbs

Song of Songs 5:15   flames dart from his mouth

                      chest as hard as rock

Consider the image of the Warrior as described in Song of Songs 5:10-16: "My lover is radiant and ruddy, outstanding among ten thousand. His head is purest gold...His eyes are like doves by the water streams washed in milk, mounted like jewels. His cheeks are like beds of spice yielding perfume. His lips are like lilies dripping with myrrh. His arms are rods of gold... His body is like polished ivory...His legs are pillars of marble...His appearance is like Lebanon...."

Job and the Song of Songs—two very different books and two exceedingly different descriptions drawn from earthly reference; yet, both give an incredible image of the eternal.

Notice, in the Song of Songs, how many references are made to precious materials. To articulate His firmness and durability, God points to a rock. A *millstone* is a large flat rock, very solid. *Gold* is a precious metal, beautiful and enduring. Gold is a permanent and stable material. It never rusts or dissolves, and it retains its beauty. *Ivory* is highly sought after; many elephants have been killed in order to obtain this rich treasure. Ivory, which Scripture uses to describe the body, is highly resilient and opaque. To illustrate His loveliness we are given *Sapphires*. Next to diamonds, there is no other jewel as hard or as beautiful. And *Marble*, recrystallized limestone, is attributed to the great strength of His legs.

Reflect on the following portions of creation and record how you see God's invisible qualities, eternal power, and divine nature. Then, in the margin, record any Scripture verse that comes to mind to support the revelation God has given you.

Mountains: _____

Ocean: _____

Thunder: _____

Waterfall: _____

Flowers: _____

What an incredible image! What a gift! Through creation, God has given us the opportunity to witness both His splendor and resolute power, revealing to us both His eternal supremacy and tender love. The Warrior is all-powerful; nothing can harm Him, and no one can stand against Him. Yet, on the other hand, He is beautiful and altogether lovely. Through creation, God affords us the privilege and benefit of peeking into the unknown, allowing us to unmask the infinite. Glory!

> End today by meditating on Job 42:5. In light of today's study, how can you now say, "My ears had heard of you but now my eyes have seen you."

Each time you experience a piece of creation, stop and ask God how it describes Him. It's all right in front of you. Look up—the heavens declare His glory—the skies proclaim His artistry. Every day creation cries out with universal speech; night after night it reveals knowledge. There is no place it does not touch; it reaches out to the ends of the earth. Creation goes forth to all peoples of the world and raises its voice to proclaim the wonders of God (see Psalm 19:1-4).

Day One: Image of God

Day Two
Behold the Vision

*"I saw the LORD seated on a throne, high and exalted,
and the train of his robe filled the temple" (Isaiah 6:1).*

Our image of God is vital. How we perceive Him is in direct response to how we envision Him. How we envision Him is reflected in how we respond to Him. Yesterday we began to behold the vision by acquiring a glimpse of the Warrior through His creation. In doing this we began to cry out as Job did in verse 42:5: "My ears had heard of you but now my eyes have seen you." Today, as we continue our pursuit of God's image, we will turn our attention to those who actually witnessed His majestic beauty.

Let's begin today by praying to receive a mental vision of Christ, then compare Matthew 17:1-8 (also see Mark 9:2-3 and Luke 9:29) with Revelation 1:9-18.

In these gospel accounts we are given a peek at the vision Peter, James and John saw of the glorified Christ. For our purposes, however, we are going to focus on John's testimony.

On the Mount, what did John see when Jesus was transformed before him?

_____

What was John's reaction to the vision that He saw?

_____

How did John record the vision of Christ in Revelation 1:9-18?

_____
_____

How did John react to the vision that he witnessed in Revelation 1:17?

_____

The Apostle John had the opportunity to not only walk with Jesus while He was here on earth, but he also had the rare privilege of beholding His glory. At least twice John beheld the vision of Christ's magnificence. As I ponder these occurrences, I find a couple of things peculiar. First, the transfiguration was mentioned in all the gospels except John's. Isn't that odd? John was the one who witnessed, but Matthew, Mark and Luke wrote about it. John doesn't even mention the event in his gospel. Why? Did he deem the experience unworthy of penning? Yet, when John saw the glorified Christ the second time, he went into much greater detail, far more than all of the other gospels combined.

Secondly, I find it interesting that when John saw Christ transformed on the Mount, John seemed to just stand there. In shock? Perhaps. In complete awe? We can assume so. Nonetheless, John seemed to be so transfixed by the image that it wasn't until he heard the voice from the cloud that he fell face down. In Revelation, the reaction appears to be the opposite. This time, when John heard the voice behind him, he turned around and saw the resurrected Christ standing before him, then he fell to the ground like a dead man.

Why do you think John reacted differently to the two events he witnessed?

I am speculating the difference came through John's image of Christ. In the first encounter John was young, possibly a teenager. He saw the miracles, the healings, the feeding of the thousands, John even saw Jesus raise the dead; but, at this point, John had a narrow view of Christ. John knew Jesus the man. The vision in Revelation came at the end of John's life while he was stranded on the island of Patmos. In the span of years that separated the two visions, John's image of Christ grew tremendously. Through the intimacy of relationship, John's perspective of Christ changed, evolving into unimaginable levels of revelation. The same is true of us; the more we spiritually mature and grow closer to Christ in intimacy, the more vivid He becomes, increasing our awareness of His greatness. The greater our revelation, the faster we fall on our faces.

Scripture affords us opportunities to visualize mental images of God's manifested glory. Some accounts are quite detailed, while others leave room for the imagination. Let's take some time and consider the response of a few other witnesses who beheld the vision.

Read Isaiah 6:1-8:

Describe what Isaiah saw?

What was his reaction?

Why do you think Isaiah responded the way he did?

Against the backdrop of purity, we see ourselves for what we really are—unclean. In the midst of God's holy perfection, Isaiah was suddenly awakened to the reality of his own corruption.

Share a time when you were so taken by God's holy perfection that you instantly became aware of your own depravity?

Day Two: Behold the Vision

The vision that loomed above Isaiah was one of enormous beauty, imposing position, and royal command. The vision was so breathtaking that Isaiah became completely undone.

Read Ezekiel 1:1-28:

What did Ezekiel see? (especially v. 26-28)

What was his reaction? (v.28)

Why do you think Ezekiel responded the way he did?

When was the last time you were astonished and overwhelmed by God's presence?

Ezekiel encountered God with an awe-inspiring visualization. Again we are given recognizable, earthly objects in order to understand what Ezekiel saw and experienced. There are times when we just can't explain it. Sometimes, our experiences go so far beyond us that all we can do is rely on the familiar to help us comprehend the unfamiliar.

After this incredible encounter with God, Ezekiel sat near the Kebar River for seven days—overwhelmed (see v. 3:15). The King James Version uses the word "astonished." No matter which word you use, Ezekiel was utterly stunned by God's appearance and presence.

One thing I often pray is for God's presence to never become common or casual. Based on what we are studying today you might think this type of prayer is ridiculous. On the contrary, if we are not careful, we can become so comfortable with routine fellowship that experiencing God becomes ordinary. When this happens, our quiet times become nothing more than ritual. We want more. We want to see God high and lifted up in awesome splendor. We want to be overwhelmed by His beauty and astonished by His glory. Amen!

Read Daniel 10:4-9:

What did Daniel see?

What was his reaction?

Why do you think Daniel responded the way he did?

I find it interesting that verse 7 tells us that the other men with Daniel did not see the vision, yet they fled and hid because they were overwhelmed with terror. Why? I believe that for those who do not know Christ, His presence can be extremely uncomfortable. I once had a neighbor who was not a believer. I tried befriending her, but for some reason, whenever she was around me she became edgy. And, on the rare occasion she came into my home, within minutes she acted like she couldn't wait to leave. One day, as she stood in my kitchen growing panicky, it dawned on me—she sensed the presence of God and it made her feel uncomfortable. As a result, she wanted to get out of there—fast.

With the men gone, Daniel was left to behold this amazing vision alone. All of his strength drained from his trembling body. He became feeble; his face grew pale, and the moment the vision spoke to him, he fainted (v. 9). Have you ever experienced the glory of God to where you actually began to feel sick? Daniel did. You see, when we behold the vision, it's not only what we see with our spiritual eyes, it's also what we experience. The closer the manifest presence of God comes, the weaker we become. Our flesh cannot handle the glory of God.

> How about you? Have you ever become so consumed by God's manifest glory that your body trembled and your flesh became weak? If yes, record what you witnessed.
>
> _____
> _____

Scripture does not tell us how long Daniel spent lying on the ground after he fainted, but we see a shift take place in verse 10 when a hand touched Daniel and set him trembling on his hands and knees. Some believe the vision Daniel saw was Christ because his description in verses 4-6 of the vision is similar to that of John's in Revelation. Others, on the other hand, believe Daniel encountered an angel; and, most likely the angel Gabriel since he had visited Daniel before (see Daniel 8:16-26; 9:21). Still others believe that there were two separate encounters by two different visions. In the first vision Daniel saw Christ (vs. 4-9), and it was this vision that caused him to become ill and to faint. And then, sometime later, Daniel was awakened by another visitation (beginning in verse 10), and this one was most likely an angel.

> I have a tendency to lean more toward the third interpretation because of what Daniel was told in verse 10:13. Regardless of the interpretation you cling to, what did the one who touched Daniel say to him in verse 10:12 to encourage him and strengthen him?
>
> 1. _____
> 2. _____
> 3. _____

The moment you let go of fear and begin to earnestly cry out for understanding (to truly know God), and to humble yourself before Him, that is the day you begin to experience deeper levels of His manifest glory. Amen!

Day Two: Behold the Vision

God wants to draw near. He wants us to learn how to handle extreme measures of His glory. The visitor told Daniel to not be afraid; in essence, he told him to be strong, to take heart, to be at peace, and to know that he was loved. When we come before the manifest glory of God, drawing closer than we've ever been before, we can rest assured that we will be welcomed and treasured. Just as Daniel was encouraged to be strong, the Holy Spirit will help us too.

Read Acts 9:1-20:

What did Paul see? (v. 3)

_____

What was his reaction? (v. 4, 9)

_____

Why do you think Paul responded the way he did?

_____

Unlike the other visions, Paul saw only an intense, brilliant light. Paul did not see the beauty and majesty of the King high and lifted up as Isaiah did; yet, Paul was suddenly awakened to the reality of his own corruption. Paul didn't encounter Christ with an awe-inspiring visualization like Ezekiel did; yet, Paul sat overwhelmed for three days and ate nothing. Unlike Daniel, Paul received a rebuke rather than encouraging words; yet, his flesh became weak under the weight of Christ's glory as he fell to the ground blind. Paul did not behold the vision the way the others did; yet, the reaction was the same. Like Isaiah, Ezekiel, and Daniel, when Paul beheld the vision, his life drastically changed.

In what way has your encounter with Christ significantly changed your life?

_____
_____
_____

End today by meditating on one of the visions we beheld today through these eye-witness accounts. As you do, ask yourself: How has my image of God expanded? In what way is my image of Christ a reflection of how I respond to Him?

_____
_____
_____
_____

Day Three

The Rider Called Faithful and True

"I saw heaven standing open and there before me was a white horse, whose rider is called Faithful and True" (Revelation 19:11).

Last week, during our ladies' Bible study, I asked the women, "Of all of the portraits of Jesus that we have examined, which one is your favorite?" Their response to my question was not surprising. With enthusiasm some loved Jesus as the Redeemer; others selected the Bridegroom as their preferred image of Christ. All of these descriptions of Jesus are wonderful, aren't they? But, I must admit, of all the images we've studied my personal favorite is this one—the Warrior.

My love affair with the warrior side of Jesus began a couple of years ago when I asked the Lord to teach me to love all of Him, not just the parts that were comfortable and charming. I do love the tender and gentle side of Jesus, but I also want to know Him as the Lion of Judah.

When I think about Jesus as that Rider on the white horse depicted in Revelation 19, the hair on the back of my neck stands on end. I become filled with awe and wonder as my spirit reverberates with the Holy Spirit. When I think about His regal posture upon that horse, His blazing eyes like fire, and His hand raised in battle; my heart begins to pound and my soul floods with joy. This is the image of Christ that I have come to trust in; the one that captures my heart and thrusts my soul into levels of risk I would never dare to embrace on my own. I am confident in this figure of Christ. I know, without a doubt, He is my Deliverer and that He will rescue me from any danger or trap set before me. No matter what burden threatens to steal my joy; no matter what fear invades my life, I know that this mighty Warrior can silence any lie and abolish any fear. He will hurl anything that sets itself up against me into the abyss, setting me free to love and be loved once again. This is my Great Warrior. This is my Hero—this is my Jesus.

Let's begin today by asking Jesus to help us love all of Him, and then read Revelation 19:11-21.

How do these verses describe the Rider on the white horse? Be specific:

_____

_____

_____

What names and titles are given to this mighty Warrior? Check all that apply:

____ Faithful and True

____ The Word

____ King of Kings and Lord of Lords

____ A name we have yet to learn

How will this Warrior judge and make war?

Who is the war against?

What will happen to His enemies?

Close your eyes and try to envision this mighty Warrior upon His horse, armed for battle, and riding with the armies of heaven. How does this image of Jesus make you feel?

In some ways, by this image of Jesus, we are reassured and comforted. He will judge the nations with the Word of God, and rule them with an iron scepter. He will destroy all who opposed His rule with the wrath of God. Sin will be devoured. Satan and his false prophet will be captured and thrown into the fiery lake of burning sulfur; and his demons will be killed by the sword of God's Word.

On the other hand, these images can horrify us, even with the knowledge of sin and Satan's demise. The representation illustrated here is frightening, gory, and abominable. To those who do not like war, or even conflict, these images can bring anything but feelings of comfort. Even the image of Jesus is one that sounds scary with His fiery eyes and robe dipped in blood.

How do the following verses bring you comfort as you try to grasp the image of the Rider on the white horse?

Romans 8:31:

Romans 8:35-39:

Psalm 37:28:

Those who belong to Christ are loved and protected. And nothing, absolutely nothing, will ever come between you and His love for you. If you know Christ as your Redeemer, and you are committed to Him in a personal relationship, you have nothing to fear. He is for you and not against you. He is your beloved Friend and gracious Protector; the One who will go to war for you and strike down anything that opposes you.

When I imagine Christ as that gallant Rider on the white horse I see a Conqueror, a Champion among champions—a Hero. When I was a little girl, my mother would say to me, "You expect prince charming to come galloping along on his white horse, sweep you off your feet, and carry you into Never-never land. Well, in essence, she was right. At that time I didn't understand the significance and neither did she; but, nonetheless, it was my young heart crying out for the Warrior, and the life that I was destined to share with Him.

Through the imagination of children's fairytales, we are given exquisite examples of our True Knight. And our happily-ever-after endings are a foretaste of the reality found in Eden's eternity.

Think about the different stories you know like: Cinderella, Snow White, and Sleeping Beauty. We, all too often, are like these fair maidens found trapped in towers of doubt and confusion, caught in the clutches of the enemy, ensnared by poisonous traps, and held prisoner by lies, fear, regret, unworthiness and failure. In many ways, we are all just like that damsel in distress who needs to be rescued by her prince.

Now, men of Christ, don't start having issues here. You need rescuing, too. We all need to allow the Rider on the white horse to charge into the darkness of our circumstances and insecurities and rescue us. We must take a leap of faith, fall into the arms of the One who loves us, and trust ourselves to this Hero called Faithful and True.

> Consider your present circumstances, what towers are you locked in? What toxic apples are you biting into? In what way(s) does the enemy have your soul held prisoner?
>
> _____
>
> _____

Locked towers, toxic apples, and deceptive schemes are strongholds. The enemy uses these strongholds to create a barrier between you and God. The purpose of a stronghold is to create an obstruction, keeping you bound, so that your relationship with God is hindered. A stronghold goes against the things and nature of God. A stronghold begins in the mind with a thought, and then festers in the soul until it manifests itself in the body.

We cannot cope with the strongholds. We cannot deal with the strongholds. We must destroy them. We have been given divine spiritual weapons in which to demolish the lies and strongholds that set themselves up against us and our relationship with God. Self-help books, counselors, and support groups will, perhaps, help you to get by, but they will not annihilate the problem.

> Read 2 Corinthians 10:3-5:
>
> What do these verses tell us about the battle we are in?
>
> _____
>
> How are we able to stand in the battle and demolish the strongholds?
>
> _____
>
> Look again at Revelation 19:15 and 21. What will the Rider use to destroy all those who oppose God's rule?
>
> _____

Day Three: The Rider Called Faithful and True

What does Hebrews 4:12 and Ephesians 6:17 tell us about the Word of God?

_____

_____

You must allow the Word of God to fight your spiritual battles. You must allow the power of guided truth to go forth in order to experience victory over the traps that are set for you. If you want freedom and victory in your life from the strongholds that are set up against you, then speak the Rider's words over your circumstances. Speak them out loud. Speak them daily, moment by moment, if you have to. Write verses on note cards. Place the cards where you will see them frequently. I keep verses by my kitchen sink and in my office. With His word (that double edged sword in His mouth), the Rider on the white horse will help you to destroy every stronghold.

> End today by meditating on Jeremiah 20:11, "But the LORD stands beside me like a great warrior. Before Him they (my persecutors, NIV) will stumble. They cannot defeat me. They will be shamed and thoroughly humiliated. Their dishonor will never be forgotten" (NLT). In this verse, how does the prophet Jeremiah describe the Lord? What happens to those who try to oppose and persecute us?

_____

_____

_____

_____

_____

_____

_____

_____

_____

_____

_____

_____

Locked towers, toxic apples, and the schemes of the enemy cannot harm you when you allow the Rider on the white horse to charge into your circumstances with the power of His word, and rescue you from whatever stronghold has you bound. Lift your head for the Warrior is fighting for you. Stand your ground, because the Rider on the white horse is standing right by your side.

Day Four
The Battle Belongs to God

"You will not have to fight this battle. Take up your positions; stand firm and see the deliverance the LORD will give you" (2 Chronicles 20:17).

There is something special, even extraordinary, about the psalms. Through the Law and the prophets God pursued man, imploring him to come and be joined to Him in an intimate relationship. The psalms, however, are man's conversations to God. They are an expression of raw emotion, zealous desire, and at times, they are downright blunt. David had a view of God that so few of us, as New Testament believers, have today. As we continue to study our mighty Warrior, we will look at Him through the eyes of one devoted psalmist.

Let's begin with prayer to our powerful Warrior, for the battle belongs to Him. Then please read Psalm 7.

What was David's understanding of God as Warrior in verse 1? How do you see his plea as an act of submission?

_____

_____

What does verse 2 tell us about what kind of battle David was facing?

_____

In verse 3-5, what does David acknowledge before the Lord? Who and what is David relying on?

_____

_____

According to verses 9-10, who does the Warrior rescue?

_____

What is David's description of the Lord in verses 10-13? How do we see the Warrior preparing for battle? Check all that apply:

_____ He is a righteous Judge

_____ He is a shield to those who are righteous and true

_____ He reveals His righteous anger

_____ He sharpens His sword, and prepares His bow against those who do not repent

_____ He prepares deadly weapons and flaming arrows

What do verses 14-16 tell us about those who plot evil?

_____

If all we knew of God was based solely on Psalm 7, what conclusions can we make concerning how God views those who submit to Him, and how He views evil?

_____

_____

If we don't, first and foremost, understand that God is our refuge and deliverer (v. 1), we won't fully embrace Him as our Warrior. David knew and understood that God, and God alone, was his protection, and only He could rescue him. This acknowledgement before the Lord was an act of submission on David's part. If we are going to experience God as our rescuer, we are going to have to submit to His authority. So often, when we are in trouble, we pray and ask for God's help; but, if we don't like the game plan, we begin to complain and then do it our way. Beloved, we will not always like the method of deliverance. God's ways are not always easy; but if we want to be rescued, we need to follow His instructions. Through Psalm 7, David gives us incredible insight into how we must submit if we want to understand God's rescuing power.

In verse 2, we begin to understand what kind of battle David is up against.

To what does David compare those who attack him? _____

What does 1 Peter 5:8 call the devil? What is his intent?

_____

_____

What does Ephesians 6:12 tell us about the battle we are in?

_____

_____

David knew this battle was beyond his ability. If God did not intervene, David felt that his soul, all of who he was, would be ripped apart spiritually.

Have you ever felt like David? Has the spiritual battle around you ever gotten so intense that if God didn't intercede you were going to be ripped apart from the inside out?   ___YES   ___NO

If yes, explain:

_____

_____

May we find encouragement in Judges 14:5-6. What did Samson come up against? Who intervened? Explain what happened?

_____
_____

As we trust in God and submit to His authority, the mighty Warrior will help us so we will have the spiritual strength to rip the enemy apart when He tries to attack us.

We must also understand, as we consider verses 3-5, that sin must be out of the picture. David opened his heart and laid it bare before the Lord. In these verses David said to God, "If I have done anything to cause this attack, then let them have their way." Remember God searches minds and hearts, and He protects the upright in heart. David asked God to search his heart and to judge him. "If I am guilty," David said, "then let them destroy me; if I am innocent then defend me."

Fill in the blanks according to Psalm 26:2, NIV:

"Test me, O LORD, and try me, _____ my _____ and my _____

This is not an easy task, but, we, too, must allow God to examine our hearts and minds to see if there is any offensive way in us (see Psalm 139:23-24).

After considering David's plea, the verdict comes, and the Warrior finds His servant innocent and the oppressor guilty. In verses 10-13, we see the Warrior become David's shield, saving him because he is upright in heart. At the same time, the Warrior, who has judged the hearts of the wicked, sharpens His sword, prepares His bow and makes fiery arrows ready for use. The Warrior defends the righteous, but to those who do evil, He reveals His wrath.

God will not tolerate sin. In fact, He hates it so much that one day it will be completely wiped from the earth. Understand: if you are living a life contrary to God's ways, and refuse to repent, God will not rescue you. God rescues those who walk in His righteousness. God extends His hand of mercy to all those who come under the headship of His Son, Jesus Christ. It is through Him that we are found righteous.

If you want to know God as a Warrior and for Him to go into battle on your behalf, then you must be willing to submit to His authority and repent of your sin. If you come to God in your weakness and say, "You are my protector. I can't do anything on my own to overcome this struggle," then you can stand firm and watch the One called Faithful and True go into warrior mode.

End today by meditating on Psalm 35:1-10. How do these verses speak to you about the aid of the Warrior and His protection from those who are too strong for you?

_____
_____

Day Four: The Battle Belongs to God

Day Five
Rally Beneath His Banner

"The camp must be holy, for the LORD your God moves around in your camp to protect you and to defeat your enemies. He must not see any shameful thing among you, or he might turn away from you" (Deuteronomy 23:14, NLT).

Yesterday we considered David's perspective of God as His refuge and shield. David knew the battle was beyond his ability, and he cried out to the only One who could deliver him.

Let's begin our lesson today with prayer to the One who is greater than the one who is in the world, and then please read Psalm 2.

Who is enraged? What are they plotting?

Who are they conspiring against and why? (v.2-3)

Yesterday David gave us the insight that if we want to be rescued by God we must submit to God's authority. If we want to be protected by God, we must be ruled by God. Regrettably, the nations do not want to be ruled by God, they do not want to submit to His authority, so they rage against Him. They plot and plan ways to try and get rid of Him.

Now let's remember, the battles we face, even the wars we see raging in the world around us, are spiritual ones. The battle for the nations began when Satan wanted to overthrow God and take over His rule. That was why God expelled him from heaven (see Isaiah 14:11-15). Now, he works through humans, and the battle manifests itself through people.

The world is not against us. The world is against God, and the sovereign rule of His Anointed One. We cannot take the battles we face personally. When someone insults us or persecutes us because of our faith in Jesus Christ, the attack is not against us but God. The world rebels against the sovereign rule and authority of God.

Many people have convinced themselves that following God is a burden. They believe coming under the Lordship of God and His Anointed One, Jesus Christ, will weigh them down with rules, and strip them of their freedom to have fun. What the people do not realize is that only under the headship of the Lord Jesus Christ can they truly find freedom.

What do the following verses tell us about freedom?

John 8:36: _____
Galatians 5:1: _____
2 Corinthians 3:17: _____

Look again at our opening verse from Deuteronomy 23:14. God wants to walk through the camp of our nation to protect it—and us. God wants to deliver us from those who threaten us, but many people today are rebelling against God trying to kick Him out of this nation. They don't want God in our schools. It is illegal to proclaim Jesus or even pray, in most, if not all, public schools; yet, so many freely use the name of Jesus Christ as a curse word. The phrases, "In God We Trust," and "One Nation Under God," are in jeopardy of being removed from our nation's vocabulary. And the really sad thing is we, as a nation, do not realize what we are permitting. Little by little, year after year, we push God out of the United States, and then wonder why terrorism threatens us. If we want God's protection, if we want this country to be free, then we must submit to God's rule as the supreme and sovereign authority over all. Without God walking within the border of this nation's camp, we will no longer be under God's protection.

> Return to our main text in Psalm 2. What is the Lord's reaction to the futile plans and rages of the nations? (v. 4-6) Why do you think He reacts this way?
>
> _____
>
> _____

God laughs not because He finds the nations' plans funny, but because they plot in vain. God has chosen His Ruler of the nations, and has enthroned Him in Zion. Isaiah 11:10 proclaims that the Root of Jessie will stand as a banner for the people, and that the nations will rally to Him.

The Hebrew word for *standard* is *nec* (pronounced nace) means "something lifted up, a standard, signal, ensign, sign, a banner." Banners and flags, used in biblical times, had several purposes, such as, worship, praise, and warfare. Banners were also used for military purposes, and were frequently used as a rallying point for God's people. This is why Jesus said in John 12:32, "I, when I am lifted up from the earth, will draw all men to myself." On the cross, Jesus became a banner, high and lifted up, a rallying point for the nations, so that all men could be drawn to Him. He is the One enthroned in Zion, the Holy One that God has chosen to rule over the nations.

> Read Isaiah 13:2-5:
>
> What is taking place in these verses? What banner is raised? Who is being summoned to the rallying point?
>
> _____
>
> _____

> Fill in the blanks according to Isaiah 5:26, NIV:
>
> "He lifts up a _____ _____ _____ distant _____; he whistles for those at the ends of the earth. Here they come, swiftly and speedily!"

Day Five: Rally Beneath His Banner

For what purposes do you think the Lord is calling His people together under His banner?

The Lord will gather His army and reclaim the nations as His inheritance. They will come and worship Him as His beloved. He will prepare them for battle, protect them like a shield, anoint them and cover them with His love.

It is written that the nations will belong to the Son of God (Psalm 2:7-9). And they will rally together under the banner He has raised, so that the people may come under His headship and find refuge and peace. And no matter what we see happening around us, there is no stopping this plan!

How does Psalm 33:9-11 confirm that God's plan will not be stopped?

It is finished (see John 19:30). The plans of the Lord will stand forever. The nations can plot, plan, and try to kick God out of the picture, but the Warrior will be victorious. We, who belong to Warrior must remember, as the nation's rage we must stand firm in the mighty armor He has given us (see Ephesians 6:10-17). We must rely on His promise that no weapon formed against us shall proper (see Isaiah 54:17). We must rise up, because the Warrior is standing with us.

Blessed are those who worship the Lord and submit to His rule, because they are the ones who will know His refuge and protection. Let us keep the camp of our nation holy, so that the Lord will not look upon us and find shameful activity. Let us submit, so He may protect us and defeat all our enemies.

End today by meditating on Song of Songs 2:4. As you ponder this verse, record the ways the Lord has placed you under His banner. Then thank Him for all He has done in your life.

The Lord Jesus is looking for a warrior bride—one who will rally beneath His cross and come under His authority. No longer hesitate; come under the refuge of His banner and worship Him.

Apply the Knowledge

In my pursuit of God as Warrior this week, the Holy Spirit has shown me …

_____
_____
_____
_____

The verse that spoke to me the most this week is…

_____
_____

In order to make this verse a reality in my life, I…

_____
_____
_____
_____

The changes I need to make in order to *know* Christ more profoundly as that Rider on the white horse called Faithful and True, the protector and Warrior over every aspect of my life are… Lord, help me to…

_____
_____
_____
_____

The hidden treasure (see Isaiah 45:3) of His Person and personality God revealed to me this week is… This higher revelation of God's presence profoundly awakens me to…

_____
_____
_____
_____

Witnessing God as a Warrior this week has changed my perspective of God from… to…

_____
_____
_____
_____
_____

Holy Spirit, help me to apply what I've learned to my everyday life, so…

_____
_____
_____
_____

Prayer for the Journey

Lord, I want to know You as my Refuge and Deliverer. I desire to fully embrace You as my Warrior. You alone are my God and my protection, only You can deliver me from those who attack me. I understand this battle is a spiritual one, and that only by Your word and great strength am I able to demolish the strongholds that the enemy sets for me. The battle is not mine but Yours. Help me to submit to Your plans, ways, and desires, so I may…

_____
_____
_____
_____
_____
_____
_____
_____
_____
_____
_____
_____

Apply the Knowledge

Session Nine
Arise, My Love
Ezekiel 37:1-10

*"I will attach tendons to you and make flesh come upon you and cover you with skin; I will put breath in you, and you will **know that I am the LORD**" (Ezekiel 37:6).*

1.) Can _____ be turned to _____ ? (Ezekiel 37:3)

2.) The bodies had _____ form, but still had _____ _____ life.
(Ezekiel 37:7-8)

3.) The _____ and _____ bring the dead to life.

4.) God would reveal the _____ _____ that would arise under the _____.

Week Ten
Know That I AM Your King of Glory

It is the prayer of my heart that we make knowing God our lifelong pursuit. Each week of our journey together we have attempted to witness God as a compassionate Father, a tenacious Friend, a devoted Husband, a forgiving Savior, a nurturing Shepherd, a merciful Healer, and a mighty Warrior. We have studied God's Word and examined what others have experienced, and we have received their testimonies as valid. We have explored for ourselves the wonders that are offered to us in an intimate relationship with God, and expectantly applied the knowledge by putting what we have learned into practice. Now, as we begin to approach our final week of study, there is a strong awe in my spirit, an anticipation that is mounting as we stand at the threshold of our next aspiration in knowing God.

This week we will examine the truth of God's word as we allow it to reveal to us infallible knowledge, and infinite beauty of the One who is King of kings and Lord of lords. Through His word, we will enter the throne room of God to behold this mighty King and witness the activity that encircles Him. Then we will endeavor to witness His supreme dominion over heaven and earth; and then open our hearts in order to pursue Him the way David did. Although we are coming to the conclusion of our study together, our relationship with this marvelous King is far from over. This is just the beginning. One day He will return to claim His Bride, and she will reign with Him forever. Now is the time to get ready for His coming. Now is the time to keep watch for His appearing. One day He will return; and, we, as the Bride of Christ, cannot be found unprepared.

I carry a sense of great anticipation as I prepare for this week of study. I hope you do, too. We have much to look forward to; therefore, let us continue in our pursuit to *know* Him.

Psalm 24:7-10

"Lift up your heads, O you gates;
Be lifted up, you ancient doors, that the King of glory may come in.
Who is this King of Glory?
The LORD strong and mighty, the LORD mighty in battle.
Lift up your heads, O you gates;
Lift them up, you ancient doors, that the King of glory may come in.
Who is he, this King of glory?
The LORD Almighty—he is the King of glory."

This week we will attempt to:

Worship around His throne
"Day and night they never stop saying,
'Holy, holy, holy is the Lord God Almighty,
who was, and is, and is to come'"
(Revelation 4:8).

Acknowledge His dominion
"The LORD has established his throne in heaven,
and his kingdom rules overall"
(Psalm 103:19).

Pursue God with a heart like David
"He…sought the LORD with all his heart"
(2 Chronicles 22:9).

Proclaim His greatness
"I will exalt you, my God the King…
his greatness no one can fathom"
(Psalm 145:1, 3).

Prepare for the King's return
"Behold, I am coming soon!"
(Revelation 22:12).

Day One
The One Who Sits Upon the Throne

"Immediately I was in the Spirit; and behold, a throne was standing in heaven, and One sitting on the throne" (Revelation 4:2 NASB).

"God is seated on his holy throne" (Psalm 47:8), and great celebration, joy and gladness surround that throne as incessant worship shouts His greatness! Have you ever stopped and truly contemplated what the atmosphere around the throne of God is like? I know we have all, at one time or another, thought about what heaven might be like. We have all thought about a place where illness, sorrow, and war will cease. But do we ever really take the time to ponder the magnitude of the celebration that takes place in heaven on a continual basis? Can we imagine, with the heart of a child, the wonder, majesty, and exhilaration as the four living creatures cry out day and night, "Holy, holy, holy is the Lord God Almighty?" Can we hear the volume of the thousands of angels who cry, "Worthy is the Lamb"?

If you've never taken the time to imagine the celebration around His throne, today you are in for a treat. Open your heart, and pray to the One who sits on the throne that you may have the privilege of being caught up in the Spirit to behold His throne, and all of the activities that encircle it.

> From the following verses, what can be determined about the atmosphere around the throne?
>
> 1 Chronicles 16:27: _____
>
> Psalm 16:11: _____
>
> Psalm 21:6: _____
>
> Psalm 36:7-8: _____

In order to grasp the richness of adoration around the throne, we must first get a revelation of the perpetual joy, gladness and pleasure that are synonymous with God's presence. Once we begin to recognize the unending ecstasy, uninterrupted happiness, and continual bliss that surround His throne, then we will begin to appreciate the grandeur of the celebration, the breathtaking display of worship, and the unrelenting admiration from those who stand in His presence.

> If you are ready to behold the throne and those who encircle it, please ardently read aloud the following set of verses, and then answer the related questions.
>
> Read Revelation 4:1-11:
>
> In verses 6-8, who are the witnesses who surround the throne of God?
>
> _____

Where are these witnesses in proximity to the throne? (v.6)

What do they cry out?

In verses 4 and 10, who are the witnesses around the throne of God?

Where are these witnesses in proximity to the throne?

What do they cry out?

Read Revelation 5:11-12:

Who are the witnesses around the throne of God? (v.11)

Where are these witnesses in proximity to the throne?

What do they cry out?

What a glorious picture is painted for us in the Word of God!

Who witnessed this incredible sight? How was he able to observe the activity of the throne room?

Can you imagine being taken up to heaven by the power of the Spirit to witness the very throne room of God? Can you fathom the opportunity to humbly stand in the presence of God and experience the volume, magnitude, and holy splendor of the winged seraphim as they cry out, "Holy, holy, holy is the Lord God Almighty, who was, and is, and is to

Day One: The One Who Sits Upon the Throne

come?" Can you grasp the passion of their unified cry as it crescendos into an offering of glory, honor, and thanksgiving, bearing witness to God's incomparable greatness and infinite beauty?

Can you picture, as John did, the twenty four elders falling face down before the One who sits on the throne? Can you see them worshiping Him with golden crowns of glory, as their unceasing cry bears witness to His inimitable and perfect domination over all things? (see Ephesians 1:18-23).

If you close your eyes and listen, can you hear the boisterous singing of the millions of angels who encircle the throne? Can you hear the voices of this eternal choir who forever sings of His authority, riches, knowledge, might, goodness and perfection? Hallelujah!

> Oh, I can hardly catch my breath. How about you? In the margin, share what revelations overtake your soul as you attempt to visualize the extent of the celebration and worship around God's throne.

And even with all of this celebration, there is still another group who witnesses the joyous grandeur and overwhelming gladness that surround the throne.

> Read Revelation 7:9-10:
>
> Who else will be included in the atmosphere of perpetual exhilaration around the throne?
>
> _____
>
> Where are they in proximity to the throne?
>
> _____
>
> What do they cry out?
>
> _____
> _____

With one voice, a vast group, too large to count from every tribe and nation, will acknowledge with great shouts of joy their release from darkness. Before the Lamb who gave them eternal freedom they will celebrate their liberation from sin, rescue from captivity, relief from damnation, and escape from bondage. Praise Him!

> How does Isaiah 61:1-3 foreshadow this great celebration?
>
> _____
> _____
> _____

Let's put this glorious celebration all together: Use the space below to draw the image depicted for us in Revelation of the throne, and the joyous activity around the throne.

Go back to the picture you just drew and include the first 3-5 words of what the different witnesses are crying out.

What stands out to you about the witnesses around the throne and their unceasing cries?

I hope you see it. All throughout this study we have, in one way or another, been talking about the importance of proximity. The angels encircle everyone present as they cry out "Worthy…." The elders worship around the throne, in front of the angels, and they cry, "You are worthy…." The peoples, from every tribe and nation, will stand in front of the throne, they will cry, "Salvation comes from our God…." But, the seraphim, who are in the center and closest to God cry, "Holy, holy, holy…." Now, if everyone present saw God, why did the seraphim have a different declaration? I believe it is based on their close proximity. Maybe I am getting a little too hypothetical, but look again at your drawing. The throne of God is in the center of the throne room. It is the core, the heart of all activity in heaven. Everything revolves around the throne of God. Every eye and ear is focused on the One who sits on the throne. He is the center of all adoration and praise.

Now, in this same center, we find the six-winged seraphim right there with Him (see v. 6), right up on Him, then the elders, then the angels. From this position, what did the seraphim witness that perhaps the angels and elders didn't? Is it possible that the seraphim had greater revelation? Think about it. What made them cry out "Holy, holy, holy," when everyone else was shouting "Worthy!"?

I don't have all the answers. I am simply suggesting that the seraphim may cry out as they do because they have a more superior point of view. They are standing right next to God; so close that they could touch Him. The seraphim have the benefit and advantage of closer proximity.

We, too, must get a more vivid and closer perspective of God, one that causes us to go from proclaiming, "Worthy" to one that begs us to cry out, from the core of our being, "Holy, holy, holy!"

> End today by meditating on Isaiah 6:1-7. What did the seraphim proclaim? What did Isaiah confess? Why do you think Isaiah felt this way? What did he witness? (v. 5) What does this teach us about what we must do in order to experience closer proximity with God?

What are you proclaiming? Are you passionately declaring "Holy, holy, holy"? What you proclaim says a lot about the closeness of your relationship with God. Understand, I am attempting to teach you a concept; I am not telling you that proclaiming "Worthy," is unacceptable. By all means, cry out "Worthy!" But more importantly proclaim, "Holy!" God wants you right there with Him, standing in the core, at the center of His throne, face-to-face. He wants that close, intimate relationship, so He may give you a more profound revelation of His infinite beauty and incomparable greatness.

Day Two
King of Heaven and Earth

"The LORD is exalted over all the nations, his glory above the heavens.
Who is like the LORD our God, the One who sits enthroned on high,
who stoops down to look on the heavens and the earth" (Psalm 113:4-6).

Yesterday we fixed our attention on the activity around the throne of God. The core of heaven is upon the throne—He is the center—the extreme essence of heaven. Everything revolves around Him. Without Him heaven wouldn't exist; and without Him the earth wouldn't exist. God is the Creator of all things and the Ruler over all things. He is enthroned as the King of heaven, and He is enthroned as King over all the earth.

According to *Webster's Dictionary*, the word *enthrone* means "to raise to sovereignty, to exalt."[55]

How do the following verses declare that God is the One enthroned?

Psalm 22:3: _____

Psalm 29:10: _____

Psalm 99:1: _____

God is enthroned as King forever over all creation. Heaven is His throne, and the earth is His footstool (see Acts 7:49). The word *king* in the Hebrew language is *melek*, and it appears "about 2,500 times throughout the Old Testament. Melek refers to human royalty as well as to Yahweh's position as king over creation and the heavenly realms."[56]

Read Psalm 97:1-6:

How is God's rule portrayed?

_____

What earthly elements are used to describe His greatness?

_____

Who and what are affected by His sovereignty?

_____

Who proclaims His rule? Who will see His glory?

_____

In Psalm 97:1-6, the psalmist portrays God as the King of all kings; the One who rules over the entire universe. Through all He has created, God has made His invisible qualities, eternal powers and divine nature known to all mankind (see Romans 1:20). All people will see His glory; and all of heaven proclaims the foundation and establishment of His rule over all things.

Colossians 1:16-17 confirms that Christ, the image of the invisible God, is preeminent over all things. List all that is under His dominion.

_____   _____
_____   _____
_____   _____
_____

In understanding the dominion of Christ as King, why is it important to understand that all things were created by Him and for Him, and that all things hold together because of Him?

_____
_____
_____
_____
_____
_____
_____
_____
_____

Without a firm grasp of Christ's dominion over all things, you will struggle with this concept and ask yourself: *If God is King over all the earth, then why is the world in such terrible shape? Why do bad things happen? Why do so many people live in poverty and suffering? If God is all-powerful, and a God of love, then why doesn't He do something?* These questions plague many of us, believer and non-believer alike. In some cases, the troublesome deliberation of these questions keeps many from entering into a relationship with God.

As we struggle with these questions, we must remember two things. First, there is opposition—God has an enemy. This enemy opposes God's rule in the world; and, because of him sin has been brought into the world. Sin is the root of misery and unhappiness. Sin, the absence of relationship with God, is often evident in a deprived country where poverty, disease, and starvation are rampant.

True, God could wipe out sin, Satan, and everything committed to sin, but that would mean that all mankind would also be wiped out. God is a God of love. He is patient, not wanting anyone to perish (see 2 Peter 3:9). He could expel the world's rebellion in a second, but He chooses not to. Instead, by the power of divine love, He chooses to exercise impartiality and loving-kindness, so that many may be drawn into His kingdom through grace by faith in Jesus Christ.

Secondly, we must remember to pray as Jesus taught His disciples to pray, "…your kingdom come, your will be done on earth as it is in heaven" (Matthew 6:10). Through His word, Jesus taught us to pray for God's dominion on earth as it is in heaven. He is training us, here on earth, to come under the control of our Lord and King. Recall from our previous lesson, God is the core—the center of heaven—and the heavens rejoice and cry out "Holy, holy, holy!" Night and day they proclaim, "Worthy is He to receive all glory and honor!" We do not declare God's greatness as Lord and King with the same level of frequency or intensity as they do in heaven.

Yes, God is enthroned, the King of heaven and earth, whether we like it or not, but we must remember to submit to His authority and dominion as those do in heaven. Therefore, let us worship as they worship in heaven. Let us surrender as they surrender in heaven. Let us serve as they serve in heaven. Let us proclaim as they proclaim in heaven, "Worthy is our Lord and God, to receive glory and honor and power, for you created all things, and by your will they were created and have their being" (Revelation 4:11).

What does Psalm 103:19-21 tell us about those who serve and worship the King in heaven? Check all that apply:

____ His angels do His bidding and act upon His word

____ All His heavenly hosts praise Him, and do His perfect will

____ All those in heaven worship Him and do exactly what He commands

What does Psalm 103:22 tell God's works (everything He has created, NLT), to do?

_____

Who or what would this include?

_____

According to Psalm 95:1-7, what are we instructed to do and why?

_____
_____
_____

Everything, from the depth of the earth, to the mountaintops, God holds all things in the palm of His hand. He made it, formed it all out of nothing. It is His, and all that He created is to revolve around Him and Him alone.

Eugene Peterson explained it this way: "First this: God created the Heavens and Earth—all you see, all you don't see. Earth was a soup of nothingness, a bottomless emptiness, an inky blackness. First, God. God is the subject of life. God is foundational for living. If we don't have a sense of the primacy of God, we will never get it right, get life right, get our lives right. Not God at the margins; not God as an option; not God on the weekends. God at center and circumference; God first and last; God, God, God." (The Message)[57]

Like it is in heaven, earth and everything in it is to praise God (see Psalm 150:6). Not as an option, but as a priority. Without God we would have nothing—we would be nothing. Therefore, let us place the King who is enthroned in heaven upon the throne of our hearts.

End today by coming before His throne by following the instruction given in Psalm 95. Meditate on Psalm 98:4, 6 and let us, "Shout for joy to the LORD, all the earth, burst into jubilant song…shout for joy before the LORD, the King" Then pen your prayer of worship below:

_____
_____
_____
_____
_____
_____
_____

Day Three
King of My Heart

"...the LORD sought out a man after his own heart..." (1 Samuel 13:14).

This morning, I had a wonderful time in the Spirit with the Lord. I felt His love and the pleasure of His touch. The only word in the English language I can think of to remotely describe this kind of intimate pleasure is ecstasy, but even then that word falls drastically short. The closer I draw to the Lord, the more He seems to share these kinds of moments with me. It is as if His Spirit descends upon my feeble soul like a shadow, and there we are, just the two of us, caught up in the pleasure of ardent love.

I have been anticipating this lesson, as I have looked forward to sharing it with you. I am fervent for the church. I pray continually for the day when she will get a heightened revelation of Christ's love for her and fall madly in love with Him. There are some in the church, I believe, who are experiencing the awareness of this intimate love. Unfortunately, there are many more who do not realize what they're forsaking. The reason many of us do not fully understand Christ's ardent love is due to our perception of Him. We, as the church, must broaden our view of Christ in order to embrace His passionate ways.

In this lesson we are going to endeavor to enthrone Christ as King upon our hearts. David knew and understood what this meant as he cried out to the Lord, "Your love is better than life" (see Psalm 63:3). David was a man who enthroned God as King upon his heart, and God knew David as a man after His own heart (see Acts 13:22b). That carries weight, my friend. Man didn't give that testimonial of David—God did.

What do you think it looks like to have a heart for God? How would you describe a man or women after God's own heart?

I believe there are several reasons why God would make such a claim about David. First of all, in Acts 13:22, God said that David was a man after His heart because he was obedient. Obedience is vital if we desire to draw close to God. But understand this about God's view of obedience: God sees the desire of our hearts. He not only sees our actions, He knows our intentions. God does not think poorly of us if we desire to do His will, but don't get it right the first time.

David was a man desperate to delight the heart of God. Still, David was not perfect; he didn't always get it right, but God knew David's heart. I have made many mistakes in my journey with Christ, but this doesn't make me a fraudulent Christian. God sees the inward observance. It is religious legalism that points its finger and screams, "Hypocrite!" whenever we mess up. We are not perfect, and God knows that. Christ does not label us frauds because we are weak. In fact, Jesus told Paul, "My grace is sufficient for you, for my power is made perfect in weakness" (2 Corinthians 12:9). If you are finding it difficult to be obedient, ask for help. Christ's strength rests on those who admit their weakness and need. What matters most is that you have a willing, submissive heart.

Although it takes a willing desire for submissive obedience to enthrone God upon our hearts, obedience will not be today's focus. For our purposes today, we will consider two other vital reasons why I think God considered David a man after His own heart: perspective and praise.

Let's begin with prayer and reveal to Christ our desire to enthrone Him as King upon our hearts, and then please read Psalm 18.

Our perspective of God is everything. How well we know and understand God's heart toward us will make a difference in how we respond to Him. How often we think of Him and ponder His greatness, will determine how we perceive Him. How we perceive Him will determine how we proclaim Him, praise Him, and pray to Him. David enthroned God upon his heart, because he had great thoughts of God.

Let's break down Psalm 18 into five sections. In each section, record the different ways you see David's perspective of God. How is he having great thoughts of God? I have given you an example to get you started.

Psalm 18:1-6:

David saw God as a source of great power and strength, a place of safety and refuge, as the One who could save him.

Psalm 18:7-15:

Psalm 18:16-29:

Psalm 18:30-45:

Psalm 18:46-50:

Is this how you think of God? Are you awed by His majesty and humbled by His omnipotence? Do you marvel at His perfection and ponder His ways? Do you think of Him as your Rock and safe place of refuge, able to save you from any situation? Are His attributes in the forefront of your mind? Has He become your Magnificent Obsession? Is God the core of your entire existence? Do you think of God as David did?

Ponder God's greatness. Consider the marvelous ways He has revealed Himself to you. Take some time and have great thoughts of God, and then record your perspective below:

David had a remarkable perspective of God; as a result, David was an extraordinary worshiper.

Look again at Psalm 18, this time, look for David's words of praise and worship offered to God. Record at least five praises in the space below along with their reference:

_____   _____
_____   _____
_____   _____
_____   _____
_____

David knew and understood the importance and impact of praising God. Look up the following verses and record David's desire to praise God.

Psalm 34:1: _____
Psalm 47:6-7: _____
Psalm 63:3-4: _____
Psalm 71:4: _____

The effect of praise offered to God is wonderful, and David rejoiced in this privilege daily. However, there is another aspect to praise you may not be aware of: God also sings praises over us. I cannot begin to tell you how joy floods my soul whenever I hear my King sing praises over me (see Zephaniah 3:17). Like sweet honey His words comfort my heart, renew my mind, and rebuild my soul. His love pours over me like a river bringing healing, fresh hope and new life. In the midst of the pain, His words of love and praise give me new insight into myself and His astonishing love for me.

Beloved, praise is a two-way street! Praise is most effective when we willingly offer praise to the King, and when we willingly receive Christ's praise over us. I learned a valuable lesson once I became acutely aware of Christ's continual praise over me and learned to accept it. For one, as a result of Jesus singing praises over me, I began to see myself in a different light. I began to have more confidence. I had more victory over my sinful nature. I began to lay hold of who I am in Christ, and recognize His heart toward me. There is power in the words of Jesus. And His healing comes pouring out whenever we take the time to stop and drink them in.

Share about a time when Jesus lovingly sang a song of praise over you. What were the effects of His praise?

_____
_____

At what other times do you want to hear praise, and from whom?

We all need a little praise from time to time. Especially as women, we need to feel loved and appreciated, don't we? Unfortunately, when we don't receive the praise we need, we can fall apart emotionally. This is all the more reason why we must rely on the praises of Christ alone to bring us the satisfaction our souls need, and why it is vital that we praise Him on a regular basis.

The Lord doesn't require praise the way we do. He doesn't need our affirmation. He knows who He is, and He doesn't need restoration and new found victory. We, on the other hand, need to hear those frequent praises from His heart in order to move from a place of hurt, devastation, insecurity and failure, and into a place of freedom in Christ.

The King wants our praises not because He needs them, but because He wants them. God greatly desires our loving worship. It is hard to believe, but God truly enjoys the praises and affections that arise from meager mortals like you and me. In fact, He loves it!

> Psalm 22:3 says the Lord is enthroned upon our praises. What do you think it means to enthrone God upon your heart with your praise?

How do you feel when you desire a word of praise and no one offers it?

Our praise of God is a reflection of the work He has accomplished in us. Like David, we must increase our perspective of God, and then allow what He has done in us and through us to come spilling out.

> End today by meditating on Psalm 150. How many times does the Psalmist tell us to praise God? _____ Who, when, where and how are we instructed to praise God?

God is the great King who deserves all our praise, and our praise is an indication of our perspective. If Christ is indeed enthroned upon our hearts, our praises will reveal it. Allow me to encourage you to enthrone Christ upon your heart today and every day. Pray continually for God to increase your perspective of Him, and then praise Him with everything that is in you. God is continually seeking out men and women who are after His own heart (see 2 Chronicles 16:9). Be one of them!

Day Three: King of My Heart

Day Four
He is My King

"I, the LORD, am the first, and with the last. I am He!" (Isaiah 41:4, NASB).

This week we have been seeking to know the King of Glory. He is the King of heaven and earth, and all things belong to Him. He is the center of all dominion and domain, and everything revolves around Him. Oh, how I hope you were encouraged yesterday as we enthroned Christ upon our hearts. It is vital that we seek after the heart of God as David did. When we do this, when we enthrone Christ upon our hearts with our praises, our circumstances and situations miraculously come into a fresh perspective.

As we draw near to the end of our journey together, it is my desire to leave you with an impression of God that will remain with you in life, an image that will encourage you no matter what you are going through. In my strength this is impossible. So, let us turn to the One in Whom all things are possible (see Matthew 19:26).

Let's begin by praying for our vision of the King to increase, so we may be overcome, yet inspired, by the view. May we be humbled by His greatness, and encouraged by His love.

Today will require a great deal of research, but it will be worth it. Look up the following verses; then fill in the blank with the word(s) that you think best completes the sentence. I have given you examples.

Zephaniah 3:15:	The Lord is the King of *Israel*
Psalm 2:6:	He is King of *Zion*
Psalm 10:16:	The Lord is King _____
Psalm 24:10	The Lord Almighty—he is the King of _____
Psalm 47:2:	The LORD Most High, He is King over _____
Jeremiah 10:10:	He is the _____ God, the _____ King
Jeremiah 23:5-6	He is the King of _____
Isaiah 66:1a:	He is King of _____
Zechariah 14:9:	He is King over the _____
Malachi 1:14:	The Lord is a _____ King
John 19:19:	The King of the _____
1 Timothy 1:17:	He is the King _____ _____ invisible
Revelation 15:3b:	He is King of the _____
Revelation 19:16:	He is _____ of Kings and _____ of Lords
Psalm 44:4:	You are _____ King and _____ God

He is the King of the Ages (Nations), the King eternal, the King of Kings and the Lord of Lords. He is the King of Righteousness, the King of Glory, the King of all things, the sovereign authority over heaven and earth. He is the King of Israel, the King of Zion, and the King of the Jews. He is my King!

Leviticus 19:2:	The Lord our God is _____
1 Samuel 2:3b:	The Lord is a God _____
Psalm 18:30:	The ways of the Lord are _____
Psalm 145:5:	The King is _____
Psalm 145:8:	The Lord is _____ and _____
Matthew 5:48:	God is _____
John 1:14b:	Jesus is full of _____
1 John 3:3:	Christ is _____
Hebrews 13:5:	Jesus is _____
Hebrews 13:8:	Jesus Christ is _____
Psalm 44:4:	You are _____ King and _____ God

He is infinitely perfect, holy and pure. He is all knowing, all seeing, gracious and loving. He is majestically powerful, yet entirely compassionate and tender. He is absolutely, and without question, flawless in all His ways. He is unchanging, indisputable; yet, completely obtainable. He is King of my heart, and faithful to all His promises (see Psalm 145:13, NIV). He is *my* King!

Psalm 119:89:	His word is _____
Psalm 136:	His faithful love _____
Proverbs 30:5:	His word is _____
Jeremiah 23:5-6	He will reign in _____
Matthew 11:30:	His yoke is _____, and his burden is _____
2 Corinthians 12:9:	His grace is _____
Hebrews 6:17:	His purposes are _____
Psalm 44:4:	You are _____ King and _____ God

Christ the King—is there any comparison? His existence is without equal. His kindness is boundless; His love endures for all time. His Word is eternal, flawless and pure. His grace is sufficient; and His purposes immutable. He is the King, the Lord our Righteousness, who reigns in wisdom, impartiality, and virtue; whose yoke is easy and whose burden is light. He is eternity's devoted King. He is my King!

How wonderful would it be if we all lived daily with this perspective of Jesus? Can you imagine what kind of world we would live in if everyone embraced Jesus the way Scripture portrays Him? This reality is called heaven.

For this entire Bible study we have been on a quest to know God, His Person and personality. In order to do this, we have been looking into some of the different aspects of relationship that God desires to share with each of us as Friend, Father, Redeemer and Husband. We have come to know Him as our Warrior who will come to our aid any time day or night. And we have considered Him as our caring Shepherd who leads and guides us through the hazards of life. Yet, in all that we have witnessed, there is still much more to Him than we could possibly dream.

It must be our daily pursuit to know Him in a fresh way. We must learn to embrace all of Him, not just the parts that feel good or make us comfortable. We must not settle. We must consider all of what the Bible teaches about Christ and not merely camp on the verses we think we can take in.

As a Bible teacher, too many times, I have encountered believers who refuse—hear me—refuse to embrace Jesus in a fresh and new way. I remember the first time I taught on Christ as the Bridegroom. I had a woman in the group who sat there, with her arms crossed, and complained through the entire lesson. Jesus is the same yesterday, today, and forever—from generation to generation—and He reveals Himself to His witnesses, making Himself known among those who chose to know Him.

To David, the once lowly shepherd who became Israel's king, God was the ultimate mighty Shepherd King who reigned in glory and splendor; yet, at the same time, He was the greatest of Lovers. To witnesses like John, and the other disciples, He was Teacher, Companion, and Miracle Worker; yet, He was the Son of Man and the Son of God who became the Savior of the world. To Isaiah, Moses, and Noah, He was the greatest of all friends, but they also knew His infinite power, wonders, and magnificence. To Paul, Christ was everything. Paul's life dramatically changed the day he encountered Christ on that Damascus road as Jesus revealed Himself in blinding greatness. And from that point on, Paul wanted to know Christ in every facet of life, and his ultimate quest was to identify with Him in both joy and suffering.

A great invitation is offered to you to come and *know* God. In Revelation 3:20 Christ says, "Here I am! I stand at the door and knock. If anyone hears my voice and opens the door, I will come in and eat with him, and he with me." This is a proposal to enter into more than you could ever ask or imagine. It is an invitation of the purest kind to come and commune with God. Without hesitation, reservation, or fear, He bids you to come and partake of Him—all of Him. And, in turn, allow Him to partake of you. Do you dare open the door and let Him in? If you do, I promise, you will never be the same.

For that reason, go ahead, "lift up your heads, O you gates; be lifted up, you ancient doors, that the King of glory may come in" (Psalm 24:7). Then, allow Him to consume you with His ways, word, beauty, power, and life, so that you may continue to know Him as never before. There is still much to be discovered this side of heaven.

End today by meditating on Jeremiah 33:3: "Call to me and I will answer you and tell you great and unsearchable things you do not know." Like the witnesses we discussed throughout this Bible study, what has God become to you? In what ways has He revealed great and unsearchable things you didn't *know* before?

What are the great and unsearchable things you still desire to know? Jesus is gloriously majestic, all-powerful, and infinitely wonderful. Nothing, and no one, can compare to Him; yet, He will mercifully reveal Himself to those who dare to seek His face and heart. In the margin, share with the King the desires of your heart to know Him more.

Day Five
The King Will Return

"Look, he is coming with the clouds, and every eye will see him…"
(Revelation 1:7).

Great anticipation fills the souls of those who wait and watch for the coming of the King. This anticipation mounted as the prophet Zechariah foretold of the coming Messiah: "Rejoice greatly, O daughter of Zion! Shout, Daughter of Jerusalem! See, your king comes to you, righteous and having salvation, gentle and riding on a donkey, on a colt, the foal of a donkey" (Zechariah 9:9). This was one of the most wonderful promises of ancient prophecy, the promise of a coming King who would bring with Him the guarantee of salvation. The prophet Zechariah also foretold that this coming King would be meek and lowly, He would be gentle and come riding on a donkey. In the eyes of those who waited, this King was a glorious promise and vision of hope.

I am excited! Let's begin with a word of prayer in expectation of our coming King, and then please read Matthew 21:1-11 and John 12:12-16.

Zechariah prophesied of a coming King. How do the verses, from Matthew and John, confirm this prophesy?

_____

_____

What were the people proclaiming as Jesus entered the city? What does this tell us about the expectations of the people?

_____

_____

"Hosanna," the people shouted, means "save now." They knew the promise, and as Jesus came riding into Jerusalem, they joyfully shouted, "Save now!" calling out for God's immediate salvation. Luke 19:37 tells us, "The whole crowd of disciples began to praise God joyfully with a loud voice for all the miracles which they had seen, shouting: 'Blessed is the King who comes in the Name of the Lord…'" The people praised God for the miracles—they knew and understood that Jesus had power. However, they had an incomplete picture of God and His plan for their salvation. They wanted to make Jesus their earthly king (see John 6:15). They wanted to overpower the influence of the Roman Empire that had them oppressed. The people took into consideration only part of the prophesy.

In the days that followed, the people's expectations were dashed. A sudden and drastic change took place in the hearts and minds of the people who, only one week prior, had hailed Jesus as king.

Read John 19:13-16:

Why do you think the people turned on Jesus?

_____

_____

When Pilate asked the people, "Shall I crucify your King?" How did the chief priests respond?

_____

Our ways are not God's ways; and His thoughts are not our thoughts (see Isaiah 55:8-9). The people took the prophesy of the coming Messiah and turned it into the plans and desires of their own expectations. And when the plan didn't come together the way they were envisioning, they turned on Jesus. Their attitude was no different than the chief priests who proclaimed, "We have no king!"

We can react that way, too, can't we? When God answers our prayers we praise Him. When we see the miracles we shout "Hosanna!" But when God acts in a way that is contrary to our expectations, or He doesn't come through in our timing, we often turn on Him. When we believe God has disappointed us, it is usually because we have a misconception about God. But Jesus wants us to know Him and accept Him for who He is, and not who we want Him to be.

Years ago, when God began to call me into a ministry of speaking, teaching, and writing, I saw a glimpse of the promise and I got excited. I thought: *This is it!* So I took the ball and ran with it. The trouble was it wasn't the fulfillment; it was only one aspect of the promise. Due to my misconception, I became overeager and tried to help God by attempting to make the fullness of the promise come faster. When it didn't work out the way I thought, I became frustrated and confused. I began to worry and doubt whether or not I had even heard from God.

I think this is what happened to the people of Israel. They heard the promises of God; they waited, they hoped, and the moment they saw the first part of the promise come marching into Jerusalem on a donkey, the way the prophet foretold, they declared: *This is it!* So they tried to take the ball and run with it. When it turned out that their plans were not God's plans, they began to doubt that this man really was their Messiah.

What did Jesus make known in John 18:36? Check the correct response:

____ I am the King

____ My kingdom has not yet come

____ My kingdom is not of this world

I love the way Eugene Peterson puts it, "My kingdom," said Jesus, "doesn't consist of what you see around you. If it did, my followers would fight so that I wouldn't be handed over to the Jews. But I'm not that kind of king, not the world's kind of king." (The Message)[58]

> What the people didn't recognize is there were two parts to Zechariah's prophesy. Compare Zechariah 9:9-13 with Zechariah 9:14-17.
>
> From Zechariah 9:9-13, list as many promises as you can:
>
> _____   _____
> _____   _____
> _____   _____
> _____   _____
>
> Now compare these promises with Zechariah 9:14-17, what does the second part of the prophesy tell us?
>
> _____
> _____

The first coming of the Messiah was fulfilled as Jesus came to Jerusalem, humble and gentle, endowed with salvation, and riding on a donkey. He came to speak peace to the nations (v.10), and to confirm the covenant in His blood (v.11a). He came to set the prisoners free (v.11b), to renew their hope, and to restore to them a double portion of what was lost (v. 12b).

The second coming, the return of the King, will bring with it flashes of lighting and the sound of the trumpet. He will appear in the sky like a storm, and every eye will see Him (v. 14).

> How do the following verses confirm the events of the second part of the prophecy?
>
> Matthew 24:27-31: _____
>
> _____
>
> 1 Thessalonians 4:16: _____
>
> _____
>
> What has the King declared according to Revelation 21:5? Fill in the blanks according to the NIV:
>
> 'He who was _____ on the _____ said, 'I am making _____ _____!'"

Day Five: The King Will Return

Look again at Zechariah 9:15-17. What will the Kingdom of God be like when the second part of the prophesy comes to pass, and the King makes everything new? Check all that apply:

____ The Lord will defend His people

____ His people will overcome their oppressors, like David slaying Goliath with a slingshot

____ His people will rejoice with celebration and laughter

____ They will be completely filled, like a bowl filled to the brim

____ His people will be set apart, like the consecrated blood used on the corners of the altar

____ The people of God will belong to Him, and will sparkle like jewels in a crown

____ They will be like Him, radiant and beautiful

____ They will flourish and thrive forever

What further insight does Zephaniah 3:14-20 and Revelation 21:1-4 give us about the Kingdom of God?

_____

_____

Hallelujah! One day the King will return to claim His people and make everything new.

No longer will we live in a world infested with sin and plagued with injustice. Christ will return to judge the earth as the King of all kings. He will abolish all sin, expose His glory, and establish His preeminence.

One day, the second part of the prophesy will come, and the fulfillment of God's promises will be complete. Jesus will come with the trumpet call, appear in the clouds, and every eye will see Him (see Revelation 1:7). This indeed will be a wonderful day, yet the gospel of Matthew warns us, "… keep watch, because you do not know on what day your Lord will come" (Matthew 24:42). "For this reason, you also must be ready; for the Son of Man is coming at an hour when you do not think he will (Matthew 24:44, NASB). Then, "Many will come from the east and the west, and will take their places at the feast with Abraham, Isaac and Jacob in the kingdom of heaven" (Matthew 8:11). Therefore, in these days, as we wait for the second part of the prophesy, we must continually keep watch and steadily prepare for His return.

Listen, can you hear the voice of the King? He is calling, "Behold, I am coming soon! My reward is with me, and I will give to everyone according to what he has done. I am the Alpha and the Omega, the First and the Last, the Beginning and the End. Blessed are those who wash their robes, that they may have the right to the tree of life and may go through the gates into the city" (Revelation 22:12-14).

"This is what the LORD Almighty says: 'I am very jealous for Zion; I am burning with jealousy for her. I will return to Zion and dwell in Jerusalem'" (Zechariah 8:2-3).

Therefore, "Shout and be glad, O Daughter of Zion. For I am coming, and I will live among you,' declares the LORD. 'Many nations will be joined with the LORD in that day and will become my people. I will live among you and you will know…the LORD Almighty" (Zechariah 2:10-11, emphasis mine).

> End today by meditating on the above verses from Zechariah 8:2-3 and 2:10-11. Are you greatly anticipating the King's reappearance? In what ways are you preparing for Christ's return?

_____
_____
_____
_____
_____
_____
_____
_____
_____
_____
_____
_____

Apply the Knowledge

In my pursuit of the King this week, the Holy Spirit has shown me …

The verse that spoke to me the most this week is…

In order to make this verse a reality in my life, I…

The changes I need to make in order to know the King, in the majesty of His splendor and greatness, more profoundly in my life are… Lord God, help me to…

The hidden treasure (see Isaiah 45:3) of His Person and personality God revealed to me this week is… This higher revelation of God's presence profoundly awakens me to…

Witnessing God as King this week has changed my perspective of God from… to…

Holy Spirit, help me to apply what I've learned to my everyday life, so…

Beloved, the journey is not over, it's just beginning. Keep pursuing God daily, continually seeking higher levels of revelation. Come after Him every day with such burning, passionate surrender and utter abandonment that it shakes the very core of your being. Ask Him to develop in you the passions of Paul, whose utmost desire was to know Christ. Pray that He would increase your perspective in order to become a man or woman after His heart. Pursue Him fervently in every aspect of relationship. Indulge in His Word. Pray in intimacy. Worship Him with longing and sheer delight. Praise Him with everything that is in you, and make it your lifelong, ultimate quest to be His witness, so you may know, believe, and understand, that He, and He alone is God.

Session Ten
One Nation—One King
Ezekiel 37:11-28

"There will be one king over all of them and they will never again be two nations or be divided into two kingdoms" (Ezekiel 37:22).

1.) The bones were the _____ house of Israel. (Ezekiel 37:11)

   a.) At this point in history, the house of Israel was _____ in _____ .

2.) God promised to _____ the two kingdoms, making the _____ become _____ .

   a.) Through God's _____ we are all one. (1 Corinthians 12:12-13)

   b.) We need to understand the importance of _____ among _____ .

3.) One _____ joined to _____ _____. (Ezekiel 37:22)

4.) _____ is what will weld us together— _____ is what will knit us together in _____.

References

Week One

[1] *Webster's Encyclopedia of Dictionaries: New American Edition* (Ottenheimer Publishers, Inc: 1978) edited by John Gage Allee, Phd, 431. All rights reserved.

[2] Reprinted by permission, *Vine's Concise Dictionary of Bible Words,* W. E. Vine (1873-1949), copyright 1999, (Thomas Nelson, Inc., Nashville, Tennessee. Pg. 135. All rights reserved."

[3] Taken from *Knowing God* by J.I. Packer. Copyright © 1973 by J.I. Packer. Used by permission of InterVarsity Press, PO Box 1400, Downers Grove, IL 60515. www.ivpress.com

[4] *Webster's Encyclopedia of Dictionaries: New American Edition* (Ottenheimer Publishers, Inc: 1978) edited by John Gage Allee, Phd, 209. All rights reserved.

[5] Ibid, 139

[6] *Webster's Encyclopedia of Dictionaries: New American Edition* (Ottenheimer Publishers, Inc: 1978) edited by John Gage Allee, Phd., 140. All rights reserved.

[7] *Webster's Encyclopedia of Dictionaries: New American Edition* (Ottenheimer Publishers, Inc: 1978) edited by John Gage Allee, Phd., 430. All rights reserved.

[8] Taken from *Knowing God* by J.I. Packer. Copyright © 1973 by J.I. Packer. Used by permission of InterVarsity Press, PO Box 1400, Downers Grove, IL 60515. www.ivpress.com

Week Two

[9] *Webster's Encyclopedia of Dictionaries: New American Edition* (Ottenheimer Publishers, Inc: 1978) edited by John Gage Allee; Phd.; 99. All rights reserved.

[10] Ibid; 198

[11] *Webster's Encyclopedia of Dictionaries: New American Edition* (Ottenheimer Publishers, Inc: 1978) edited by John Gage Allee; Phd.; 39. All rights reserved.

[12] *Webster's Encyclopedia of Dictionaries: New American Edition* (Ottenheimer Publishers, Inc: 1978) edited by John Gage Allee; Phd.; 163. All rights reserved.

[13] *Webster's Encyclopedia of Dictionaries: New American Edition* (Ottenheimer Publishers, Inc: 1978) edited by John Gage Allee; Phd.; 297. All rights reserved.

[14] *Webster's Encyclopedia of Dictionaries: New American Edition* (Ottenheimer Publishers, Inc: 1978) edited by John Gage Allee; Phd.; 341. All rights reserved.

[15] *Webster's Encyclopedia of Dictionaries: New American Edition* (Ottenheimer Publishers, Inc: 1978) edited by John Gage Allee; Phd.; 109. All rights reserved.

[16] Ibid, 109

[17] Reprinted by permission. *Vine's Concise Dictionary of Bible Words,* W. E. Vine (1873-1949), copyright 1999, (Thomas Nelson, Inc., Nashville, Tennessee. Pg. 97 All rights reserved."

Week Three

[18] *Webster's Encyclopedia of Dictionaries: New American Edition* (Ottenheimer Publishers, Inc: 1978) edited by John Gage Allee, Phd, 155. All rights reserved.

[19] *Webster's Encyclopedia of Dictionaries: New American Edition* (Ottenheimer Publishers, Inc: 1978) edited by John Gage Allee; Phd., 319. All rights reserved.

[20] *Webster's Encyclopedia of Dictionaries: New American Edition* (Ottenheimer Publishers, Inc: 1978) edited by John Gage Allee; Phd.; 82. All rights reserved.

[21] *Webster's Encyclopedia of Dictionaries: New American Edition* (Ottenheimer Publishers, Inc: 1978) edited by John Gage Allee; Phd.; 39. All rights reserved.

Week Four

[22] Taken from *Praying the Names of God* by Ann Spangler. Copyright © 2004 by Zondervan, Grand Rapids, Michigan; 219-221. Use by permission of Zondervan. www.zondervan.com

[23] Taken from *All the Divine Names and Titles in the Bible* by Herbert Lockyer. Copyright © 1975 by Zondervan, Grand Rapids, Michigan; 125. Use by permission of Zondervan. www.zondervan.com

[24] Taken from *Encyclopedia of Bible Characters: The Complete Who's Who in the Bible*; Gardner, Paul D. Editor, Copyright ©1995 (Zondervan, Grand rapids, Michigan) pg. 258. www.zondervan.com

[25] Ibid, 321, 378

[26] *Expository Dictionary of Bible Words*, by Renn, Stephen D (Editor), 2006 by Hendricks Publishers, Inc., Peabody, Massachusetts, 792. Used by permission. All rights reserved.

[27] *Expository Dictionary of Bible Words*, by Renn, Stephen D (Editor), 2006 by Hendricks Publishers, Inc., Peabody, Massachusetts, 559-560. Used by permission. All rights reserved.

[28] *Expository Dictionary of Bible Words*, by Renn, Stephen D (Editor), 2006 by Hendricks Publishers, Inc., Peabody, Massachusetts, 219. Used by permission. All rights reserved.

[29] *Webster's Encyclopedia of Dictionaries: New American Edition* (Ottenheimer Publishers, Inc: 1978) edited by John Gage Allee, Phd, 431. All rights reserved.

[30] *Webster's Encyclopedia of Dictionaries: New American Edition* (Ottenheimer Publishers, Inc: 1978) edited by John Gage Allee, Phd, 198. All rights reserved.

[31] Ibid, 79

[32] *Webster's Encyclopedia of Dictionaries: New American Edition* (Ottenheimer Publishers, Inc: 1978) edited by John Gage Allee, Phd,; 408. All rights reserved.

[33] Ibid, 408

Week Five

[34] *Webster's Encyclopedia of Dictionaries: New American Edition* (Ottenheimer Publishers, Inc: 1978) edited by John Gage Allee, Phd, 307. All rights reserved.

[35] *Webster's Encyclopedia of Dictionaries: New American Edition* (Ottenheimer Publishers, Inc: 1978) edited by John Gage Allee, Phd, 431. All rights reserved.

[36] *Expository Dictionary of Bible Words*, by Renn, Stephen D (Editor), 2006 by Hendricks Publishers, Inc., Peabody, Massachusetts, 407. Used by permission. All rights reserved.

[37] Mason, Patty, *Experiencing Joy: Strategies for Living a Joy Filled Life* (Liberty in Christ Ministries, Nashville, TN, 2012)

[38] *Webster's Encyclopedia of Dictionaries: New American Edition* (Ottenheimer Publishers, Inc: 1978) edited by John Gage Allee, Phd, 101. All rights reserved.

Week Six

[39] Taken from *All the Divine Names and Titles in the Bible* by Herbert Lockyer. Copyright © 1975 by Zondervan, Grand Rapids, Michigan; 47-48. Use by permission of Zondervan. www.zondervan.com

[40] *Webster's Encyclopedia of Dictionaries: New American Edition* (Ottenheimer Publishers, Inc: 1978) edited by John Gage Allee, Phd, 435. All rights reserved.

[41] *Webster's Encyclopedia of Dictionaries: New American Edition* (Ottenheimer Publishers, Inc: 1978) edited by John Gage Allee, Phd, 86. All rights reserved.

[42] *Webster's Encyclopedia of Dictionaries: New American Edition* (Ottenheimer Publishers, Inc: 1978) edited by John Gage Allee, Phd, 169. All rights reserved.

[43] Ibid, 296

Week Seven

[44] Learn about my story by reading; *Finally Free: Breaking the Bonds of Depression without Drugs* (Liberty in Christ Ministries, Inc.), 2011.

[45] *Webster's Encyclopedia of Dictionaries: New American Edition* (Ottenheimer Publishers, Inc: 1978) edited by John Gage Allee, Phd, 205. All rights reserved.

[46] *Webster's Encyclopedia of Dictionaries: New American Edition* (Ottenheimer Publishers, Inc: 1978) edited by John Gage Allee, Phd, 80. All rights reserved.

[47] Ibid, 274

[48] Ibid, 232

[49] *He Speaks to Me: Preparing to Hear from God* by Shirer, Pricilla; (2005) (LifeWay Press, Nashville, Tennessee) pg. 91. All rights reserved.

[50] *Webster's Encyclopedia of Dictionaries: New American Edition* (Ottenheimer Publishers, Inc: 1978) edited by John Gage Allee, Phd, 45. All rights reserved.

Week Eight

[51] Taken from *All the Divine Names and Titles in the Bible* by Herbert Lockyer. Copyright © 1975 by Zondervan, Grand Rapids, Michigan; 174. Use by permission of Zondervan. www.zondervan.com

[52] Taken from *All the Divine Names and Titles in the Bible* by Herbert Lockyer. Copyright © 1975 by Zondervan, Grand Rapids, Michigan; 174. Use by permission of Zondervan. www.zondervan.com

[53] Taken from *Praying the Names of God* by Ann Spangler. Copyright © 2004 by by Zondervan, Grand Rapids, Michigan; 74, 77. Use by permission of Zondervan. www.zondervan.com

[54] Taken from *All the Divine Names and Titles in the Bible* by Herbert Lockyer. Copyright © 1975 by Zondervan, Grand Rapids, Michigan; 17. Use by permission of Zondervan. www.zondervan.com

Week Ten

[55] *Webster's Encyclopedia of Dictionaries: New American Edition* (Ottenheimer Publishers, Inc: 1978) edited by John Gage Allee, Phd, 127. All rights reserved.

[56] *Expository Dictionary of Bible Words*, by Renn, Stephen D (Editor), 2006 by Hendricks Publishers, Inc., Peabody, Massachusetts, 560. Used by permission. All rights reserved.

[57] Scripture taken from *THE MESSAGE*, Peterson, Eugene H. Copyright © 1993, 1994, 1995, 1996, 2001, 2002. Pg. 19-20. Used by permission of NavPress Publishing Group.

[58] Scripture taken from *THE MESSAGE*, Peterson, Eugene H. Copyright © 1993, 1994, 1995, 1996, 2001, 2002. Pg. 1959. Used by permission of NavPress Publishing Group.

Preparing to Lead

Welcome to *Know That I AM God*. I am overjoyed to have this privilege to serve you. Thank you for your willingness to take the time to be a part of the lives of others. With all my heart, I know, firsthand, how God can completely change and alter a life. I pray for you, dear brother or sister in Christ, that the God of Glory will equip you and anoint you with His blessing and power, as you co-journey with the precious souls He has entrusted to you during this study.

You are an ambassador of Christ (2 Corinthians 5:29), a guide for those on this quest to know God in a richer, more intimate way. Your success as a leader will depend on your consistent commitment to this study, your willingness to complete the weekly lessons, and the encouragement you offer the group to do the same. Therefore I am confident you will take the time to invest in this study, so you can be a vessel God can use to impart into the lives of others. Be devoted in attending all weekly gathering sessions; make sure all necessary preparations and details are taken care of; and, be sensitive to the needs of those around you and God will bless this season abundantly for His glory.

Each week, after you have completed the weekly lessons from the workbook, read through the leader's portion and the discussion questions. Ponder the questions for yourself prior to your next gathering, and write down anything God communicates to you in your time of preparation. There will be no right or wrong answers to these questions, they are designed to provoke a deeper level of thinking, and, hence, stir deeper levels of closeness in each of the aspects of relationship God desires to share with us. Prepare any special instruction in advance that will enhance your time together. It is my sincere hope, through this Leader's Guide, to remove much of the guesswork by giving you clear guidelines that will help you make the most of your group time; while, at the same time, enhancing the learning experience for the group. It is my goal to offer you tips and suggestions that will support you and benefit the group, making your time together rich in both God's Word and His presence.

Before the Guests Arrive

- **Order all necessary materials in advance.** As you prepare for this study determine how many participants you will have, and order one workbook for each member. You may wish to order 1 or 2 extra workbooks in case there are any last-minute attendees. You can order the workbooks online by going to: www.LibertyinChristMinistries.com or www.Amazon.com

- This Bible study does not have an introductory session; therefore, **distribute the workbooks one week prior to your first Bible study class** and instruct each participate to read the introduction and do the first week's homework before your first meeting.

- **Make sure you are able to retrieve and view each of the 10 video sessions.** This video series, which accompanies this Bible study, comes in a DVD format. Each video teaching is between 15-25 minutes in length. You'll find workbook pages specifically designed for each weekly video session. The purpose of these videos is to enrich the weekly lessons, while giving greater depth of study. The video teachings are taken from the book of Ezekiel, where God continually declares, and *"...you will know that I am..."* Through the Prophet Ezekiel God revealed His ultimate glory, and showed His people that He and He alone is God. Since each video teaching is between 15-25 minutes in length, you should have ample time for group discussion, prayer, and worship while giving you the flexibility to accommodate either a longer or shorter gathering time.

- **Obtain all other necessary materials**, such as pens, name tags, video viewing equipment, candles, and CD player prior to each week. Check the Leader's Guide to see if there are any special instructions or additional items you will need to have on hand for the following weekly session.

- **Pray for each guest member by name**, and continue to pray for them each week.

- **Arrive at least 10 minutes early.** Arrange the room as needed. An intimate setting works best, placing chairs in a circle. If possible, keep the group size small (somewhere between 6 to 10 people). If a larger group exists, then prayerfully consider making arranges for a second group leader.

- If you desire to serve refreshments, keep it simple. Juice and coffee, and/or a light snack (grapes, cheese cubes, finger food). Snacks served prior to the meeting, or at the very end of your gathering time, offer a valuable time for fellowship.

- As a personal touch, if the church or home you are hosting in permits, set the atmosphere by lighting candles and playing instrumental music softly in the background. This will generate a wonderful atmosphere in which to worship and connect with God.

Help the Guests Feel Welcomed and Valued

I have been doing Bible studies for many years, and I know from experience that women, especially, drop out of studies when they do not feel valued. Here are some suggestions to help your group feel valued and welcome:

- Arrive early and make certain everything is in place before they arrive, so you can be ready to greet each guest warmly and affectionately.
- Learn each person's name as quickly as you can. For at least the first two weeks, have name tags available. Calling people by their first name makes them feel esteemed and valued.
- Again pay attention to group size. The size of the group makes a huge difference and offers flexibility for individual attention, while giving everyone ample opportunity to share during discussion time.
- When someone in the group shares, make eye contact and smile.

  At first, if the group members are unfamiliar with each other, there may be prolonged periods of silence during your times of discussion. Keep in mind that some people are intimated or afraid to let their feelings and thoughts be known. Do not let yourself become uncomfortable during the wait. Relax, smile, and allow the Spirit to stir their hearts. If the prolonged silence goes for more than a minute, or no one is making eye contact with you, then you will need to share a personal experience in relation to the discussion question. This will help to inspire others to participate.

- If, on the other hand, the opposite happens, and there is one, or maybe two people who seem to monopolize the discussion, then say something like: "Does someone else have a thought?" or "Does someone else have something to share?" Do your best to keep the conversation flowing among the whole group.
- If time permits, go through all of the discussion questions listed for each week. Try to keep the group on track. Remember, you are the guide, the tour director for this trip, and it is your support, encouragement, and leadership that will help to keep the discussion running smoothly.
- If someone in the group has a special need, be understanding and give him/her time to open his/her heart and share his/her burden. If this person takes a great deal of time revealing needs or begins to cry (if a woman) go over to her, touch her lightly and ask the others in the group to rally around her in prayer. If it is a man, be supportive and again take the time to pray over him as a group. Then, during the week, continue to pray for this person.
- During the week, send one or two special notes or emails to the people in your group. Perhaps someone shared something that touched your heart or added value to the group, thank him/her, praise him/her, and let him/her know that what he/she shared was appreciated. Rotate each week in sending out special notes, until each person has received at least two special notes from you during the course of the study.
- If someone misses a session and did not call you or someone in the group to let you know that he/she would not be in attendance, follow up with a note or a warm phone call. Let him/her know he/she was missed.
- If you are uncertain if someone in the group has received Christ as his/her Savior a good question to ask is: "Have you placed your trust in Jesus or are you still searching?" If this person says that he/she received Jesus ask: "Would you share your testimony?"
- In Week One there is an opportunity to invite the group to share personal testimony of how they first came to the cross. If someone in the group shares that he/she has not made that decision, do not push them. Offer encouragement. Listen! Be sensitive. Respond only as the Holy Spirit leads you. Throughout the study, continue to build the relationship. Invite him/her on a special outing (coffee, lunch, etc.). Encourage questions and commend any inquisitiveness. God may open the way for you to have the extreme privilege of leading this dear soul to Christ.
- Thank you again for your willingness to be an instrument God can use to impact the lives of others. May the God of Glory bless you and keep you as you serve those He has entrusted to you.

Leader's Guide

Week One
The Challenge to Know

Song: *I Wanna Know You Like That* by Anthem Lights

Begin with prayer

Leader's Note: *The Holy Spirit desires to do a powerful work in the lives of those who seek Him. During your gathering times, follow the leading of the Holy Spirit and submit to any direction or course of act He gives you. If you feel God is leading you to ask a question, or to respond a certain way, please comply. This Leader's Guide is just that—a guide—feel free to deviate if you become aware of the Spirit's prompting to do so. Give the Holy Spirit the room He needs to work among you.*

Read Aloud:
This week we began the guest to know God more intimately than we do now. This study is not designed to offer facts, but to cultivate deeper levels of awareness with God, so we may know Him personally, believe Him with absolute resolve, and understand His heart. We began our journey by first recognizing the significance of being God's witnesses, and that we will not move forward in our journey unless we have a firm foundation grounded in the basics of prayer and God's word. In Day Two we came to the conclusion that we will not know God unless we first come to the foot of the cross. Then, we examined our hearts in order to test our motives and expose any wrong motivations for our pursuit of God. We discovered that the fear of the Lord is the beginning of knowing God, and how possessing an appropriate fear of the Lord will help us to draw closer. And, then finally, we examined the evidence of knowing God by revealing the evidence of Christ's likeness in our lives, and how that likeness will impact the world around us.

Discussion Questions:

1. How has this week's study impacted your pursuit of God? In what way(s) have you been challenged in your walk with Jesus? What stood out to you this week and why?

2. In what way(s) have you *Applied the Knowledge* to the weekly lessons offered this week? How do you think your obedience to *Apply the Knowledge* will change your pursuit of God?

3. When examining the motives of your heart in Day Three, which question did you struggle with the most? Why?

4. Read Exodus 20:18-21. Share about a time when inappropriate fear kept you from drawing closer to God. How did Christ help you to overcome that fear?

5. Have each participant, one-by-one, turn to the person on their right and share with him/her one evidence of knowing God that is prevalent in his/her life.

6. In what way(s) would you like to know God better? What are you hoping to gain from this study?

7. (**Video**) Put yourself in Ezekiel's place, how do you think that kind of an encounter with God would change your life? Of the things that Ezekiel struggled with after his encounter, what would be the most difficult for you to deal with?

Share your testimony: How did you begin your quest to know God by first coming to the cross of Jesus?

Leader's Note: *If someone in your group shares that he/she has not yet come to the cross for salvation, do not push or make them feel uncomfortable by trying to convert them on the spot. Encourage him/her for the desire to learn more about Jesus by coming to the study. Remember to respond with compassion as the Holy Spirit leads you. God may open the way for you to have the extreme privilege of leading this dear soul to Christ.*

Leader's Note: *Other opportunities for salvation appear in weeks five and ten. Be patient, and wait for the timing of the Lord.*

End with a time of worship and prayer

Week Two
Know That I AM Your Father

Song: *Adoni* by Avalon

Begin with prayer

Leader's Note: *God desires to reveal His tender Fatherly heart to His hurting children. In order to give Him the room to move in people's hearts, remember to always follow any prompting or leading of the Holy Spirit.*

Read Aloud:
With the foundation and basics of our pursuit laid, we continue our quest to know God by viewing our heavenly Father's heart through the eyes of Jesus—the only true witness. What a tender week this has been as the Father revealed His longing for each of us to come under the protection and shadow of His wings, to abide in His presence. What love and persistent care He has shown through His desire to equip, train, and prepare us through acts of pruning and discipline, so that we may share in His holiness, and reap the fruit of His righteousness and peace. And if that were not enough, the Father gives us a most valuable and precious gift—His Holy Spirit—giving us the power to both know Him and to be His witnesses to the ends of the earth.

Discussion Questions:

1. What have you gained this week from your pursuit of God as your tender-hearted Father? How has your attitude or view of the Father changed?

2. How has examining the relationship with your earthly dad helped you to relate to your heavenly Father? How has your relationship with your dad hindered your relationship with God as Father? How has the Holy Spirit spoken to your heart this week in an attempt to mend any hurt, or restore the relationship either between you and your earthly dad, or your relationship with God as Father?

3. In an attempt to heal the pain of her childhood, the Father tells Patty stories. In what way(s) do you see the Father reaching out to you in order to restore what was lost in childhood?

4. Share about a time when you strayed away from the Father's protective care. What was it like to be out from under His protection? What was it like to return home, to come back under the shelter of His wings?

5. How has the Father's pruning shears produced fruit in your life? How has His discipline brought holiness, righteousness and peace?

6. End your gathering time together by praying for the Father's gift to be more evident in all of your lives.

Leader's Note: *Either pray as a group or break up into smaller groups of two or three. First ask each participant to invite the Holy Spirit to search his/her heart and to repent of anything He reveals. (The group may wish to do this quietly in their hearts.) Read the Scripture verses below out loud, then pray and surrender to the work of the Holy Spirit as you ask Him to flood your lives.*

Read prior to end prayer:
"So I say to you: Ask and it will be given to you; seek and you will find; knock and the door will be opened to you. For everyone who asks receives; he who seeks finds; and to him who knocks the door will be opened (Matthew 7:7-8). Which of you fathers if your son asks for a fish, will give him a snake instead? Or if he asks for an egg, will give him a scorpion? If you then, though you are evil, know how to give good gifts to your children, how much more will your Father in heaven give the Holy Spirit to those who ask him!"
(Luke 11:9-13).

Week Three
Know That I AM Your Friend

Song: *Friend of God* by Phillips, Craig and Dean

Begin with prayer

Leader's Note: *God desires to mend broken hearts and restore what was lost through damaging relationships, so His people can find the freedom to draw closer to Him in friendship with confidence. Therefore, offer encouragement and follow any leadership the Holy Spirit gives you.*

Read Aloud:
What a true and faithful friend we have in Jesus! This has been a glorious week full of His love. As we have looked at friendship through God's eyes, He has shown us His incomparable grace, and the intensity of His longing to be near us. What depth of suffering He was willing to go, all for the sake of being our Friend. In our pursuit this week, God has shown us His desire to be our constant Friend—the one we can laugh with, cry with, and share everything with. Jesus is our truest Friend, the One who will never leave us, forsake us, or betray us by being unfaithful. This week, we also learned to recognize some of the obstacles that can hinder or cause us to remain distant in our friendship with God. Then, we completed our week of study by witnessing the genuine beauty and steadfast companionship of this one-of-a-kind Friend.

Discussion Questions:

1. What has hindered you the most in your friendship with God? How do you see God working to overcome these hindrances?

2. How has the Holy Spirit moved your heart closer to Jesus in friendship this week?

3. At what point in your life did you first recognize God's offer of friendship? How would you characterize your friendship with God?

4. How do you see the Holy Spirit developing in you the 5 characteristics we studied in Day Four found in those God calls friend?

    Leader's Note: *Righteousness, Blameless, Humility, Obedience, Believing God*

5. Which characteristics of friendship found in Day Five mean the most to you? Why?

6. How will you continue to *Apply the Knowledge* from this week's lessons in order to bring greater levels of intimate friendship with Jesus into your life?

7. (**Video**) What true friendships has God brought into your life as a result of your friendship with Jesus? What means the most to you about these godly friendships? How have your true friends brought words of encouragement and words of caution into your life?

End with a time of worship and prayer

Week Four
Know That I AM Your Bridegroom

Leader's Note: *Before the guests arrive, set the atmosphere for romance. If permitted, light candles and put on soft, worshipful instrumental music. Add any other special touches you feel will speak to hearts and convey romance.*

Song: *Dance with me Lover of my Soul* by Paul Wilbur

Begin with prayer

Leader's Note: *God desires to lead His beloved into the most intimate of all relationships. This concept may be difficult for some, especially if they have been deeply hurt in marriage. We must remember that God is not man, and therefore will not react like man. Jesus is the Bridegroom of the church, and His ultimate desire is to be joined with His church as one. Again, remember to give the Holy Spirit full rein by following any guidance He gives you.*

Read Aloud:
All throughout Scripture we see the pursuit of God for His beloved. We see the imagery of the covenant marriage woven throughout Scripture, from beginning to end, like a golden thread. This week, we focused on Christ's passion and tenacious love as we observed His heart through a few men who knew and understood the heart of God, and His desire to be the eternal Husband of the church. We witnessed Christ's heartbreak through Hosea, and His unwillingness to give up on the ones He loves. Through Moses we witnessed the promise of a better covenant fulfilled in the man Christ Jesus. And through Boaz we saw the kindhearted kinsman redeemer whose desire was to right all wrongs. And, finally, through the eyes of Solomon, we saw Christ—perhaps like we've never seen Him before—as a Lover. I hope you are keeping an open mind, Beloved. There is much more to Christ than we could ever hope to know, and there is more to the relationship He desires to share we us than we could ever ask or imagine.

Discussion Questions:

1. In what way(s) do you see the sacred romance being revealed to you through God's Word and the world around you? In what way(s) has Holy Spirit awakened your heart and soul to the wonders of the sacred romance, offered to us through covenant relationship?

2. In what new way(s) has the Holy Spirit broadened your perspective to witness Christ as the Bridegroom? How has this new perspective helped you to perceive, recognize, understand, and know Christ more deeply and intimately?

3. At some point, we've all been like Gomer—unfaithful. Share about a time when the Lord remained faithful to you even in your unfaithfulness.

4. In what way(s) have you seen Christ intervening in your life the way Boaz intervened in Ruth's? How has He acquired you, given you new life, and changed your lineage?

5. Solomon wooed his beloved in the Song of Songs. How do you see this sacred poem paralleling the heart of Christ and His desire to woo His beloved.

6 In what way(s) are you experiencing the wooing of Christ in your life?

7. (**Video**) What false lovers are you dealing with in this season of your life? How do you think the knowledge of giving away payment to the false lovers of fear, worry, doubt and unbelief will change your attitude or perspective?

End with a time of intimate worship and prayer

Week Five
Know That I AM Your Redeemer

Song: *Redeemer* by Nicole C. Mullin

Begin with prayer

Leader's Note: *How I pray that everyone would know the wonderful salvation our Redeemer brings. If there is someone in your group who you suspect has not yet received Jesus as his/her Savior by grace through faith offer encouragement. Listen! Be sensitive. Respond as the Holy Spirit leads you.*

Read Aloud:
One of the most important aspects of relationship with God involves our personal revelation of His great love and delight for each of us. Beloved, in order to understand the emotional make-up of God's heart, we must allow the revelation of His love to penetrate our hearts. We must come to a place in our relationship with Him where we see ourselves as He sees us—as the apple of His eye. Yes, He is the holy and just God of the Old Testament. He is the same yesterday, today, and forever (see Hebrews 13:8). Nothing has changed, and neither has His longing to be with us. Therefore, in order to make a way for us to be with this holy and just God, He sent His Son to die for us. This redemption of God's grace given to us by faith has made a way for us to come into intimacy with Him. Into a place where we can enjoy God and He can enjoy us. And it is the unrelenting desire of God's heart that you know this place of ultimate pleasure with Him.

Discussion Questions:

1. What challenged you the most this week in your pursuit of God? How has the Holy Spirit opened your heart to receive more of God's redemptive grace in your life?

2. In what way(s) has God opened doors so you can share His love and redemptive grace with a world that does not know Him?

3. Share a testimony of forgiveness: How has the Lord helped you forgive someone who hurt you deeply? What does it mean to you to know that God has forgiven and redeemed you through His Son Jesus Christ?

4. Are you utterly convinced of God's heart toward *you*? Do you believe that He takes great delight in you? Why or why not?

5. Do you believe God is a safe place? Has God become your hiding place? Why or Why not?

6. **(Video)** How has seeing the true heart of the Redeemer helped you to witness the Bridegroom more clearly? How do you think this perspective will change your heart in how you see Christ and those who are lost?

End with a time of worship and prayer

Week Six
Know That I AM Your Shepherd

Song: *Jesus My Shepherd* by Robin Mark

Begin with prayer

Leader's Note: *God desires to protect us and tend to all our needs. There may be some in your group, however, who have not received the promise that the Lord is my shepherd, the One who will provide in all situations. God desires to break down the fences of doubt, so His sheep will come to Him willingly and trust Him to be their protector, provider and sustainer in all of life. Therefore, as you see the Holy Spirit moving and working in people's hearts, be sure to give Him the room He needs to touch and change their lives.*

Read Aloud:
David was our guide for our lesson time this week, as he allowed us to draw close enough to understand something extraordinary about His God. From his viewpoint and personal experience as a shepherd, David knew and understood the heart of God, and he shared this perceptive with us in Psalm 23. As we examined this profound psalm, we first saw the depth of David's understanding as he proclaimed: "The LORD is my shepherd; I shall not be in want" (v. 1). As we made our way through the psalm, we began to witness our Shepherd the way David did: As the One who watches over His sheep as protector, provider, and complete sustainer of life. He is the mighty Shepherd who guards His flock from danger, and the tender, gentle Shepherd who feeds, loves and guides His lambs. He is one of a kind. David knew it, and I pray we know it, too.

Discussion Questions:
1. What is your greatest struggle or hindrance in coming to the Lord every day in order to gather and partake of His manna? Spend some time brainstorming for creative ideas that will help in overcoming these struggles or hindrances.

Leader's Note: *For example: if time is an issue, we may want to rise 30 minutes earlier or cut 30 minutes out of our television viewing time. Another thought may be to give up something you are doing if it doesn't bring you peace or joy. A lack of joy and peace, when serving the Lord, is a sign that this task may be something the Lord does not want you to do. Pray and ask God what you should get rid of. Being too busy is a relationship killer. We must schedule our lives around God, not schedule God around our lives.*

2. Are you learning to rest in the presence of the Lord? What is your greatest struggle in learning to "be still and know that He is God" (see Psalm 46:10). How do you daily practice His presence, giving the Shepherd the opportunity to feed your soul throughout the day?

3. Which of the Shepherd's tools do you find more comforting the "rod" or the "staff"? Why? How do you see the Holy Spirit helping you to submit to both of these tools?

4. How do you see the Shepherd using His Staff to unite you with Himself and His body (the church)? In what way(s) have you witnessed the guidance of the Holy Spirit in your life?

5. In Day Four, we looked at some of the ways our Shepherd guards us in our lives and the things that He protects us from. What do you believe the Shepherd is currently guarding or protecting you from?

6. How has witnessing God through David's eyes changed your perspective of God this week? How has this perspective increased your desire to know and trust God more?

End with a time of worship and prayer

Week Seven
Know That I AM Your Healer

Song: *The Hurt and the Healer* by Mercy Me

Begin with prayer

Leader's Note: *This may have been a beautiful week for those who know the power of God's healing touch in their lives. For others, this week may have been challenging and deeply distressing if they feel God has not come through by answering their prayers for healing, whether in their lives or in the lives of loved ones. If someone in your group is struggling, reassure them that God is good, and, if he/she lets Him, God will bring good out of every situation. God is sovereign, and there will be some things we will not understand in this life. We must remember that God has a plan and a purpose for our pain and why He sovereignly chooses the way He does. Beloved, God does heal—if not in this life, then in the next.*

Read Aloud:
This week we witnessed the Healer in action as He healed the sick and mended the brokenhearted. We also witnessed the great faith of a man who understood faith from the standpoint of authority; and we learned that, without faith, we will not witness the miracles that God desires to bring into our lives. Our study then shifted to suffering, as we looked for the joy found in our circumstances, and in our preparation for eternity with Christ. Then we learned that as Christians, we are never alone in our suffering, and that God can use our suffering to comfort others. Finally, we looked at the fervent cry of Paul's heart, a man who greatly desired to go to the extreme with Jesus. Paul truly wanted to know the riches of Christ through the fellowship of both intimacy and suffering, and he was willing to pray some dangerous prayers in order to experience this profound partnership.

Discussion Questions:

1. As I shared in our lesson time this week, I first met Jesus as Healer. How did you first meet Jesus? Share a testimony of how the Healer worked in your life? How does the testimony of others bring you encouragement?

2. How has God increased your faith in your life? Was there a time when circumstances were bleak, but you found extraordinary strength through Jesus to exercise great faith? Share your story.

3. How does focusing on Christ and the reward of eternal completion help you to see your trials from a new perspective? What joy do you find in knowing that you're being made ready to stand before Christ?

   Leader's Note: *If someone shares that he/she is having difficulty in finding joy in his/her circumstance(s), and that the trial is too much to bear, take some time to offer him/her comfort. If led by the Spirit, pray over this person. Have the entire group join in this time of prayer.*

4. What has God brought you through that He is now using to comfort someone else? Explain how God comforted you, and then used your time of suffering to comfort another.

5. Do you yearn to know Christ as Paul did? Have you prayed this week to know Christ more—to know Him as Paul did in intimacy, suffering, and power? What transformation do you see taking place in your heart and attitude as a result of this type of prayer?

   Leader's Note: *If someone says that he/she is having trouble praying as Paul did, reassure him/her. This is dangerous praying, and he/she will need to first pray for the strength of Christ to help him/her in his/her weakness. If lead by the Spirit, pray as a group that everyone would desire to know Christ as Paul did.*

6. (**Video**) How is the Healer rebuilding what was destroyed in your life?

End with a time of worship and prayer

Week Eight
Know That I AM

Leader's Note: *You may wish to do a little extra homework this week in order to learn more about the wonderful, matchless Name of Jesus and the many Titles of God. Good resources for this pursuit are:* All the Divine Names and Titles in the Bible *by Herbert Lockyer, and* Praying the Names of God *by Ann Spangler.*

Song: *Your Great Name* by Natalie Grant

Begin with prayer

Leader's Note: *God desires to reveal much through His incomparable Name; so, as always, remain open and responsive to the leading of the Holy Spirit.*

Read Aloud:
As I studied the Names of God this week, it was life altering for me. I pray it was for you as well. There is much more to the Name of God than any of us realize, and when we stand on His Name and all we are promised in His Name, we find victory and power well beyond anything we could ask or imagine. Therefore, let us forever sing, shout, and proclaim "Hallelujah!" which means "Praise ye Jah!"

Discussion Questions:

1. As we studied the Names of God this week, what new wisdom or insight have you gained about the Person and personality of God? How will this new understanding affect your relationship with Him?

2. In what way(s) has grasping the Names and characteristics of God brought you to a new level of comfort and safety?

3. The name of Jesus appeared 600 times in the four gospels, because the name Jesus truly meant something special to the early disciples. Like the first disciples, *who* and *what* is Jesus to you?

4. In what new way(s) are you invoking God's Name in prayer? What has been His response to your call?

5. **(Video)** Romans 1:20 says "For since the creation of the world God's invisible qualities—his eternal power and divine nature—have been clearly seen, being understood from what has been made…" How have you witnessed Elohim in creation? How have these revelations brought you into greater depths of understanding of the Person and personality of God?

6. There are over 675 Names and Titles of Jesus in the Bible. Ask the group to break up into smaller groups of 2 to 4. Take about 10 minutes. Ask each group to record as many Names and Titles as they can think of. Return to your full group and have each smaller group share what they came up with. List all the Names on a flip chart, or something that everyone can see. Once each group has shared their lists, ask each member to select one Name or Title from the list that is special to them and why that Name carries great value to him/her.

Read Aloud:

Revealed in His Word
Author unknown

Genesis:	He is the Breath of Life
Exodus:	The Passover Lamb
Leviticus:	He is our High Priest
Numbers:	A consuming Fire
Deuteronomy:	He is Israel's God
Joshua:	Salvation's Choice
Judges:	Israel's Guard
Ruth:	The Kinsman Redeemer
Samuel:	our trusted Prophet
Kings and Chronicles:	He is Sovereign
Ezra:	He is the true and faithful Scribe
Nehemiah:	He is the rebuilder of walls and lives
Esther:	He is our courage
Job:	our Timeless Redeemer
Psalms:	our Morning Star
Proverbs:	our wisdom
Ecclesiastes:	the time and the season
Song of Songs:	the Lover's Dream
Isaiah:	the Prince of Peace
Jeremiah:	the weeping Prophet

Lamentations:	the cry for Israel
Ezekiel:	the call from sin
Daniel:	the Stranger in the fire
Hosea:	the forever faithful
Joel:	He is the Spirit's power
Amos:	He is the strong arms that carry
Obadiah:	He is the Lord our Savior
Jonah:	the Great Missionary
Micah:	the Promise of Peace
Nahum:	our strength and our shield
Habakkuk and Zephaniah:	He brings revival
Haggai:	He restores that which was lost
Zechariah:	We see Him as our Fountain
Malachi:	He is the Son of Righteousness rising with healing in His hands

And that's just the Old Testament

Matthew, Mark, Luke and John:	He is our God and our Messiah
In the Spirit-filled book of Acts:	He is the Son of God rising with the Spirit of fire in His hands.
Romans:	He is the Grace of God
Corinthians:	the power of love
Galatians:	freedom from the curse of slavery
Ephesians:	our glorious Treasure
Philippians:	the servant's heart
Colossians:	He is God and the Trinity
Thessalonians:	our calling King
Timothy, Titus, Philemon:	He is our Mediator and our faithful Pastor
Hebrews:	Everlasting Courage
James:	the One who heals the sick
1-2 Peter:	the faithful Shepherd
1-2-3 John:	The God of love
Jude:	The God who preserves and protects
Revelation:	in the end, when all is said and done and time will be no more: He was, and is, and will always be. The King of kings and the Lord of lords; the prince of Peace and the Son of Man; the Lamb of God and the Great I AM. He is the Alpha and Omega, the God our Savior. He is Jesus Christ our Lord.

End with a time of worship and prayer

Week Nine
Know That I AM Your Warrior

Song: *Mighty Warrior* by Randy Rothwell

Begin with prayer

Leader's Note: *For some, especially women, the Warrior side of Jesus may seem intimidating, but God wants us to know, understand and enjoy all aspects of relationship with Him. If someone in the group appears to pull back during this week of study and gathering time, reassure her that Jesus is on her side and desires to protect her in all circumstances. He is a Warrior she can count on to stand with her in the battles of life.*

Read Aloud:
There before me stood a mighty Warrior. His appearance is like jasper and carnelian. His face like lightning, and shone like the sun. His eyes are like flaming torches, His arms and legs like the gleam of burnished bronze, and His body like polished ivory decorated with sapphires. He is radiant and ruddy, outstanding among all others; nothing on earth is His equal. His strength and form are graceful. No one can subdue Him; He is a creature without fear. His position is firm, His stance immovable. The sword has no effect on Him; iron He treats like straw. From His mouth came flames of fire, His breath set coals ablaze. All who oppose Him are brought down in defeat. He is invincible, unstoppable, commanding, and a true conqueror—a champion among champions—a hero unlike any other. This is Jesus.

Discussion Questions:

1. As we've witnessed the Warrior in action this week, how has your perspective of Jesus changed? How has this new perspective changed how you respond to Him?

2. How has the Holy Spirit opened your spiritual eyes to behold the image of the Warrior within the boundaries of His creation? How has this imagery of creation changed your image of Christ?

3. How has the image(s) described by Isaiah, Daniel, Ezekiel and John enlarged your perspective of the Warrior? Can you relate to any of these witnesses? If so, which witness, and how do you relate to their experience?

4. Share about a time when you were captured and in need of rescuing? How did the Warrior charge into your circumstances and save you?

   Leader's Note: *If anyone in the group is struggling right now in a stronghold or spiritual battle, rally around that person and call upon the Warrior on their behalf.*

5. Through Psalm 7, David gave us two valuable insights: If we are going to be rescued by God, we must first understand that He alone is our Rescuer. Secondly, if we want the Warrior to act on our behalf, then we must be willing to submit to His plan of deliverance. Of these two insights, which is the most challenging for you? Why?

6. How do you see the Warrior at work in you? In what way(s) is He bringing you under His banner of love and transforming you into His warrior bride?

7. (**Video**) In what way(s) have you witnessed dead, dry bones coming to life? Who are you still praying for that they may know life in Christ?

Leader's Note: *If someone in the group has lost someone to both physical and spiritual death, do not allow him/her to blame themselves or God. Remind the group that when it comes to salvation God has His part; He will be faithful to convict the person of sin and to reach out. You have your part; you must show those around you the love of Jesus by being a good example of what it means to follow Jesus and to share the good news of the gospel. BUT the person you are witnessing to also has his/her part; he/she must receive life. God has given us free will, He does desire that none should perish, but He will not force anyone to receive Him.*

End with prayer for those who are still spiritually in the valley of dead, dry bones.

Leader's Guide: Week Nine

Week Ten
Know That I AM Your King

Song: *Who is This King of Glory* by Third Day

Begin with prayer

Leader's Note: *What a journey this has been! I'm so glad you joined me. The good news is this is not the end; rather it is just the beginning of a glorious pursuit to know God in ways we've never known Him before. Be sure to applaud your group for their efforts through this 10-week study, and encourage them to continue daily on this lifelong pursuit to know, believe and understand that He and He alone is God (see Isaiah 43:10). As always, give God full dominion and rein over your gathering time.*

Read Aloud:
We have focused a great deal this week on the perception of God. How we perceive God will have a direct effect on how we respond to Him. If we have great views of God, as David did, we will worship Him, praise Him and obey Him in the way for which He longs. I hope you received a great perspective of God this week as you witnessed the center of all worship in heaven. I pray that His magnificence was engraved on your heart in a fresh way as you pondered the King of all kings. May our view of Christ continue to grow daily, as we allow the Holy Spirit to broaden our vision of God to embrace all of Him. There is more to this great King than we could ask or imagine, and we must prepare for His return. There will be a day when the sky will roll back like a scroll, and He will return in all His glory to take His bride home, just as the Prophet Zechariah explained. On that day, all peoples, from every tribe and nation, will stand before the Lord and shout His praises with all of heaven.

Discussion Questions:

1. How will your worship of the King change as a result of witnessing the continual worship taking place around His throne? Just as God is the center of heaven's praise, how has God become the central part of your life?

2. How has witnessing God as the King of Glory changed your perspective? How do you see this new perspective changing your walk with Jesus? How will this new perspective change your life?

3. (**Video**) In what ways do you see the One King bringing together His church as one Nation?

4. For ten weeks, we have been on a quest to know God. What have you learned about God that you didn't know before? In what way(s) have you *Applied this Knowledge*, so that what you've learned did not stay head knowledge, but became life changing heart knowledge?

5. How has this Bible study enhanced your walk with Jesus? How have you drawn closer to God in intimacy as a result of your quest to *know* Him?

6. What do you still desire to know?

   Leader's Note: *Encourage the group to continue in their quest to know and witness God. Remind them that this is a lifelong pursuit. Encourage them to keep asking, seeking and knocking (Matthew 7:7-8). When they are ready, God will open the door and reveal a new part of His Person and personality.*

7. Where will you go from here? How has your level of hunger to *know* God increased? Only God can satisfy our spiritual hunger, but what choices will you make so your hunger may be fueled and fed?

Thank your guests for joining you on this 10-week journey, then end your time together with worship and prayer.

What are the Desires of Your Heart?

You were created for a purpose! *Transformed by Desire* is a journey of awakening and discovery that will help you identify the truest desires of your heart, while revealing to you the desires of God's heart for you. God has implanted desires and dreams in your heart that only Christ can fill. God wants you to tap into those desires, the ones that will radically transform your life. Dare to dream. Dare to hunger for more. Dare to answer the question: **What are the desires of my heart!?**

This 10-week Bible study includes a Leader's Guide and the 11-week video series, *A Journey of Transformation*.

Transformed by Desire Bible Study
is in-depth and perfect for personal quiet times,
book clubs, churches, or small group Bible study.

Ask for it wherever books are sold,
or order on-line at www.libertyinchristministries.com

Speaking to the Needs of Women

Patty Mason is a passionate communicator who speaks to the emotional needs of women, inspiring them to find hope, healing, and freedom for their souls. Each of her topics are heartfelt, biblically sound, and pertinent to the needs, lives, and struggles of today's women.

To invite Patty to your next event, email her at
Patty@libertyinchristministries.com

Or visit her website:
www.libertyinchristministries.com

Made in the USA
Charleston, SC
08 September 2013